PRAISE FOR *HYPER*

"In *Hyper* the interior life of a misunderstood boy is honored with lyric language. Tim Denevi has written a memoir about emotional vulnerability and recovery in the literary tradition of Styron and Susanna Kaysen. This is a powerful, literary book about childhood medication and its human cost. It's also a lasting story about mind, heart, and soul."

—Stephen Kuusisto, author of *Planet of the Blind*

"Intriguing . . . A well-written, easy-to-read journey of one man's experience living with ADHD and the history of the disorder. Parents may see their children in Denevi's story, and adults may see themselves in the childhood accounts that are shared here."

—*Library Journal*

"Haunting."

—*Nature*

"In his remarkable book *Hyper*, Tim Denevi tells the story of his childhood struggles with ADHD and his evolving understanding of this puzzling disorder. His narrative captures the essence of his daily struggles and features the disarming poetic rhythm of an extraordinarily talented writer. Over the past decade, I have often been asked to recommend books for parents and professionals who are trying to better understand ADHD. I have always responded with the titles of the three classics by Hallowell, Levine, and Ratey. Now, there are four. *Hyper* is full of blazing insights, wisdom, information, and inspiration. It is a significant and singular contribution to our field."

—Richard Lavoie, author of *It's So Much Work to Be Your Friend* and *The Motivation Breakthrough*

"Frank, moving, and instructive."

—*Booklist*

"Enlightening . . . Readers with ADHD will find affirmation of their own thoughts and emotions, while those without the condition will experience revelations."

—ADDitude

"At once both memoir and social history, *Hyper* chronicles what it was like to grow up as a kind of guinea pig for the treatment of ADHD in the 1980s. With hard-won clarity and excruciating honesty, Timothy Denevi has written a fascinating and sometimes disturbing account, never self-pitying but consistently illuminating and riveting."
—Robin Hemley, author of *Nola: A Memoir of Faith, Art, and Madness*

"Excellent."

—*Publishers Weekly*

"Timothy Denevi is a wonderful, true storyteller, drawing us into his own perilous childhood while taking us through vast changes in cultural attitudes, from a time when doctors described ADHD kids as feeble-minded threats to civilization up to the present triumph of congressional recognition of their right to treatment and education. *Hyper* is informative, moving, and entertaining—quite a feat."
—Robert Shapard, editor of *New Sudden Fiction* and *Flash Fiction Forward*

"Tim Denevi tells two stories—episodes in the history of the diagnosis and treatment of ADHD and episodes of his own life, from early childhood to maturity. He shows us how terribly difficult (and time after time, inadequate) has been the scientific and therapeutic effort to alleviate the suffering of children and youths. And with immediacy and clarity he narrates his own past anguish and bafflement (and that of his parents) as they all three tried to make sense of his impulses and vulnerabilities. Over time, they found their way to everyday ordinary human success at life, and Tim Denevi has found the way to write about it—a very impressive success indeed."
—Reginald Gibbons, author of *Slow Trains Overhead: Chicago Poems and Stories*

hyper

A Personal History of ADHD

Timothy Denevi

SIMON & SCHUSTER PAPERBACKS
New York   London   Toronto   Sydney   New Delhi

Simon & Schuster Paperbacks
An Imprint of Simon & Schuster, Inc.
1230 Avenue of the Americas
New York, NY 10020

First Simon & Schuster trade paperback edition September 2015

SIMON & SCHUSTER PAPERBACKS and colophon are registered trademarks of Simon & Schuster, Inc.

For information about special discounts for bulk purchases, please contact Simon & Schuster Special Sales at 1-866-506-1949 or business@simonandschuster.com.

The Simon & Schuster Speakers Bureau can bring authors to your live event. For more information or to book an event contact the Simon & Schuster Speakers Bureau at 1-866-248-3049 or visit our website at www.simonspeakers.com.

Interior design by Aline Pace

Manufactured in the United States of America

10 9 8 7 6 5 4 3 2 1

The Library of Congress has cataloged the hardcover edition as follows:

Denevi, Timothy.
Hyper : a personal history of ADHD / Timothy Denevi.
pages cm
1. Denevi, Timothy—Mental health. 2. Attention-deficit-disordered adults—Biography. 3. Attention-deficit hyperactivity disorder—Complications. I. Title.
RC394.A85D46 2014
616.85'890092—dc23   2013042085
[B]

ISBN 978-1-4767-0257-5
ISBN 978-1-4767-0258-2 (pbk)
ISBN 978-1-4767-0259-9 (ebook)

For my mother and father

If you can think of life, for a moment, as a large house with a nursery, living and dining rooms, bedrooms, study, and so forth, all unfamiliar and bright, the chapters which follow are, in a way, like looking through the windows of this house. Certain occupants will be glimpsed only briefly. Visitors come and go. At some windows you may wish to stay longer, but alas. As with any house, all within cannot be seen.

—JAMES SALTER, *Burning the Days*

I have been corrected on some points, mostly of chronology. Also my mother thinks that a dog I describe as ugly was actually quite handsome. I've allowed some of these points to stand, because this is a book of memory, and memory has its own story to tell. But I have done my best to make it tell a truthful story.

—TOBIAS WOLFF, *This Boy's Life: A Memoir*

CONTENTS

hyper

1

The Evil Logic of Clenched Hands

It's late afternoon, suddenly evening. The shadows in dense fingers along the wall. As if in a dream the color begins to drain from the wallpaper. The door is gauzy, the carpet insubstantial. Puzzle pieces litter the floor like flat, monstrous teeth. Or maybe not. In truth the details are a blur; for minutes I've been standing near the door, sobbing, screaming, the world reduced to darkness and light beneath the thing I feel.

Northern California, 1984: I'm five years old. It's my very first complete memory: I was having dinner with my parents and one-year-old sister and refused, when asked, to give something up. A toy car, baseball card—it doesn't matter; I was ordered from the kitchen and into my room. All I needed to do was serve the time-out.

But the memory never changes. What I wanted is gone, I've lost it forever, and perhaps the last identifiable emotion is something deeper than anger, a sense of desperation akin to homesickness; there's no way back to the place I just left.

Later, standing in the middle of my room, I'm voiceless, tensed, my face briny with sweat. There's pain; I've been dragging the corner of a building block across my chest. It's still in my fist, the color of sand. I drop it, look up. As if for the first time, I see them: my parents.

They're enormous. My father, Mike: his dark hair, the slope of his neck and shoulders, mustache; he's crouching, trying to catch my eye.

"Timmy!" he shouts.

For an instant they seem like strangers, a reflection. I feel a terrifying crush of loneliness, something I hate to recall even now. But I'm not the only one who's been shouting.

My mother, Patty, is sitting next to him, her cheeks thinly drawn as if she's been attempting to speak the entire time. Her eyes are small and bright. Huge lashes. She's crying.

And like that the tantrum is over. The room is measured and still. Once again I'm me: a skinny, sensitive boy who can be bargained with.

>>

What would you do? Your child won't stop screaming. Maybe he's sick, exhausted—any trigger could have started it. Then, miraculously, he calms down. Later you talk to him, emphasizing that such behavior is unacceptable, that there are consequences for his actions, and that most of all you love him very much. Of course you wonder how you might have handled it differently. He has had problems before, serious ones, but this is something altogether new.

By this point my parents had been married for almost a decade. There's a story they like to tell about their college days, right after they first started dating. A party at Santa Clara University, the early 1970s: My mother walks into a crowded dorm room. My father is sitting down. Already he's a standout baseball player, and on his lap is a preening, blond-haired girl, a freshman, who seems to be nuzzling him. My mother screams. Not at my father. She's telling everyone else to leave. The girl looks up—"Do you think I should go too, Mike?" But before he can answer, my mother is dragging her by the ponytail into the hallway. Only after the room has cleared out does she turn to my father and slap him. ("What was I supposed to do?" he likes to say. "The girl sat on my lap.")

Another story: they're seniors. For the last four years they've had an on-again, off-again relationship—recently they've broken up. My mother is going out on a few dates, my father is miserable. And yet, they still spend a lot of their time together. My father has been drafted by the Kansas City Royals. This particular afternoon he's just finished practice. In a few weeks he'll be reporting to a minor-league affiliate in Florida.

"I was thinking we should get married," he says to her.

She straightens up. "Are you fucking kidding me?"

"Come on," he says happily, impulsively. "You know I can't live without you."

And it was true, for both of them, has been ever since. But then my parents have always had too much in common. They were born, unbelievably, on the same morning of the same year—February 19, 1953—at Bay Area hospitals forty miles apart. Both my grandfathers were authoritative, first-generation Italians, parlaying whatever advantage they could find—the GI Bill, an athletic scholarship—into college and, later, moderate financial success. Both my grandmothers were Irish, beautiful, mildly alcoholic, and between them raised nine children in three decades.

Growing up, my mother wanted to be an actress. At Santa Clara she acted in plays, her black hair down to her waist. Even today the family home is decorated like a personal stage: crucifixes, family photos, and poems about dogs. But now, in her early sixties, she has only enough energy to engage the people closest to her. It wasn't always that way.

My father loved everything about baseball. At nine, the youngest on the team, he won the local Little League championship with a bases-loaded double. He was drafted at eighteen by the Chicago Cubs but went to college instead. He grew up surrounded by a large, excitable family, and I have a feeling he probably had more in common with me than he'd like to admit; but his mother, Jo Ann, would ignore his most egregious behavior, while his father, Pietro, would swing at him with an open hand. He hated high school; his father was the football coach. But he loved Santa Clara, and his coaches there adored him. Following an All-American senior season, he settled with my mother on a four-year plan to make it into the major leagues. Five years later, he was injured and demoted from Triple-A, so he came home to take a job in the real estate business. My mother was already pregnant with me.

»

The San Francisco Bay Area, 1984: That September we were part of a family gathering in Los Gatos. The commotion! My Italian aunts and uncles speaking in loud voices, eyeing one another from behind their drinks. I kept running from group to group, shouting until I was shaking, hoarse. Then I wandered into the silence of the garage and saw, perched on a shelf, an enormous fishing pole.

I froze. I'd never seen anything like it: the slacked line, the fleshy handle. I could hear family members behind the door. The air was heated, dirty. I stared at the object for what felt like minutes. It didn't move. And then I understood: this was some sort of marvelous tool, textured, intricate, meant above all to be held in your hands. I climbed the bench and was reaching for it when my father walked in.

"Oh!" he said. "*Goomba!*"

In the whirlwind of the party he'd been eating and drinking, keeping track of my sister, and socializing. Who knows how he ended up in the garage precisely at this moment, but he was genuinely happy to see me—discovering his young son in the midst of such an earnest mission. A light switched on. I was scooped off the counter and carried outside.

The afternoon, its dried canvas of grass and juniper bushes. Uncles and aunts crowded along the patio, talking with bright, hurried gestures. I started shouting about the garage. I had been so close: the lure, the feathered tip, the hem of mysterious wire. I kicked and twisted, my fury amplified by a complete lack of power. Nothing helped. It was happening again.

"Hey," my father said. He looked around for my mother.

The sky was a domed, colorless vault. The grass emptied of texture. I writhed, screamed, clicked my jaw. Shadows advanced and retreated, the ghosted angles of hands. My own voice buzzed, a reminder of something meaningful. But the world was cheap; it receded. The best way I can describe it now is in terms of a religious experience: the departure, however brief, into a space where something so limited as people—their bodies—couldn't possibly matter.

Then the backyard was silent, windless. Aunts and uncles stood over me, blocking the sky, a fabulation of adulthood, mouths and noses etched into their faces.

Suddenly my mother broke through the crowd. She'd been changing my sister, noticing, finally, the silence in the backyard. And just like that I was taken up and away—a clutch so overwhelming that I could feel her earring on my cheek, its metallic chill.

》

My mother always talked about my colicky first few years. Sleepless nights, ear infections, antibiotics and cold medicines, digestion problems, and at eight months old a serious case of pneumonia. I was born early, hyperreactive to light and sound. She was sure I couldn't digest dairy; the special replacement formula cost over $100 a month. When my sister, Katie, arrived I started preschool in Los Gatos, but on the very first day I bit another boy on the ankle. I couldn't sit still long enough to fall asleep during nap time or share with the other children. My mother consulted the teachers, planned strategies, and talked to friends, but no matter what she tried, my irritable behavior continued; it was, if anything, getting worse.

A year before the onset of my tantrums my mother had written to National Jewish Health (NJH) in Denver. She'd read about something called the Feingold diet, a treatment for behavior problems caused by allergic reactions to food additives put forth by Benjamin F. Feingold, MD. It was all the rage back then, though the evidence and methodology behind it had already been refuted. Nevertheless, in June we drove across a third of the country so that the doctors at NJH could put me on a liquid diet. After a week new foods were introduced; I'd spend whole days eating only carrots, then potatoes. It was like this for two months, until they finally determined that I wasn't allergic to anything; my constant oversensitivity to the world, its agitation of people and places, couldn't be explained by any physical discomfort.

Today a diagnosis would have been clearer. Attention-deficit/hyperactivity disorder (ADHD) has become the most studied childhood condition in the world. The latest *Diagnostic and Statistical Manual of Mental Disorders* (*DSM*)—published in editions over the past fifty years by the American Psychiatric Association—now divides ADHD into three subtypes: inattention, hyperactivity-impulsivity, and both.

To be diagnosed under the hyperactivity/impulsivity subtype, a child should meet six out of nine possible symptoms:

1. Often fidgets with or taps hands or feet or squirms in seat

2. Often leaves seat in situations when remaining seated is expected (e.g., leaves his or her place in the classroom)

3. Often runs about or climbs in situations where it is inappropriate

4. Often unable to play or engage in leisure activities quietly

5. Is often "on the go" or acts as if "driven by a motor" (e.g., is unable to be or uncomfortable being still for extended time)

6. Often talks excessively

7. Often blurts out answers before a question has been completed (e.g., completes people's sentences; cannot wait for turn in conversation)

8. Often has difficulty waiting his or her turn (e.g., while waiting in line)

9. Often interrupts or intrudes on others (e.g., butts into conversations, games, or activities; may start using other people's things without asking or receiving permission)

Listing these now is like running into someone who's wearing an outfit identical to mine—as a child I met every single one of the criteria—but how do you evaluate such behavior as being inconsistent with normal development?

The most comprehensive approach today involves gathering information from everyone involved. The goal is to limit the biases of each person—parent, child, teacher—in order to accurately judge the situation. Doctors should employ scales and aptitude tests, interview parents and teachers, review school records and grades, and eventually conduct observations in multiple environments. Of course there are shortcuts to a diagnosis, but before the physician in charge can label it ADHD, the assessment should include a decent amount of evidence-based evaluation.

》

In the fall of 1984 my parents took me to see Dr. Atkinson, our family pediatrician in Los Gatos. He was a short, wiry man in his early fifties with a blooming paunch. The tantrums had been going on for months—similar to the first, often triggered by objects. I was moody and excitable. Dietary causes had been dismissed. Atkinson's first intention was to rule things out, the most frightening of which, given my symptoms, was epilepsy. He ordered a series of tests.

I remember a weekend afternoon with my father. My mother was off with my sister somewhere. We were at the local hospital where I was being examined: the waiting room, forms, doctors, my histrionics as a nurse drew blood. I'm not sure if there's anything in the world my father hates more than this type of situation; he has never been—and I say this without judgment since the same can be said of me—a patient man.

Before we left they needed a urine sample. We were herded into a small bathroom. Through the thin walls we could hear shuffling, wet coughs.

"I want to hold the cup please," I told him.

"We're almost done."

"But Daddy."

"Yeah."

"I said *please.*"

He sighed and handed me the sterile cup, and it accidentally slipped from my hand into the toilet.

I looked up, aware of the consequence; it was the last straw. My father was staring back. Then he laughed. Maybe he snorted. He was seeing it: the walk down the corridor, the explanation, the additional delay. Were the situations reversed—had he, a quarter of a century earlier, made this type of mistake—his own father might have slapped him across the face. Instead, he bent over the toilet and fished out the cup.

"No big deal," he said.

"But it's dirty," I replied.

He squinted. "You're right." Quickly, he rinsed the cup in the sink and held it inside the rim of the toilet. "Aim and fire."

I pulled down my pants, but I couldn't pee. I was terrified; at any moment a doctor could burst in and yell at us for taking too long.

He began moving the cup from side to side. "Try and hit it."

"Hit what?"

"The target."

And just like that I was peeing all over his hand, into the cup, onto the harsh floor.

"I win!" I shouted. "Daddy, you lose!"

My young father. I'm proud of him. And I don't mean it condescendingly. I can understand what he must have felt: taking your son to the doctor, the nurses, the demands, the broken boundary of privacy—the goal always being not to freak out your child; after all, he's sensing things more keenly than you are. In truth, the simplest maneuvers convince: a game, a distraction. But only if you can find a way to remain calm yourself.

At the dinner table that evening the phone rang.

My mother answered it. "Wait," she said. "What?"

"Who is it?" my father asked.

She covered the receiver. "The hospital. It's about the tests."

My father rose to join her and quickly explained about the contaminated cup, how he didn't think, at the time, that it would be a big deal.

"I ask you to do one simple thing." She uncovered the receiver. "I'm sorry. What were you saying?" She listened. Eventually she hung up. Then she pointed a finger at him.

He held up his palms.

"Everything's fine," she said. "But listen to me: this is serious. I can't handle it without you."

And that was all it took—as if he'd been waiting for this moment ever since we left the hospital. "Shut up!" he shouted, pointing back. "Don't say another word!"

Instantly she was at him. Then came the accusations: *You're lazy! You overreact to everything! You're an asshole! You're a stupid fucking idiot!*

My sister was screaming. The phone was knocked ajar, sounding in waves. Finally my father stormed off.

I've tried to explain my parents' fury as the flip side of their love. They've always been able to draw closer together than any couple I've known, but their intense feelings cut both ways; antagonism comes in a series of escalations, the pace increasing during periods of stress. Don't get me wrong; they've never left bruises, and no one has ever had to call the police. The goal of each is simply to make the other believe—and back down; it's like watching a knife leave a trail of blood while tracing the shape of a heart.

»

What precisely is ADHD? To begin, it's a mental disorder. Dr. Russell A. Barkley, a professor in the Department of Psychiatry at the State University of New York Upstate Medical University, is perhaps the foremost contemporary expert on ADHD; over the last three decades he has written more than fifteen books on the subject. In his introduction to Lisa Weyandt's 2001 *An ADHD Primer,* he explains, "ADHD constitutes a failure or serious deficiency in a mental mechanism that is universal to humans (a psychological adaptation in the evolutionary sense), in this case, response inhibition and self-regulation. And it produces harm."

And so, we have a norm, i.e., the way most people act, and a deviation: impairment. But how do we explain the cause of such behavior without relying on more trying terms—catchalls such as "personality" and "temperament" eventually leading to the most inclusive concept of all, "identity," which in my opinion is really just a modern way of saying "the soul"?

To begin again: the term "attention deficit/hyperactivity disorder" is used to describe a range of behavior that's both irregular and harmful. It's different than, for example, the term "cancer," in which the malignant cells and the broader category of the disease go by the same name. ADHD, like most psychiatric disorders, doesn't include in its title a reason for how things came to be; instead it's a classification based on symptoms. So how do we define it without simply offering a list?

Dr. Barkley calls it "the most recent diagnostic label for children presenting with significant problems with attention, impulse control, and overactivity." In *What Causes ADHD?,* the clinical psychologist Joel T. Nigg describes it in terms of "a framework for identifying children who are impaired in meeting their developmental milestones." And Dr. F. Xavier Castellanos, director of research at the NYU Child Study Center, says, "People with ADHD can do anything; they just don't do it quite so well. It's a disorder of efficiency, or inefficiency, as much as anything, I believe."

Of course ADHD is a controversial diagnosis, and the dissent goes beyond the vocalizations of more extreme groups such as the Scientologists, who tend to discount the validity of mental illness altogether. Dr. Lawrence Diller, in his popular book *Running on Ritalin,* characterizes it as "a condition that psychiatry has only recently defined—in fact, is still struggling to define—and for which it has a long list of symptoms but no firm explanation." However, Dr. Peter Breggin, author of multiple books on the subject, thinks ADHD is a marketing ploy: "The drug companies, like the tobacco industry, like the alcohol industry, are highly competitive, and are always searching out new markets. . . . What medicine and psychiatry have done is to take essentially behavioral problems—problems of conflict between adults and children—and redefine them as medical problems."

Part of this controversy has to do with the question of the disorder's origins. Is ADHD a physical condition, like Down syndrome, rooted in a testable source? Or does it arise from a combination of factors, more along the lines of, say, Posttraumatic Stress Disorder? Or, could it be the result of our contemporary environment—the demands we've placed on children and their natural inability to meet our concept of "the norm"?

According to recent studies, about 3–8 percent of US children can be considered ADHD, or one or two in a classroom of twenty. It affects boys at a much higher ratio, around 3:1, though sources vary. Prevalent across the social and economic strata of society, it's not strictly a Western or American or contemporary phenomenon. The age of onset tends to be around three or four, though symptoms can surface earlier. Those with ADHD often suffer from other disorders, a situation called "comorbidity," including anxiety, depression, Tourette syndrome, dyslexia, and bipolar disorder. For a long time it was believed that upon reaching adulthood, the symptoms would naturally diminish, but follow-up studies that started in the 1980s now reveal that most children continue to experience some degree of impairment throughout adolescence and for the rest of their lives.

The first person to approach the symptoms and causes of ADHD in a modern, scientific manner was the early-twentieth-century physician George Frederic Still. He appears in surviving portraits as a hawkish figure, incomplete, like a man returning from some disastrous mission to the tropics: slicked hair, pencil-thin mustache, his body concealed beneath robes and a dark, flowing cape.

During a 1902 presentation at London's Royal College of Physicians, Still outlined the findings of a study on the behavioral difficulties of twenty children. He identified several symptoms of the present-day ADHD diagnosis.

"The notable feature in many of these cases," he said, "is a quite abnormal incapacity for sustained attention." He argued that such behavior could be explained by "a defect in moral control."

Still was born in 1868 London, that happening capital of the Victorian universe. He attended Cambridge; was fluent in Greek, Latin, Hebrew, and Arabic; professed a hobby of reading ancient texts in their original languages; and was knighted. He is considered the father of English pediatrics, the first to define and categorize a host of juvenile ailments, including a form of arthritis that bears his name: Still's disease. And while he was no doubt a product of his time and place, his ethical wording tends to provoke a complaint common against doctors in general: their failure to see illness—its suffering—from the perspective of the person actually being diagnosed.

»

In the spring of 1985, after the initial medical tests, my pediatrician, Dr. Atkinson, ordered a round of evaluations at Stanford University Medical Center, a kind of group therapy that I remember, most strikingly, for its pair of note-taking doctors.

These psychiatric professionals were charged with assessing my behavior. During hour-long sessions I was kept in a pen with two other children—an asphalt outdoor playground with a high chain-link fence. We were all five years old. The boy had an enormous head, his teeth were spaced unnaturally, and he wore heavy black glasses that never fell from his face, even though he couldn't stop moving, much less yelling. In contrast, the girl hardly ever spoke. She was small and frail; whenever I talked to her she'd gaze at my knees or at something behind me, her eyes surfacing as if through water. At the time I didn't understand any of it—especially why I'd been grouped together with *them*—and each new session began to feel like a mistake: soon enough the people in charge would come to their senses and realize I shouldn't be here.

These sessions lasted for about two months. On one of the last afternoons I was standing against the fence when the boy sprinted past me, heading for the girl who'd been trying, delicately, to pedal a tricycle. He grabbed the tricycle and lifted it upward, spilling her onto the blacktop. Then he leapt against the fence and began to shout.

Both doctors quickly intervened, one leading the girl inside. The other, writing on his yellow legal pad, turned to me and said, without looking up, "Timothy, would you like a turn on the tricycle?"

The tricycle was my favorite object on the playground. He knew this, of course. It was the other boy's favorite, too. Whenever things got dull, the tricycle tended to appear. But I couldn't move from the fence. The doctor kept scribbling. The boy hadn't stopped shouting. The second doctor emerged from the entrance, her eyes narrowed, keenly, on me. It was as if she could draw out and study my most alien aspect. I knew it had to do with my tantrums, and then I realized that both of these adults were waiting for me to throw one; they were betraying me. In the distance the tricycle gleamed. I was overcome with helplessness, the way I always was right before a tantrum.

Just then the session ended. My mother arrived, smiling. (They had asked her not to stay and watch.) She was always happy to see me, but this time I couldn't look at her. In the car she kept asking me how it went. I nodded, then shook my head.

"Are you hungry?" she said. "Should we stop for ice cream? Do you feel hot? Can you please tell me what's wrong?"

"What's happening?" I finally asked. "Am I sick?"

She was trying to keep her eyes on the road. "Honey," she replied. "Why would you say that?"

»

The therapy sessions ended the summer I turned six; I was about to be diagnosed and treated for the first time. Just before that I spent a week-end afternoon at a friend's house. Tony Androcetti was a boy from an Italian family very much like my own. He was dark-haired and quiet. His parents were older. We were in the backyard playing a game with a metal baseball bat: one of us would spin around, holding the bat at arm's length, before toppling to the ground. I loved it—the momentum, the dizziness, the object itself, the pine tar along the handle. During Tony's turns I would circle at an unsafe distance, wanting, even though I knew better, to reach out and snatch the bat away.

Then it was my turn. I twirled, giggling, and fell backward. But sud-denly my hand was empty. The world was swooning. I couldn't stand. There was a sound like the far-off call of a siren. It was Tony, a few feet away, his hands against his face. He pulled them aside. His right cheek, just below the eye, was already blue and swollen.

I ran inside, feeling dizziness, adrenaline; for a moment I was wor-ried I might be having a new kind of tantrum. I found Tony's mother watching television in the living room. Libby: she wore the eyeliner and red lipstick of a woman from a department store.

"Come outside!" I yelled, and she followed me.

In the backyard, Tony was sitting up, his cheek purpled, the bat alongside him. She ran across the lawn and cradled her son. Then she looked up at me and shouted, "What the fuck is wrong with you?"

I sat down in the grass next to the bat. I was waiting for a tantrum like a storm on the horizon, large enough to flood out the afternoon. But as Tony's mother lifted him up and retreated inside, the world didn't drain of color.

From the house I could hear shouts, a choked sob. It had been an ac-cident, of course, something I understood even then. Up until that point, the tantrums had felt like accidents too, arriving and departing beyond my control. They'd been occurring regularly enough, perhaps once a month, each a bit less intense than the one preceding, or so it seemed. I hated them and was always confused as to what had brought them on. But this time, when Libby said, *"What the fuck is wrong with you?"* I could no longer separate my actions, purposeful or not—good or bad— from the thing that defined me. I was crushed. What *was* wrong?

»

In the same 1902 presentation on hyperactive children at London's Royal College of Physicians, Dr. George Frederic Still, bless his cape-wearing heart, tried to walk the line.

"There is a defect of moral consciousness which cannot be accounted for by any fault of environment," he said.

He argued that the origins of hyperactivity stemmed from a lack of "volitional inhibition." Kids acted this way because they didn't have the willpower to be good. He went on to suggest that this limitation might be rooted in biological causes. Like many of his contemporaries, the good doctor was a social Darwinist; he believed that lower classes and racial minorities were inferior, physically, to those of more civilized breeding—someone who could speak five languages, for example. In Still's view, moral control represented "the highest and latest product of mental evolution": a trait that hadn't developed in impoverished children, not to mention all those bothersome savages the empire had yet to enlighten. He noted the physical abnormalities of a number of his patients: large head sizes and compulsive ticks that he referred to as "the stigmata of degeneration." In the end he theorized that the problem was centered in the brain; these children were developmentally impaired because of their inferior breeding or because they had suffered "nerve-cell alteration" through some past trauma.

Let me say this about George F. Still: His outlook was regrettable. In his robed portraits, his face was that of a leering uncle. But he does seem to have stumbled in the direction of a more scientific explanation for what we now call ADHD.

At the time, Sigmund Freud's theories of mental illness were in ascendancy. The ego, the unconscious, neurosis, repression, and a multitude of complexes were meant to explain our actions in an environmental light; Freud believed that the root cause of a behavior such as hyperactivity resided within the mystery of human experience, as opposed to the physical structure of the equally mysterious organ tasked with processing it.

Still's theory on physical causes represented a fresh starting point for future researchers. The encephalitis epidemic of 1918 offered additional evidence: children who managed to survive the disease—their brains swelling horrifically—exhibited many of the symptoms he'd outlined, along with a host of others. Further support was provided by frontal lobe ablation studies: observations of monkeys with lesions along these hemispheres. Researchers began developing the link between behavior and biology. In 1947, Dr. Alfred Strauss, a psychiatrist and neuroscientist working in Racine, Wisconsin, identified hyperactivity as one of the most prominent symptoms of children who'd suffered documented damage to their brains; as for all other cases of hyperactivity—i.e., those lacking documentation—he claimed that such behavior could be the result of minimal brain damage (MBD, also known as "minimal brain dysfunction"), which was undetectable with certain instruments at his disposal. This was perhaps the first official term to describe hyperactive children.

With MBD, the brain of the hyperactive child is seen as a static thing, broken at some point in the past and incapable of developing in any measurable capacity. The therapeutic goal becomes the management of immediate surroundings. Which makes MBD a prognosis in the strictest sense: a prediction of how things will go. It's as if the problematic behavior was sunk into a child's very core, where biology meets personality: identity beyond repair.

Today we know that the millions of American children diagnosed with ADHD did not contract it as a result of blows to the head. In Dr. Alfred Strauss's time, brain damage was thought to be a much more unified concept—one with overarching symptoms, the most common of which was considered hyperactivity.

》

The summer I turned six, Dr. Atkinson completed his series of tests. Then he referred me to a psychiatrist in Los Gatos for a final evaluation. Dr. Frank Smythe—a skinny man in his sixties—was, in my mother's words, "the biggest asshole ever." She couldn't stand the way he talked down to her. Local psychologists didn't like working with him either because he never incorporated anyone else's behavioral input. Briefly, he examined me. Then he offered his diagnosis: In 1985, more than half a century removed from encephalitis epidemics and ablation studies, this man told my mother that I was suffering from minimal brain damage.

She didn't freak out, as I'd like to imagine, didn't pull at her hair and shout, *Not Timmy's brain!* She knew enough already to ignore what the term implied: that I was suffering from some trauma inflicted on my frontal lobes. And while it was absurd of Smythe to use the term, older doctors at the time would still employ it as a catchall description for hyperactivity, in the way that ADD is now often used in place of ADHD, despite the fact that Strauss's theory had long since been debunked.

Throughout the 1960s, tension persisted between the organic and environmental explanations for ADHD; meanwhile, medical research looked for causes within the brain's structure and nervous system. The second edition of the *DSM* labeled it "Hyperkinetic Reaction of Childhood," a term that implied familial and social causes. Then in 1980, the *DSM-III*—a revolutionary document in the world of psychiatry—helped solidify the long-developing view that the causes of mental suffering could reside, at least in part, within the human body's chemistry.

Hyperactivity was completely reclassified as a subtype under the newly coined (and since revised) Attention Deficit Disorder. Additional diagnostic criteria were provided—a detailed, categorical approach that could be employed by all levels of medical professionals, including pediatricians. As a result, funding for research increased dramatically; now doctors had a more coherent framework in which to recognize and treat the symptoms, though how they utilized such information was another matter entirely.

Dr. Smythe had a treatment in mind, but first he wanted to run one more test: a sleep-deprived electroencephalogram (EEG) to measure brain patterns. My parents were tasked with keeping me awake an entire night. I still remember their extraordinary proclamation: No bedtime! I thought of it then as a reward, even though I couldn't figure out what I'd done to deserve it.

The night started off well enough. My father had recently purchased a VCR, promoting its life-changing applications to anyone who would listen ("Hey Timmo, now you can watch *Scooby-Doo whenever you want!*"). So he rented movies and invited over his best friend, Carlo Silvera, who'd played baseball and football with him at Santa Clara. Carlo was Catholic, from a Portuguese family and, as my mother always liked to point out, was raised by women; she enjoyed his careful but no less emotional perspective on life.

We ate a large dinner. My sister fell asleep. I snacked on candy. My father drank beer. Around eight my mother went to bed; she'd take the late shift. By eleven I was nodding off. More candy. Movies ran in a continuous flicker. Then jumping jacks, twenty questions, even a game of tag. Soon enough I was being shaken awake at intervals by my father, a sensation like falling through the heft of the world, then being yanked all the way back to a life that, until then, had been delicately, if inelegantly designed. And I was overcome by the same emotion I'd felt on the Stanford playground: once again the known universe had reversed itself, except this time it was instigated by the people I knew best, which heightened the sense of betrayal.

"I want to go to sleep," I said to my father.

His eyes were heavy, blinking, the television a distant murmur. "What?"

"Daddy."

"Yeah."

"Am I in trouble? Are you mad at me?"

He looked up from the TV. "Say that again?"

"Please!" I stomped my foot. My wrist caught a beer bottle. It clinked against another and another until one fell to the floor and shattered.

My father jumped up. So did Carlo Silvera.

"Why don't I take him outside for a bit?" Carlo said.

Just then my mother emerged in the kitchen light, her nightgown an unearthly yellow. I knew what was about to happen. Desperately, I wanted to apologize—for the broken glass, my attitude, the tantrums in general. Even then my concept of right and wrong had a distinctly Catholic slant, something I'd gleaned from Sunday school. If only my parents would yell at me instead of each other, everything could go back to normal.

She glanced at the bottles on the counter. "How many beers have you had?"

"Not enough?" My father smiled at his own joke.

"You're so drunk you're breaking things?"

"Go back to bed," he said. "We're handling it."

"I can see that."

He pointed at her. "Go back to bed!"

In the next moment they both started shouting, each finding fault with the other's approach to the problem—me—while Carlo picked me up and headed out the front door. I wanted to run in between them and yell, "Look!" And somehow reveal the boy I really was. Maybe then they'd stop trying so hard to fix me. But Carlo and I were already moving toward the sidewalk. The horizon was distant, its arch of lights: downtown San Jose, the mountains beyond. I'd never been outside so late at night.

"When I was your age," Carlo said calmly, setting me down, "I used to climb onto the roof of our house. Have I ever told you about that?"

He'd grown up only a few miles north of here. His father was a boxer who died young from brain damage inflicted in the ring. Carlo was raised by his mother and Portuguese grandmother, who were even more emotional than my Italian relatives. As a child he was willful. So were the women in charge. When the fights got really bad—everyone shouting, crying—he'd simply crawl out the window and spend the night on the roof where the women couldn't reach him.

"In the morning when I came down, they acted like nothing happened," he said.

I was walking alongside him, listening, barely awake. Then I heard my name. "Timmy." We turned around. My mother was standing outside in her nightgown, calling us both.

The next morning, we arrived at our local hospital just as the sun was coming up. I hadn't slept. I was, to put it mildly, a mess. My mother no longer remembers Smythe's explanation for ordering the test. It was probably an attempt to eliminate any remaining possibility of epilepsy, but she thinks that he was actually looking to confirm his diagnosis that I had a damaged brain—which is how she explained it to me at the time, in a watered-down version, of course.

I was taken into a white room. The EEG scanner sat in the corner.

"I don't like that thing," I said.

The nurse planted sensors along my scalp and across my forehead and temples, the wires trailing back to the machine.

I turned to my mother and said, "It's going to read my mind."

"Timmy!"

"Turn it off," I told her.

"Honey, everything's okay. It's just a test."

She patted me on the back and began to sing softly. And then I saw myself from a distance: a small, scrutinized shadow. Something oily was being hooked and drawn out of my chest.

I opened my eyes, blinking. There was nothing I could do; the machine was ruthless. It was looking into the deepest part of me. And I understood the message being transmitted along the veil of wires, spoken as if in my own tongue: *I am evil.*

»

If we've spent the last hundred years working toward a medical model of mental illness, where, exactly, have we arrived with ADHD?

Technology has helped to sketch a crude map. Thanks to advanced forms of neuroimaging, we have a better idea about which regions of the brain influence hyperactivity: the prefrontal cortices, the structure responsible for big-picture stuff; the basal ganglia, its subcortical weave housing our comprehension of consequences and our impulsivity, along with the ability to interrupt behavior like a tantrum; then the corpus callosum, a ribbon of thick fibers connecting the hemispheres; and finally the cerebellum, involved in among other things timing, patience, and the ability to learn from mistakes.

However, a complex behavior such as hyperactivity does not originate in a single region but rather in how those regions interact, their communication facilitated by neurotransmitters like dopamine, serotonin, and norepinephrine. The brain, in its assemblage of clearly labeled destinations, is much better characterized as the result of its own multiple pathways. Such combinations are finite but at times our most essential organ can seem like the perfect paradox: too intricate, perhaps, to perceive the extent of its own intricacy.

But over the last two decades, studies have begun to show disparities in both structure and transport. Dr. F. Xavier Castellanos has found that in ADHD children overall brain volume is less, by about 5 percent, a reduction that increases to 10–12 percent within key structures like the prefrontal cortices, basal ganglia, and the center of the cerebellum. There's also a deficit in communication: how neurotransmitters are used and stored, especially dopamine, which is thought to modulate the complex circuits of reward-response behavior. So while the brain is constantly changing, and a toddler can seem hyperactive and inattentive compared to a six-year-old, and a teenager compared to an adult, certain vital pathways appear to be developing at a slower rate in children with ADHD.

Two decades of research by the Harvard Medical School psychologists Stephen V. Faraone and Joseph Biederman, including an analysis of over twenty previous studies of twins with ADHD, show that the disorder is overwhelmingly inherited—nearly 80 percent, which is greater than most forms of mental illness.

"For comparison," Dr. Russell A. Barkley writes, "consider that this figure rivals that for the role of genetics in human height."

Which is not surprising—after all, the development of the brain, like eye color, ear size, or the inglorious hook of a nose, follows a template established the moment we first become ourselves. The pertinent genes are thought to govern neurotransmitters: their transport, reuptake, and creation in key areas of the brain. And yet, unlike Down syndrome or Huntington's disease, where the cause can be tested, the genetic origins of ADHD may never be isolated in a single source. As with all neural mechanics, the triggering mechanism is interaction. It's called the G x E effect: the complex exchange between our genes and the environment.

Which gives way to the non-biological aspect of the equation.

"These types of genetic influences on ADHD are probabilistic, not deterministic," Dr. Joel T. Nigg writes.

Our brains develop along a genetic blueprint, but they can also change shape according to the events they're processing. To quote a common metaphor: Biology loads the gun, environment pulls the trigger. Or, as the developmental neuropsychologist Dr. Bruce F. Pennington states, "We do not have evidence that the social environment in general, or parenting practices in particular, can directly cause ADHD. At the same time, there is no doubt that the social environment influences the course of ADHD—especially whether ADHD develops into another disruptive behavior disorder, such as conduct disorder."

So the G x E interaction helps explain most cases—but not all. The remainder fall perilously close to earlier misconceptions, and allow us now, from the enlightenment of our contemporary perch, to offer a begrudging shout-out to Still, Strauss, and all the rest of those dead white doctors who spent their days slicing ever so thinly the organic roots of

ADHD: up to 20 percent of children suffering from the disorder may have acquired their symptoms from external issues like low birth weight, maternal smoking, fetal alcohol syndrome, lead exposure, and, in some rare cases, head injury.

Is it enough, then, to say that hyperactivity is the result of a genetic predisposition that's influenced, but not caused, by the environments we find ourselves growing up in? It makes sense on an intuitive level: all you have to do is gaze up at the many branches of your family tree. Mine? The uncles in legal trouble; cousins struggling to finish high school; a whole host of athletes, blue-collar workers, and salesmen. They are not simply the byproducts of social factors; they share personality traits—engaging, impulsive, unpretentious, and mildly manic—that have been carried forward for generations.

〉〉

After my sleepless night's EEG, Dr. Smythe prescribed five milligrams of methylphenidate—Ritalin. Dr. Atkinson would oversee its administration. My mother had heard about the drug; she thought it was a new approach to treating hyperactivity, but she was hesitant to put me on it. She was worried about my response to drugs in general, a sensitivity she shares. Already I'd had a paradoxical reaction to the over-the-counter antihistamine Benadryl; when she gave it to me for a cold, I spent hours jumping around my room, even though the main side effect is drowsiness. I also broke out in hives after taking the antibiotic amoxicillin. And these were familiar drugs. She'd never had any experience with Ritalin. The whole idea confused her.

"Why would a child who can't sit still become *calmer* on a stimulant?" she asked Smythe.

He explained something about "contraindications" and moved on.

Eventually, despite their reservations, she and my father agreed to try it.

During the first week I was kept at home. Outside of day care—the structure, its demands—it was difficult to tell just how well the Ritalin was working. But every evening, I became extremely irritated, refusing even the simplest requests. After a few days my mother called Dr. Atkinson's office. He said it was a rebound effect: the suppressed symptoms were returning more forcefully as the drug left my system. He compared it to how people tend to feel tired when the sugar or caffeine they've ingested wears off.

On the fifth day—with my father at work and my two-year-old sister playing in her bedroom—my mother asked me to come to the dinner table. I wanted to finish the television show I was watching. I wasn't hungry.

"Leave me alone," I told her. She spoke softly, counting to three. "Shut up!" I shouted. She reached down. I began to scream, writhe. I probably weighed about forty-five pounds, small enough to be subdued. But I jumped to my feet and darted from the room. She found me at the silverware drawer, grabbing a butter knife.

My mother approached from behind. I wheeled around. She stopped. I placed the knife against my wrist.

"I'm going to kill myself," I said.

In the next instant my mother wrapped her arms around me. She held on until I stopped struggling. Then she called Dr. Atkinson and left a frantic message. She also called Dr. Smythe. His receptionist took her information. And she waited.

》

How would you respond if your own son, in the midst of taking a stimulant for hyperactivity, told you he was going to kill himself? Ritalin may be the catalyst, but in what sense? Could it be a matter of dosage—the "rebound" effect exacerbated in some extreme manner? How does a six-year-old even know about suicide?

My mother says I looked like a robot. As I stood in the kitchen with the butter knife at my wrist, my eyes were blank, my body rigid. This was nothing like the previous tantrums—it wasn't *me*—and she recognized the difference.

The next day we drove to Dr. Atkinson's office. Dr. Smythe had still refused to call her back, claiming through his secretary that such issues should be dealt with by her pediatrician. In fact, my mother never spoke to him again.

Dr. Atkinson gave me a brief physical examination—tapped knees, a light to the eyes, ears, some hearty coughs. Afterward I sat in an adjoining waiting room that always smelled like suntan lotion, no matter the season.

"Okay," my mother said to the doctor once I was out of earshot. "Tell me why this happened."

Dr. Atkinson began explaining the "rebound" issue again: how my reaction, in this context, was normal enough.

"You think a six-year-old threatening to kill himself is normal?" she said.

He asked if she might want to keep her voice down. A number of variables could have led to my behavior, and the worst thing she could do now, he said, was to abandon the course of treatment they'd spent so long preparing.

"Are you kidding me?" she said.

He wanted to try a lower dosage. Maybe breaking the pill in two and taking it at intervals would soften the impact. If this didn't work there was also Dexedrine: an amphetamine that was supposed to last longer than Ritalin.

"No," she told him. "He's not some guinea pig."

"His problems aren't simply going to disappear," he replied.

She stood up to leave. And with a flourish, she turned to Dr. Atkinson and asked, "Have you been listening to a word I've said?"

Let me say this about my suicide threat: it's a blank spot. When I was told about it the next day, I don't think I understood what I had done or what it meant. I do remember the uneasiness in my father's voice when he sat down to talk to me about it, but, try as I might, I can't recall the emotion. It lacks shape; unlike the earlier tantrums, there's no point of departure, no return. To tell you the truth, in the aftermath of the incident I remember feeling better, which had everything to do with my mother. Somehow she had managed, in the brilliant way that parents have of stabilizing the world, to make me believe that Ritalin was to blame—for all of it.

»

The following week, we stayed home together, my mother and me. My sister was at day care, my father working. I remember it like a vacation. Something had gone wrong. We'd tried to fix it. But it had made whatever was wrong worse. Now we weren't doing anything at all: no more doctors, tests, therapy, pills—even the variable of preschool had been removed. In the mornings we'd watch cartoons together, eat cereal, build forts, and fill in coloring books. My mother would tell lengthy, imaginative stories. In the afternoons, following a nap, we'd walk outside and pick dandelions from the heated sidewalk. It was as if we'd struck a truce: there were still skirmishes over minor issues—nap time, dessert, television—but really, for this one week, I could do whatever I wanted.

It was the end of August. I was about to start kindergarten at St. Lucy's, a Catholic school five miles up the freeway from our house. My mother needed to get back to work; we missed the money from her retail job. I knew it was temporary, that my problems weren't magically cured. The EEG scan had been the climax: the evil logic of clenched hands, grating teeth, profound and irredeemable in the most simplistic way—something that even for a six-year-old was more comprehensible than you might imagine.

On one of our last afternoons together, we were still wearing our pajamas, an extravagance allowed after my nap. The summer light was shadowed in clear shapes along the carpet. The radio was playing a Madonna song, "Lucky Star," just as my father was coming home from work, carrying my sister; he looked up to discover me and my mother in the living room, dancing. My sister screeched, struggling to join us. It felt spontaneous; I hadn't even realized how much fun we were having until that moment. And as the lyrics rose precipitously my mother flashed an enormous smile, a gesture for my father, for all of us.

"Patty?" he said. Madonna's childlike, theatrical voice. My mother clapping to the beat.

Finally my father smiled. He swung my sister, offered me a high five. When the song was over, we followed my mother into the kitchen and, just like any other night, we ate dinner together as a family.

2

Reflection in the Low Linoleum Glaze

In 1985, stimulants weren't the only treatment option for ADHD. That summer my mother heard about a child psychiatrist, Laurie Hamilton, who'd developed her own system of therapy specifically aimed at hyperactive children. My mother contacted Laurie and told her about my reaction to Ritalin, and an appointment was set; I'd begin seeing Laurie the same week I started school.

On my first day of kindergarten, my father left early to drop off my sister at day care. My mother and I took our time getting ready; we ate cereal and watched cartoons just as we had the week before.

St. Lucy's was located between strip malls and a clamoring stretch of interstate. I'd been attending Sunday school there for a few years. It was where I developed my all-or-nothing sense of good and evil. Most of the building dated from the 1950s: a low-slung structure of hallways and classrooms arranged around concrete courtyards. The parking lot and basketball courts merged into an expanse of haphazard lanes that led to the kindergarten entrance. My mother worked at a retail store across the street.

We were already a few minutes late. The main courtyard was empty. I stepped out of the car wearing new corduroys and a collared shirt, the school's stiff uniform. The morning fog hadn't cleared, and the blacktop was darkened, slick, the buildings a distant blue. For a moment it felt like we were crossing over water.

"Isn't this exciting?" my mother said. She pulled me gently by the hand. But as we neared the door, I let go. I could hear voices.

"You're going to leave me here?" I asked.

My mother bent down, eyes level to mine, her necklace a brief cascade. "Timmy," she said. "I'm happy to stay as long as you want."

She pushed the door open to reveal a large crowd inside. Child after child drifted by me, adults too, like faces on the same circling body. We crossed the carpet, past small tables, toys gathered in bins, and alphabet posters along the wall. Everything smelled like crayon wax.

A tall boy walked up to me. He smiled, his two front teeth jutting outward, and said, "I'm Brendan." Two more boys joined us. Their names were Tim Shelley and Tim Gallo.

"Three Tims!" I shouted.

They were looking up at Brendan, who was a full head taller than me. I nodded at him. He nodded back. I reached up and touched the hair just above his ear. He laughed.

"What are you doing?" asked one of the Tims.

But I was already gone, touching each of the chairs, tapping crayons, and dragging my palm against the wall. For the next few minutes I circled the entire classroom, making contact with everything.

Finally I felt a hand on my shoulder. It was my mother's. "Timmy," she said. "Timmy, look at me." Gently, she placed a name tag on my chest. "You be sure to tell the teacher if you don't feel well. Okay?"

"What do you mean?"

"You know, if you're having a tough time with anything."

Behind her Brendan Tanger was holding up his hands. The Tims were jumping to reach them. I ran toward them.

"Timmy," my mother said.

Brendan offered me his palm: a high, backlit target. I jumped, slapping as hard as I possibly could. My mother walked over to my teacher and introduced herself; already they were discussing the new therapy I was about to begin.

》

When I first started therapy with Laurie Hamilton, she was in her thirties. She had grown up in the town next to ours. In the 1970s, as a psychology graduate student at Stanford, she was struck by the increasing number of children being prescribed stimulants, so she wrote a grant request to the National Institute of Mental Health (NIMH): for her dissertation she wanted to compare medication to a therapy that she'd tailored for hyperactivity.

Laurie's program worked in three ways:

1. Parents met with her weekly to go over child-management techniques such as behavior charts, reward systems, and conflict resolutions, with a goal of establishing an all-encompassing structure that depended on support from the teacher;

2. Every day a note decorated with *Star Wars* characters went home from school documenting behavior on a scale from 1 to 5. This note included categories like "sits still," "takes turns," and "refrains from shouting out," and a section at the bottom was reserved for comments;

3. In therapy sessions held on the school grounds, she worked directly with the children, teaching a curriculum of more than thirty individual techniques for anger management, relaxation, impulse response, and self-control.

Laurie hoped this new treatment would prove that stimulants were un-
necessary. She studied eight boys, ages nine to eleven, over a six-month
period. Some of the subjects improved so drastically that they were able
to discontinue Ritalin. Others saw their doses reduced. A few, however,
actually needed to be on higher amounts of medication, which was difficult for her to accept. But Laurie was pragmatic, and if her therapy didn't
yield results, she was willing to work alongside a psychiatrist she trusted
to find the right titration and provide continual feedback on Ritalin's effectiveness.

My biggest problem was the tantrums. I was still experiencing them
every so often—the last had occurred a few months earlier—and my
mother was worried that whenever her phone rang at work, it was a nun
calling to inform her that I'd been screaming for minutes on end.

At St. Lucy's, each grade consisted of a single teacher and anywhere
from fifteen to twenty-five students. Pat Hartinger taught my kindergarten class. She was a tall, long-necked woman maybe a decade older than
my mother, her hair cropped short at the back. Her shoulders were like
a swimmer's, surprisingly broad. When she smiled you could see her
gums. At the time she seemed enormous.

One morning during our first month, we were working at tables—but
allowed to move around the room as we pleased—when Mrs. Hartinger
announced that it was reading time. We sat down quietly on the carpet.
As she narrated from a large book with glossy pictures, I started to tap
my foot. I shifted positions, sighed, clicked my tongue. Even the slightest
movement felt like a release. From what? The setup was exhausting, the
sustained attention, but I found the story interesting enough. For a moment I'd hang on every detail. Then I'd roll on my side like a house cat
and stretch both legs. It went on this way until suddenly Mrs. Hartinger
stopped reading. The other students turned to look at me. I stood up.

"She's not finished," someone said.

There must have been similar moments in day care and at home with
my mother. Restlessness in six-year-olds is expected to a certain degree,
and the structure of a kindergarten classroom takes this into account.

Still, at that instant I felt like I did after the tantrums—jarred back into a version of the world that I didn't know I had left.

"We're almost done," Mrs. Hartinger said.

I sunk to the carpet. This time I stared intently at the pictures. Rabbits! They were huge, impeccably dressed, their faces serious and toothy. I imagined a farmhouse and the garden.

"But which one's the uncle?" I heard myself saying.

Again, the teacher stopped and my classmates glanced around, confused.

Finally it was time for a break. Everyone headed outside through the bright glass doors. Mrs. Hartinger asked me to stay back.

"Do you understand why the other kids got upset?" she asked.

I nodded hastily. More than anything I couldn't bear being separated from the group. But she was standing over me, a canopy of shoulders and white elbows in the morning light.

"Is this going to go on my note home?" I asked.

She arched her neck. "I think we can wait until the end of the day to decide." Then she straightened up, and I sprinted away.

>>

When it comes to a disorder like ADHD, it's important to remember that "treatment" is a relatively modern concept. Up until recently, extreme behavior was explained along one of two lines: the moral view and the biological view. From the moral point of view, a person is mentally ill because he or she is inhabited by a demon. From the biological point of view, the brain is infected by a disease or damaged beyond repair. Either way, the prospect of a cure falls outside the scope of human agency. It was only a few hundred years ago when afflicted adults and children were chained or collared in their homes, beaten, thrown into pits—caged and separated from everyone else.

Eventually, spurred by the Enlightenment values of the eighteenth century, individuals with varying degrees of mental illness were removed to asylums. The goal wasn't simply isolation; a calm, structured environment was meant to be therapeutic. And starting in the nineteenth century, these settings offered the chance to apply what we now call psychotherapy: the establishment of a close relationship between a doctor and a patient that could lead to increased self-awareness through the power of suggestion.

But by the twentieth century, most asylums were overcrowded and poorly run, such as the notorious Georgia State Sanatorium at Milledgeville, which would grow to house eight thousand patients.

"Psychiatry was at a dead end," the medical historian Edward Shorter writes in *A History of Psychiatry.* "Its practitioners were concentrated for the most part in asylums, and asylums had become mainly warehouses in which any hope of therapy was illusory."

Enter Sigmund Freud. In retrospect his timing was perfect. Freud was born in Austria in 1856. After considering a career in law, he decided to attend medical school at the University of Vienna, where he conducted research into the reproductive organs of eels. He also published a paper on cocaine's therapeutic applications. Eventually he settled into the field of neurology, which at the time was focused on the treatment of psychiatric conditions such as hysteria.

In the 1890s, Freud began formulating his famous version of psychotherapy—psychoanalysis—while seeing members of the Viennese middle class for various neuroses. Based on the notion that repressed traumatic experiences, usually sexual, can create unconscious complexes and influence behavior in damaging ways, his treatment sought to unearth the source of this trauma and redirect the resulting emotions. In adults he employed techniques like dream analysis and free association. He would meet with his patients in a demure residential office, where they would recline on a leather chaise lounge, six times a week for fifty minutes a day. Such intimacy was revolutionary: a style of interaction that was impossible in the asylum.

Freud was one of the first psychiatrists to emphasize the importance of childhood experiences. He usually did so as a way of explaining the onset of neurosis and psychosis in adults. But over his career he also treated a small number of children for their behavioral problems. In a 1909 case study titled "Analysis of Phobia in a Five-Year-Old Boy," Freud introduced us to Hans, a "little Oedipus" living with his parents and younger sister in Austria. For more than a hundred pages Freud documented how Hans was suffering from a repressed erotic attraction to his mother that had manifested, consciously, as a fear of animals . . . and their enormous penises.

"The reason he was afraid of horses now was that he had taken so much interest in their widdlers. He himself had noticed that it was not right to be so very much preoccupied with widdlers, even with his own, and he was quite right in thinking this."

Freud and Hans's father, also a psychoanalyst, analyzed the boy's dreams, particularly those about a "crumpled giraffe," which they interpreted as a symbol of an oversize vagina. But their clearest window into the child's behavior arrived in the form of "play therapy." They took notes as Hans used a penknife to slice apart the legs of his favorite rubber doll, Grete. Freud concluded that he and the father must explain to Hans the process of birth: "So long as the child is in ignorance of the female genitals, there is naturally a vital gap in his comprehension of sexual matters." A birds-and-the-bees conversation took place, and the boy, after a brief argument, accepted the explanation; his unconscious desires were transferred to his conscious mind. From then on, Freud assured us, Hans was no longer afraid of the many well-endowed horses clomping through the streets of Vienna.

In 1909, psychoanalysis was starting to gain worldwide notice. That year, Freud and Carl Jung visited America for the first time. Play therapy would eventually be applied to all types of childhood disorders, including ADHD. The analyst would observe a young boy in a sandbox and deduce subconscious motives—how a decision to scoop here or there revealed a deeper environmental cause. It's similar to what I personally experienced in 1985, in that terrifying pen at Stanford University: the doctors trying to evaluate my unconscious mind. I was the same age as little Hans, separated by seventy-five years, a period of time that would witness Sigmund Freud's approach to therapy rise and fall as the dominant treatment for mental illness in America.

»

During my initial months at St. Lucy's, my parents and I met with Laurie on a weekly schedule. The behavior-rating scores on the notes home hovered in the lowest range. Out of the fifteen or so children, I was the slowest to adjust. Still, when it came to the classroom, I had yet to experience one of the severe tantrums that had defined the previous year. Not that they'd vanished.

I remember a winter morning, the sky backlit; I was sprinting ahead of everyone through the big glass doors. It was our first break of the day, and I loved the transition, rushing from our heated classroom to the deep-set panorama of the playground.

At this point I was spending most of my time with Brendan Tanger, the child I first met with the two Tims. But during these outdoor breaks, I most wanted to be near the Tims. Every recess I'd run up to them and start babbling. Usually they'd ignore me.

Tim Shelley was birdlike and pale, with freckled cheeks. He didn't talk much. Tim Gallo's large Italian family had lived in San Jose for generations and owned several grocery stores. In class he liked to help Mrs. Hartinger pass out supplies. He was an appealing, cooperative boy with dirty hair and black eyes, his skin always darker at his neck.

I spotted the two Tims in a corner of the playground and ran up to where they were kneeling over something in the gravel. "S. D. G.!" I shouted—our last initials. It was how I greeted them.

They didn't respond. They were poking at a dragonfly, its wings peeled from its body, the trunk vibrating like some fantastic machine.

Tim S. brushed it with his finger. I was reaching too.

"Don't," Tim G. said.

I hardly heard him. The bug was beating itself into the dirt.

Gallo stood up and pushed me back. I staggered, recovered. He shoved me again. His face was tight and angry. I understood what it meant—I was seeing myself, starkly, from his perspective.

"Be nice!" I yelled. I started crying.

Tim G. laughed. So did Tim S. And then it happened, in a fresh way: the sky shrinking down, the playground shadowed. The Tims were colorless. I couldn't bear how far away they seemed: a clean, inaccessible sense of distance. I jumped up, clawing and screaming, and the next thing I knew I was being lifted off the ground by Mrs. Hartinger: she'd descended, with her strong wrists, to pry us apart.

»

Like most mental disorders, ADHD has its core symptoms: impulsiveness, inattention, and excessive motor activity. But it's also a developmental condition, best understood in comparison to the standard behavior of a child's specific age group. In *Interventions for ADHD*, the educational psychologist Phyllis Anne Teeter writes, "Development in the middle childhood stage is characterized by complexity and increased expectations for self-control, cooperation, compliance, and independence."

She's talking about the ages of six to twelve. For hyperactive children, the developmental lag—the way the disorder causes them to differ from everyone else—interferes with the overall process of maturation in two main areas: social and academic. As a result, "a number of secondary problems can emerge—aggression, low self-esteem, academic failure, depression, and/or social isolation."

So ADHD has two sets of symptoms. The first can fuel the second; together, they can create an enormous amount of conflict. It's an important distinction in terms of treatment; when I was prescribed Ritalin, the goal was to target the core symptoms, but Laurie's system shifted the focus to secondary symptoms: the area between my initial response to the world and how everyone else reacted to it. Her management techniques emphasized the steps I could take when my behavior instigated conflicts with my parents, teachers, and peers.

She and I continued to meet once a week throughout my first year of school. We'd walk along the perimeter of the playground, a half-hour session consisting mostly of dialogue. She tended to ask open-ended questions, and with her dark, stylish hair and sharp chin, she resembled an academic aunt. I resented our sessions on principle—being separated from everyone else—but before I knew it, I'd be telling her all the things that had happened since we last met.

By the spring, I found myself getting into a fistfight every month or so. They were often centered on the Tims, took place outside the classroom, and were broken up by Mrs. Hartinger. Recapping them to Laurie, I made sure to emphasize exactly what the other boys had done. She'd listen patiently.

"But how did you feel in the moment?" I remember her asking during a session just before school got out for the summer.

"What do you mean?"

"Well," she said, shading her eyes. "Can you describe it to me?"

At this time of year the playground was especially dry. Smog blurred the shadows in the mountains. Above, the sky was the color of the sun. "I know I need to think before I act," I said, something I'd heard from my father.

She laughed. "But isn't that a little difficult?"

I shrugged. At the end of our sessions I would always start to focus on the school door, antsy to get back inside, even if, once there, I immediately wanted to be out on the playground again.

"The next time you get upset," Laurie said, "you might want to try something I learned from athletes when they get angry on the field."

"Really?"

"Direct from the soccer players themselves on the San Jose Earthquakes. For ten seconds I want you to tense a muscle and then relax, exhaling deeply."

I tried it out, starting with my hands, moving to my arms, shoulders, forehead, jaws, legs, feet, and chest.

"Pretend you're a balloon," she said. "Slowly reach your full size. Now hold it. Keep the balloon filled up, ready to burst. Now release the air, slowly."

By the time I finished, we were standing near the entrance.

"How do you feel?" she asked.

"Fine." It was true. The playground was bare and bright, the doors no longer a magnet.

"Try it the next time you find yourself getting upset at one of your classmates," she said.

》

Laurie's approach to ADHD was based on the psychotherapeutic method: like Freud, she was seeking to foster a sense of intimacy that would allow for suggestion. The detail and focus of her system, however, went much further than an informative chat on human reproduction.

Freud's play therapy represented one of the earliest formal attempts to treat ADHD. Its goal was to cure primary symptoms. But from the very beginning, his methods failed to have an effect on the many disorders we now understand to be influenced by biology. The singular environmental cause he was searching to unearth and transfer didn't actually exist. And no amount of awareness—sexual or otherwise—would make a child fidget less.

But in the first part of the twentieth century there weren't many options. The asylum-style approach was still being used, and in the most extreme cases, troubled young children were removed from society altogether and placed in residential centers. One of the best funded of these was the Emma Pendleton Bradley Home (now Bradley Hospital) in East

Providence, Rhode Island, founded by the wealthy George Bradley in 1931 and named after his neurologically impaired daughter. Its mission was to care for impoverished boys and girls with psychiatric and behavioral conditions.

George's great-nephew Dr. Charles Bradley was its medical director, and a large number of children displaying ADHD-like symptoms came under his care. Bradley started looking beyond psychotherapy for treatment and ran extensive medical diagnostics on his patients, including an extremely painful procedure called a "pneumoencephalogram," in which cerebrospinal fluid was drawn from the skull and replaced with air to better highlight the shape of the brain in X-rays. The aftereffects included debilitating headaches, which Bradley medicated with Benzedrine, a type of amphetamine, thinking it might increase the regeneration of spinal fluid.

Amphetamine was first isolated in an 1887 Berlin laboratory by the Romanian researcher Lazăr Edeleanu. A stimulant, it was initially prescribed for ailments as diverse as heart blockage and seasickness, and by the 1930s the drug was available under the trademark Benzedrine in bronchial inhalers. One of its known effects was an increase in blood pressure, which was why Dr. Bradley thought it would help with the spinal-tap headaches.

The headaches continued nevertheless, but it soon became apparent that the children taking the drug were performing much better on their schoolwork. So Dr. Bradley set up a controlled study to determine the extent of this phenomenon, which was subsequently published in a 1937 issue of the *American Journal of Psychiatry.* One dose of twenty milligrams of Benzedrine was administered orally to twenty-one boys and nine girls, five to fourteen years old. The medication was taken in the morning and would last, in some cases, for up to twelve hours.

"The behavior and school performance of many of the 30 children who received the drug underwent a dramatic change," he wrote, "characterized by increased interest in schoolwork, better work habits, and a significant reduction in disruptive behavior."

Almost two thirds of the participants finished their homework more quickly and accurately. Others showed social improvement like diminished moods swings and better attitudes. A few offered spontaneous remarks: "I start to make my bed and before I know it, it is done." And: "I feel peppy." The children themselves noticed the effects and called the medicine "arithmetic pills."

"To see a single dose of Benzedrine produce a greater improvement in school performance than the combined efforts of a capable staff working in a most favorable setting," Bradley wrote, "would have been all but demoralizing to the teachers had not the improvement been so gratifying from a practical viewpoint."

A pediatrician by trade, Dr. Bradley had studied in Philadelphia before completing his residency at Babies Hospital in New York. There's a picture of him in a 1998 article in the *American Journal of Psychiatry*. In it he is gazing at a slight angle to the camera, his face handsomely proportioned: rimless glasses, clear forehead, hair combed neatly back. It's a strikingly modern angle; in his dark suit and patterned tie, he resembles an actor—someone captured, briefly, in the role of a prewar psychiatrist—the diligent eyes, wry lines of the lips; in his hands, an open book. You might think the photographer caught him by surprise, until you realize he's looking directly at you.

Dr. Charles Bradley's ultimate goal was to improve the daily well-being of his patients. But certain aspects of his findings troubled him. He wondered why the Benzedrine had made hyperactive children calmer—"It appears paradoxical that a drug known to be a stimulant should produce subdued behavior"—though he speculated that it might have to do with the nervous system, which he thought might affect "voluntary control." A large section of his article was devoted to documenting the side effects. Six of the children suffered sleep disruptions; "loss of appetite and nausea at the time of the morning meal were observed in a few"; three patients were found to cry more frequently; "two others were noted to wear worried expressions quite foreign to their usual appearance"—one of whom "was at times fearful of death." Out of the thirty treated, a single child "responded to the medication by becoming more hyperactive, aggressive, and irritable."

"In spite of the attractive results," he concluded, "it seems wise to await more complete knowledge of the action of Benzedrine before recommending its clinical use in behavior problem children."

»

At the heart of any treatment for mental illness is a simple equation: How do you achieve the most good while inflicting the least amount of harm? Like Dr. Charles Bradley, Laurie Hamilton was seeking to improve my day-to-day functioning. But instead of applying a single therapy, she adapted a wide array of methods to treat ADHD. And yet, after nearly a year, my primary symptoms remained. I'd still fidget at my desk, shout out whatever I was thinking, and leave my seat impulsively. The fistfights had taken the place of the tantrums—at their core was the sense of a terrifying descent—and the trigger was other children: the way they grew annoyed at my behavior or rejected my presence altogether.

But now I was responding to these symptoms differently. Following a conflict, I didn't immediately assume that there was something wrong deep inside of me, as I'd done a year earlier with Tony Androcetti and his mother. I still had a feeling that I was different than everyone else, sure— especially when the Tims and I started arguing or Mrs. Hartinger kept me inside during recess—but not in the sense of *good* and *evil.* Laurie had introduced a nightly system she called "star charts": each evening, my parents would draw attention to something I'd done well—listening, speaking nicely to my sister, cooperating at bedtime—and plant a star-shaped sticker on a cardboard sheet that listed the days of the week. Once I accrued a dozen or so stars, I was rewarded with a toy of my choosing. My mother would then tack up the completed chart, and soon the walls of my room were covered with them: rows of shiny stickers that measured my good deeds, implying that my actions, like everyone else's, could be good and bad—and didn't always define who I *really* was.

At least my behavior hadn't grown any worse, thanks in part to Mrs. Hartinger. She always filled out the comments section at the bottom of the daily report, she never raised her voice, and during the fights she dealt with the Tims and me equally. She'd probably had a boy like me every year for the past twenty, but she seemed to enjoy offering the extra effort that Laurie's treatment required. My achievements became her own.

It was the summer after kindergarten, 1986, and at Laurie's suggestion, I enrolled in athletic day camps; for two months I played baseball, basketball, and soccer. In the midst of so much physical activity I got along well with other children. Every night my father would pitch me Wiffle Balls in the backyard. He'd just started a new job at a health club. In August we went together to see the San Francisco Giants at Candlestick Park: some of his best friends were still in the big leagues, traveling like movie stars across the country. At the end of the last inning we walked down to the dugout, and one of my father's old minor-league coaches appeared near the on-deck circle, smiling. After a moment he tossed a baseball to me, which I snatched out of the air as if it were a coin.

I returned to St. Lucy's in the fall for first grade: the scabs of gum on the linoleum; a trilling water fountain; and always the sunlight, blue and layered, a whole corridor of it beneath the windows' high gauze. Everyone was taller and leaner. I felt unaccountably fresh, as if I'd spent the summer shedding puffy layers of skin. During one of our first lunch periods Brendan Tanger and I played against the Tims in basketball, and Gallo actually seemed to enjoy the challenge.

The next morning we were lining up for recess when Gallo and Shelley walked over.

"Hi!" I said. "Maybe today we can mix up the teams? Or not. Whatever you guys think."

"Your hair looks like a bowl," Gallo said.

"What?"

He turned to Tim Shelley. "I bet he puts a bowl on top of his head and then cuts it himself." With his two front fingers, he mimicked a pair of scissors snipping across his forehead.

Shelley laughed.

"Okay," I said. I didn't know what any of this had to do with basket-ball.

"Your hair's stupid," Gallo told me.

For a moment I was too shocked to respond. I couldn't get past the way I'd just felt: finally they'd come over to see me.

Tears appeared in the corners of my eyes, but Gallo walked off before I could say anything, with Shelley trailing behind him. I stood quietly, my face wet, feeling crushed by the difference between what I wanted and the way things actually were. There was nothing I could do to change it. They had planned this. Their minds were made up.

Then it was recess. I slipped into the hallway. I felt emptied but directed. The playground was flat, lightless. I ran up behind Gallo and slammed into him. He crumpled to the ground.

Suddenly I understood where I was, the world and all its details. Was he hurt? Would he tell the principal? How could we ever be friends now?

"I'm sorry!" I shouted. "Please!"

Tim Gallo picked himself up, his wrist trembling, his elbow blackened by the concrete. He walked off—toward the basketball court and its crowd of watching children—and managed to respond in the most damaging way of all: he never looked in my direction.

》

For first grade, my teacher was Mrs. Kay O'Connor. She was about forty-five years old, bookish and delicate, a pair of enormous glasses positioned on her face; sometimes when she glanced around the room, the lenses would catch the sunlight, veiling her eyes with the briefest reflection. In class she seemed almost grandmotherly.

For my mother, Mrs. O'Connor represented the ideal Catholic ed-ucator—calm and spiritual, more concerned with that one inattentive sheep than the other twenty coloring so earnestly at their desks. Her class resembled a standard version of elementary school. Now there was assigned seating, homework, and lessons in phonics, math, social studies, and penmanship. On certain weekdays we would read aloud in groups, organized according to ability.

The reading sessions were participatory; I was either talking or waiting to talk, which is all I ever really wanted to do. Mrs. O'Connor placed me in the most advanced group. She also let me use graph paper to help me with the penmanship lessons, which were especially difficult. On the notes home she'd write things like: *Reminded him three times to raise his hand today and in the afternoon he did so.*

My reading group consisted of five well-behaved girls, each of whom tolerated me with the exasperation of older sisters. The two Tims were in the middle level. Brendan Tanger was in the lowest. This was the setup throughout the year. One spring afternoon, after we finished a session and returned to our seats, Gallo came up behind me.

"That's a girl's book," he said.

I turned to face him.

He pointed to the cover in my hand. *The Baby-Sitters Club.*

"Girl's book!" Tim Shelley chimed.

"Shut up," I said, trying to keep Mrs. O'Connor from hearing.

Gallo smiled. "You like to read stuff for girls."

He was right. I found the book enthralling. Who were these babysitters? Why had they formed such an exclusive club? And how, exactly, would they manage to solve the continuing mystery of the phantom caller/jewel thief? I somehow hadn't bothered to wonder if maybe, with the frilly cover, this book might be meant for a different audience. But Gallo knew a single comment could undo me, and this seemed like a good bet. Eventually, wildly, I was bound to react.

I held the book at my hip and glared at him. His eyes were placid. Finally I turned away. But *The Baby-Sitters Club* was gone from my hand. It took me a moment to realize that Tim Shelley had snatched it.

"Give it back!" I shouted. The tears were coming on. "You're stupid, both of you. You're in the stupid reading group!"

In the next moment Mrs. O'Connor was standing beside me. The classroom reordered beneath her searching adult gaze. She led me into the hallway.

"Go to the bathroom," Mrs. O'Connor said in measured tones. "Wash your face. Take your time."

»

What makes a treatment "successful"? How do you weigh improvement against adverse effects? And at what point might the goal of a therapy come at too high a cost?

Dr. Charles Bradley was considering these questions more than seventy-five years ago. At the time, however, no one else was connecting the dots. The 1930s and 1940s would mark a quiet period of research into childhood disorders. Up until 1955, fewer than a dozen studies were published on stimulants and children, including Bradley's own 1950 follow-up in which he and other doctors at the Bradley Home reproduced his earlier results. Instead, these decades were dominated by psychoanalysis.

Sigmund Freud died in 1939. Throughout the 1930s, many of his European followers had fled the rise of Nazism and come to the United States, increasing the numbers and prestige of their American counterparts. Analysts founded advocacy organizations such as the Group for the Advancement of Psychiatry, whose members would come to staff 75 percent of the American Psychiatric Association's committee posts and occupy the academic chairs at major universities like Yale. From these positions of power, they were able to control the departments of psychiatry at schools across the country, including the University of Pennsylvania and Johns Hopkins; compose popular textbooks like *A History of Medical Psychology*; and sit on the examination boards that awarded degrees in psychiatry and medicine, thus solidifying their influence.

According to Freud, there was only one type of mental illness— repression—the severity of which existed along a continuum that spanned from a child's phobia to full-blown schizophrenia. Its ultimate cause was rooted in our response to environmental influences. And despite continuing medical studies, there was no hard evidence to prove otherwise.

By 1950, the two main treatment options—Freudian psychotherapy and asylum-style residential care—had failed to alleviate the symptoms of disorders like psychosis, mania, and depression. Then, in 1951, a French naval doctor in Paris named Henri Laborit began experimenting with a new drug, chlorpromazine, to help calm his more "anxious, Mediterranean-type" patients for surgery and to keep them from going into shock. Chlorpromazine, an antihistamine, had been provided to Laborit for testing by the French pharmaceutical company Rhône-Poulenc.

Dr. Laborit soon found that chlorpromazine worked exactly as he'd hoped; it prevented shock. His patients appeared detached and subdued during the surgical process. Eventually he persuaded some psychiatrists to employ the drug, and they discovered that it alleviated the primary symptoms of psychosis so effectively that schizophrenics who'd been living in an asylum for years were actually able to return to their previous lives. These results were presented at a meeting of the Société Médico-Psychologique in 1952.

By 1953 asylums in Paris had been transformed; patients were being released and former custodial techniques like straitjackets and padded rooms were no longer essential. In American mental hospitals, psychiatrists started treating their most disturbed patients with chlorpromazine, where it became known by its trade name Thorazine. The drug's success led to the development and testing of other effective medications: lithium for mania, and imipramine for depression. Research increased, buoyed by the emerging belief that—with the right penicillin-esque drug—everything from madness to fidgeting could finally be cured.

The first detailed study of chlorpromazine's effects on hyperactive children was published in a 1956 issue of the *American Journal of Psychiatry.* Herbert Freed, chief of the Child Psychiatry Research Unit of the Philadelphia General Hospital, and psychologist Charles A. Peifer assigned the drug in oral dosages to twenty-five "hyperkinetic, emotionally disturbed children" who had been "combative with their classmates and teachers." The trial period lasted from four to sixteen months and included placebos. They observed the children's behavior and also ran a battery of tests, including the Rorschach—a series of inkblot interpretations often used in psychoanalysis—and reported varying improvement in twenty-one cases—or 84 percent. But it's important to look at their definition of success. Classroom behavior improved because "the quieter child makes less demands on the environment." The same was true with interpersonal relations: "Learning is facilitated when teachers are not frustrated." As for the Rorschach results, the children's initial interpretations of "fighting cats" were replaced with "crawling cats"—which supposedly represented a decrease in hostility.

In fact, the less-combative behavior was really just the result of sedation. Chlorpromazine, when applied to non-schizophrenics, causes a reaction similar to what Dr. Laborit's patients experienced during surgery. Freed and Peifer noted this, citing the children's "placidity" and drowsiness. In full-blown adult schizophrenia, the psychosis is so severe that the drug, in its intensity, works to bring patients back toward their baseline personality. For hyperactivity, it was simply a knockout punch—with potentially catastrophic consequences; the doctors failed to note that chlorpromazine's most serious side effect is a loss of muscular control, known as tardive dyskinesia, that's characterized by debilitating bouts of twitching and shaking.

Freed and Peifer's study took place nearly half a century after play therapy was first initiated with little Hans. It was the polar opposite of Freud's approach. While psychoanalysis might offer a minimal chance at improvement, at least it avoided causing long-term physical harm. Chlorpromazine, in contrast, could effectively treat primary symptoms but with a blunt force that threatened a child's individuality and well-being. Their 1956 article included one final observation: "It has been suggested that chlorpromazine has ushered in a new era of psychiatric treatment."

»

Laurie Hamilton had been seeing hyperactive children in private practice for more than half a decade before she began working with me. She knew from experience that her therapy wasn't going to magically cure behavior like fidgeting and blurted questions. As I started second grade, we continued to concentrate on secondary symptoms, particularly how the Tims were responding to me. Together we talked about context. It was normal, she said, for boys to fight. But such a concept was alien to me. My sister, Katie—a bossy and loving five-year-old—didn't suffer from my behavior problems. And no one was more popular than my parents. Friends seemed to be present everywhere they went. It didn't quite square with how often they fought with each other, but at least there were fewer fights about me. I was eight years old: skinny, tan, my hair draped across my forehead like (it's true) a bowl. And every few months I became a newer version of myself. It was the heart of childhood. If you were to ask my mother and father to name their favorite stretch of time in our history together, they might very well answer these first few years of school. I still got into fights, but I also spent weekend afternoons at Brendan Tanger's house, traded baseball cards, played Nintendo, and excelled in Little League.

Laurie and I also reexamined the anger-management techniques she'd introduced to me in kindergarten, especially the soccer players example—taking deep and clenching breaths. We discussed teasing. If the Tims were deliberately trying to get me upset, then wasn't ignoring them a better way of winning the battle?

After our sessions, I'd briefly see the world from her point of view: *Who cares what everyone else thinks?* Not that the realization ever stuck; the next time Shelley and Gallo made fun of my shoes or my backpack I'd find myself as upset as ever. But at least now, I'd try to walk away or go find Mrs. O'Connor; I understood that the goal was to keep things from getting worse. And so far at St. Lucy's, my teachers had been outstanding.

»

To this day I still have nightmares about my third-grade teacher, Pamela Kovalenko. I'll be dreaming about some familiar landscape—my office, my backyard—when out of nowhere she'll appear, wearing a drab sweater and looking lost. Then she'll see me and flash a grin, her teeth a window of bright bone. In the dream, I am terrified; in the next moment I realize that she's terrified too.

My first memory of our time together is from a morning lesson. She was trying to explain the instructions for our math worksheets, but I kept asking unrelated questions like "What does the 'USSR' on the map stand for?" and "Why do some of the lowercase letters have different shapes than the uppercase ones?"

The other children laughed. Mrs. Kovalenko would pause tensely, then move on. It was my first week in her class. Already I was overwhelmed by the new classroom's decorations: presidential portraits, a growth chart behind the pencil sharpener, the alphabet above the chalkboard, and the brightly colored geographical maps near the windows. My attention was wandering, yes, but really I felt the same as always; the other students and the teacher were far away until suddenly their world surged across mine.

When we finally started the worksheets, Mrs. Kovalenko sat down at her desk, exhausted. I figured I'd better focus. I was answering the first problem when something damp struck my neck.

I turned around. Tim Gallo was looking straight ahead. From the front of the room, Tim Shelley was watching us. On the ground was a lump of binder paper, heavy with saliva. I uncrumpled it. The lines were blank. I balled up the paper, angrier than ever at Gallo, and reached back for my return shot but stopped midthrow when I noticed my new teacher standing beside me.

Mrs. Kovalenko looked normal enough: a sweater top and sagging socks, her brown hair in a ponytail. At the time she was in her late thirties, but up close she seemed much older. It was a matter of shadows;

they added extra wrinkles to her forehead and chin. Parallel creases descended from her eyes to her lips, emphasizing her meaty nose. Beneath the bright ceiling lights, her face was incredibly pale.

"He threw it at me first," I said, pointing to Tim G.

"Is that true?" she asked him.

He shook his head.

She turned back to me. "Wait outside."

"What?" I glanced at Gallo; he was genuinely shocked.

"Now," she said.

I waited for her outside the classroom. Finally the door swung open and I began pleading my case. But her back was turned; she was dragging my desk into the hallway.

"A half-hour," she said.

"I'm supposed to sit out here?" Behind her, the classroom was vibrant and sunny.

She slapped the worksheet down in front of me. "I have twenty-five other students," she said. Then she was gone, behind a closed door, and I was left to stare at my reflection in the low linoleum glaze.

»

Have we perhaps established that children with ADHD, once they enter school, place a tremendous amount of strain on the available resources, especially their teachers, to the point where basic classroom functioning can become a struggle? The 1950s doctors who experimented with chlorpromazine on hyperactivity may seem monstrous now, and fair enough, but their ultimate goal wasn't to devise the most effective means of drugging children into submission; they and other researchers were looking for a less-drastic treatment than seclusion in a residential center—and for something more effective than psychotherapy.

In light of the pharmacological breakthroughs to treat disorders such as depression, mania, schizophrenia, and anxiety, it was inevitable that Charles Bradley's findings would be revisited. In 1957, the new medical director of the Bradley Home, Dr. Maurice Laufer, published in collaboration with his colleagues a pair of papers on "hyperkinetic" behavior in children. Throughout both, Laufer provided a diagnostic description for hyperactivity, speculated on a possible developmental problem within the brain (as opposed to prior trauma), and compared the effects of different types of amphetamines, such as Benzedrine and Dexedrine. The results confirmed Charles Bradley's earlier work: drug therapy could diminish primary symptoms in a large number of hyperactive children. Laufer's second article in the *Journal of Pediatrics* mentioned the effectiveness of a new stimulant, methylphenidate.

Methylphenidate was synthesized in 1944 by the Italian chemist Leandro Panizzon while working for CIBA, a Swiss pharmaceutical company. He called it Ritalin after his wife, Rita. They both tried the drug and though it didn't have much impact on him, it made her feel upbeat and outgoing. His wife had low blood pressure, and she liked to take it before a tennis match.

Ritalin's chemical properties were nearly identical to amphetamine's, despite its claim to be a milder form of stimulant; however, it entered and left the patient's system in a smoother fashion, which made it an appealing alternative to Benzedrine and Dexedrine. In 1955 it was introduced to the American market as an antidepressant for older patients. An early advertisement in the *American Journal of Psychiatry* shows an elderly woman, her eyes cast downward, standing before the magnified profile of a doctor. "In chronic fatigue and mild depression," the accompanying text reads, "try a gentle stimulant with few side effects." The Food and Drug Administration amended Ritalin's usage indications to include behavior-problem children in 1961, but it was still mostly being prescribed to adults.

The first major report on the usage of Ritalin for ADHD was published in 1962 in the *American Journal of Psychiatry.* Dr. Leon Eisenberg and Keith Conners of Johns Hopkins University documented eighty-one children from foster homes and a psychiatric treatment center, none of whom were "diagnosed as brain damaged, defective, or overtly psychotic." The study was controlled—half the participants were given a placebo—and double-blind: no one involved knew who was receiving the drug. It was the most rigorous clinical trial in the history of child psychiatry at the time.

Eisenberg and Conners found that Ritalin improved hyperactive behavior as successfully as other stimulants, and with less adverse reactions. They speculated that it helped instigate "an activation of inhibitory controlling systems." Its main side effect was appetite loss, followed by nail biting and anxiousness. Like Dr. Charles Bradley, they advocated "caution in the application of the drug in clinical situations."

Keith Conners was a young psychology professor and former Rhodes Scholar when the article was released. Leon Eisenberg had been researching childhood psychiatric disorders for years. In 1956 he'd published the first detailed, long-term study on autism. His evidence-based approach stood in contrast to psychoanalysis; at a 1962 meeting of medical educators, a crowd of analysts shouted him down from the podium after he'd challenged their methods. In his view, midcentury child psychiatry had failed to take into account both biological and social factors. He was famous for stating, "It's time to stop pulling drowning kids out of the river and start heading upstream to see who is pushing them in." Eisenberg's parents were Jewish immigrants from Russia, and he'd struggled to get into medical school because of prejudice toward his background. In a photograph from a 1960 national awards ceremony, he appears tall and athletic, his glance cast sideways. He's standing alongside his colleague, the famous psychiatrist Leo Kanner, and smiling modestly. He looks at ease, in a bow tie and black suit, as if he's about to cycle through a few introductory jokes and then deliver a precise ethical critique of his field.

Eisenberg refused to believe that the roots of behavior could be reduced to something as biological as a virus or bacterium—and treated his patients accordingly. In a 1960 study, he proved that tranquilizer drugs caused more harm than good for children suffering from anxiety disorders. He saw childhood mental illness as another form of exclusion, and he was searching for the best available means to help his patients escape the confinement of the "training school for delinquents," which is how he described the youth psychiatric center he worked with in his 1962 study on Ritalin.

Throughout the 1960s, Eisenberg and Conners studied the effects of medication on ADHD. They both received grants from the newly created Psychopharmacology Research Branch of the National Institute of Mental Health, and their findings continued to influence treatment trends. By the close of the decade, psychiatrists were choosing stimulants over other options like psychotherapy to treat ADHD; a 1970 congressional report estimated that the medication was being prescribed to between 150,000 and 200,000 American children.

By this time, Ritalin had been clinically proven to help alleviate impulsiveness, lack of attention, and excess motor activity in up to 75 percent of patients—without sedating them into submission. But the decades-long drive to achieve these results had overshadowed a more basic question: Was there a way to improve a hyperactive child's functioning without focusing exclusively on primary symptoms?

》

While *psychiatry* attempts to treat abnormal behavior, *psychology* is best understood in a broader sense: the science of why humans act and think in such diverse ways. As a clinical discipline, it harkens back to the nineteenth-century work of William James.

Born in 1842, James was the eldest son of an eccentric theologian. His younger brother, Henry, would become one of the world's most famous novelists. William initially studied painting and biology, but after a severe bout of depression he settled on teaching philosophy at Harvard. In 1890 he wrote *The Principles of Psychology,* a 1200-page textbook that drew upon science, history, metaphysics, and personal experience to examine the mechanics of human behavior. His more clinical approach helped distinguish the emerging field of psychology from philosophy.

Throughout his career he emphasized actions and their results, and while he and Sigmund Freud both believed that human functioning was a response to our environment, James was more pragmatic; in his 1884 essay "The Dilemma of Determinism," he went so far as to describe the word "cause" as "an altar to an unknown god."

In the early 1900s, a researcher from South Carolina named John B. Watson expanded upon James's work to establish behaviorism: the theory that all human actions are conditioned responses to environmental stimuli. At first, Watson found his proof in animal trials that were similar to Ivan Pavlov's famous study on dogs, but in 1915 he took a research position in child development at Johns Hopkins University, where he tested his concepts on orphaned infants. In his most well-known experiment, an eleven-month-old named Little Albert was presented with a white rat. Initially, the boy and animal played happily together. But during their next meeting, just as the rat emerged, Watson banged a hammer against a steel bar. He proceeded to do this each time Albert reached for the animal. Soon enough the child would break down screaming at the sight of white fur.

Watson's proposed treatment for a mental disorder was his proof: conditioning. He claimed that with his approach he could train any random infant to become "a doctor, lawyer, artist, merchant-chief, and yes, even a beggar-man and thief." He was eventually ousted from his position at Johns Hopkins, though not for terrorizing children; he was caught having an affair with a graduate student.

During the 1950s, Harvard psychologist B. F. Skinner would help shift behaviorists' attention to consequences; his theory of operant conditioning claimed that patterns of action tend to be repeated if they're reinforced. To modify undesirable behavior, he created a contingency system of rewards and punishments. This was the beginning of "behavior" therapy, a new treatment that would eventually serve as the foundation for my very own 1980s star charts. At the time, however, it was applied to more extreme cases like mental retardation, and the focus remained on primary actions.

Then, in 1961, Albert Bandura of Stanford University studied how children respond to aggression in his "Bobo doll experiment": For about a minute an adult would interact happily with a large, inflatable, clown-faced doll located in the corner of a room while a child watched. Suddenly this adult would begin to kick, hit, and toss the doll—and finally smash it in the head with a mallet. The child, left alone in the room, was inclined to mimic what he'd just seen.

The results helped support Bandura's concept of social modeling: most behavior is a learned *reaction* to what we see in other people, as opposed to an unconscious response. A successful treatment, then, should go beyond the baseline symptoms of a disorder and target the way everyone involved interprets the situation.

At Stanford, Bandura employed this broader approach. He expanded Skinner's version of behavior therapy to include relaxation, anger-management, and communication techniques; by the time Laurie Hamilton began her doctoral work there, Bandura and his colleagues were applying this new treatment in a standardized trial to adult patients suffering from issues such as depression, anxiety, and overeating. Laurie adapted it to hyperactive children.

So by the 1970s psychiatry and psychology were offering two distinct alternatives to Freudian psychoanalysis: drug therapy and behavior therapy. Drug therapy attempted to target and reduce core symptoms. Behavior therapy took into account a question best summarized in 1967 by the psychologist Gordon L. Paul: "*What* treatment, by *whom,* is most effective for *this* individual with *that* specific problem, and under *which* set of circumstances?"

Laurie's emphasis on adaptability and individuality had worked well, in my case, because my parents were willing to exert the effort her system demanded. And my first teachers had also gone the extra mile. They saw the additional work as money in the bank, since full-blown dysfunction can actually take a much larger toll than any system of notes, charts, and relaxation techniques.

»

Pamela Kovalenko was new to St. Lucy's. I have no idea if she had any previous teaching experience, if she had heard of ADHD, if she knew about Ritalin, or if she'd ever worked with a child psychologist to help improve child behavior. In any event, I'm sure she hadn't encountered anything like Laurie's method.

During the first week of third grade, Kovalenko called my mother in for a conference and told her that my specific therapy for hyperactivity amounted to special treatment. She refused to let Laurie observe an afternoon class. She stopped filling out the daily note. I was told I couldn't use material aids like graph paper to help my penmanship; the next week she returned a book report I'd written with the comment: *Can't Read.* For the fall spelling bee, I lost in the second round on a dispute between "flower" and "flour." Her explanation: "You should have asked me to use it in a sentence." She began keeping track of the number of times I left my seat or spoke out of turn, and my desk was being dragged out into the hallway on more days than not.

In October, I was sitting down for a reading session when she called me over. "I want you to work with Brendan today," she said.

"What? Why?" We had remained in the same basic groups for the last few years; I was still surrounded by precocious girls while Brendan Tanger, far and away the nicest boy in class, was the worst reader.

She shrugged.

"That's not fair," I said.

"What's not fair?" She was looking directly at me. Her sooty eyes! Mashed nose! The bloodless patties of her cheeks! She was an unbelievably fleshy woman, but only in her face, which made her appearance all the more frightening.

It was the end of the day, the shadows of other children grazing the wall. I sat down next to Brendan, who didn't even have his book out. He was staring blankly. So was I.

》

That fall, the nuns who ran the school emphasized the benefit of Laurie's therapy to Mrs. Kovalenko; perhaps this was one of those situations where dragging desks into the hallway only made things worse? My mother met with her again, my father too—"That's one weird bird," he said afterward—but nothing changed. There was only one third-grade class at St. Lucy's, and, by all accounts, my teacher had taken it upon herself to dismantle a treatment we'd spent years establishing.

From my mother's perspective, Pamela Kovalenko was a very literal woman. She didn't have any children of her own, was physically rigid: the kind of person who straightens at loud sounds, who doesn't laugh at a joke because she never really understood it in the first place. And let's not forget: my behavior was annoying. I'd wander the room, touch other students, and say whatever popped into my head—disrupting an environment that she struggled, every day, to control.

So it might make sense if this woman, already sensitive to the blare of my personality, saw Laurie's therapy as an elaborate excuse. Maybe she thought ADHD was a bogus condition altogether. There was acceptable behavior and if by third grade a child still lagged so far behind the rest, it was high time to bring down the big Catholic hammer. Had she perhaps gone to parochial school herself, a product of some late-1950s environment in which students weren't allowed to write left-handed, let alone ask questions every five seconds? Regardless, it was soon clear to everyone involved just how much this woman disliked having me in her classroom. And there's not much you can do about that.

Winter came and I stopped trying to prove that I was smart, honest, or even sorry about my behavior. I didn't finish my homework, which had never been a problem before. My report card was a massacre. Usually I'd find myself in the hallway before lunch. I spent hours there, despondent, drawing crude warplanes on the backs of my worksheets, and when I finally did rejoin the class, I'd sulk quietly at my desk—the only time Mrs. Kovalenko and I ever got along.

Tim Gallo watched all of this. At first, he was merciless. I was already on edge, and after one of his comments or tossed pencils I'd start screaming—exiled again to the hallway. But I could always get revenge on the basketball court. And I was angrier than ever, crashing into him at every turn.

One January afternoon, I was waiting in the parking lot for my mother to pick me up when he and Shelley walked over. I knew what this was about; earlier in the week I'd elbowed Gallo in the nose under the hoop. Now it was payback. And this time they weren't alone. He had somehow recruited two shaggy-haired fifth graders.

I took off running. They followed. Up ahead: a chain-link fence. I wheeled around. They were converging. Gallo, dark-eyed, alert; Shelley at his side; the fifth graders a few feet off.

"Hey," one of the larger boys said, his mouth loose. I'd seen him before, playing tackle football on the blacktop.

I thought maybe I could get away. I ran at Shelley and hit him in the throat. He went down, and I was tackled from behind. The fifth graders held my arms, and Gallo began kicking me in the side. It hurt, but worse than that was the sensation of being pinned. I started screaming. They held on. Gallo put an elbow to my throat. It was like the tantrums: a full-body shake. The world was domed and colorless, the basketball hoops barring the sky. For an endless moment I was washed completely from my body.

The whole thing must have lasted about a minute. Suddenly the boys above me turned their heads toward the parking lot. In the curve of my vision, I could see movement: my mother was running at us, her necklace throwing off big beads of sun.

The two fifth graders scattered. So did Tim Shelley. Gallo remained. He glanced up, confused, and my mother shoved him aside. Earrings, sky, a clack of heels. Finally I was pulled up to my feet. Instead of going home we headed for the school's third-grade classroom.

"Kovalenko!" my mother was screaming. But the door was closed. Outside it, in a pool of afternoon light, parallel tracks marred the linoleum: remnants of my desk's most recent forced march.

»

Like drug therapy, Laurie's version of behavior therapy was rooted in testable sources: she'd conducted a randomized trial and compared her results to previous studies. Such testing has its limits, especially in terms of focus and interpretation, but from the beginning, both treatments were subjected to the scientific method.

Freudian psychoanalysis, however, had never produced repeatable, evidence-based results. And starting in the late 1960s, a series of studies by the Harvard neuroscientist Seymour Kety would further undermine its efficacy. Kety was researching identical twins in Denmark adopted at birth; he was seeking to evaluate the role of environmental influences on mental illness, and he chose Denmark because this country kept an extremely detailed record of each citizen's history, including, in cases of adoption, biological parentage. By comparing rates of hospitalization and treatment between separated twins and their family members, he found that schizophrenia was ten times more likely to afflict biological relatives, especially brothers and sisters. Subsequent studies of twins proved the biological factor at play in a variety of disorders, from mania to agoraphobia. Still, Freud's followers refused to reexamine his original thesis that all aberrant behavior was the result of past trauma. And while a few older psychiatrists might recommend psychoanalytic evaluations in addition to other measures, psychoanalysis was declining as a treatment option. Freud's theories would become, as Edward Shorter writes, "objects of disbelief, not so much disproven—for they were incapable of disproof—but relegated to the same scientific status as astrology."

In the meantime, a technical understanding of just how stimulants acted on children continued to evolve. In his 1937 study, Dr. Charles Bradley had first questioned why Benzedrine seemed to produce paradoxical "subdued behavior" in hyperactive subjects. Nearly thirty years later, a study by the doctors Bernard Weiss and Victor G. Laties titled "Enhancement of Human Performance by Caffeine and the Amphetamines" addressed the drug's effect on *everyone*. They agreed that stimulants increased focus and diligence, and that these improvements occurred regardless of whether a user was tired or rested.

Amphetamines, even in pill form, can produce a sense of euphoria. And with the concurrent explosion of recreational drug use in the 1960s, the danger of abuse was apparent. In 1965, Ritalin was effectively banned in Sweden after reports of widespread abuse, and fear of a similar epidemic was growing in America. For three decades psychiatrists had told the public that mental illness was environmentally caused, and in that light, drug therapy was perceived as just another form of repression: it kept children in line but failed to do anything about the assumed experiential roots of ADHD. Technology still couldn't provide evidence of the disorder's organic basis or how stimulants affected brain chemistry.

All of these concerns became front-page news in June 1970 when the *Washington Post* published an article titled "Omaha Pupils Given 'Behavior Drugs.'" Staff writer Robert Maynard reported that 5–10 percent of the children in Omaha were taking stimulants such as Ritalin.

"How it works is still the 64-dollar question," said Dr. Byron B. Oberst, a local pediatrician.

Maynard described cases of children swapping their pills on the playground and teachers calling parents at home to promote the drugs. "Many medical authorities" were concerned about the potential for abuse. A regional politician named Ernest Chambers said, "I don't want my child growing up believing that as soon as things aren't going right, they can take a pill to make it better." The article ended on the unsettling case of a hyperactive child who, while taking stimulants, left his finished homework on the dinner table for his parents to check, along with the note: "Thank you, mother, I feel much happier."

Maynard's story generated an enormous amount of publicity. After reading it, Congressman Neil Gallagher of New Jersey promised a congressional hearing. Similar pieces soon appeared in other media outlets, including the *Saturday Review.* In September, a House of Representatives subcommittee recommended a new set of rules to govern stimulant use, and a month later Congress passed the Comprehensive Drug Abuse

Prevention and Control Act; Ritalin and other stimulants were designated as Schedule III narcotics, which limited the number of refills a patient could receive. The following year, the Drug Enforcement Administration (DEA) went a step further and classified Ritalin and amphetamine as Schedule II. In addition to tightened prescription regulations, a quota would be set on the annual amount of Ritalin that a pharmaceutical company could produce. From then on, the DEA monitored the distribution and usage of stimulants much more closely.

Nevertheless, in 1971, the first advertisement recommending Ritalin for childhood hyperactivity appeared in the *American Journal of Psychiatry*. It was a double-page spread. On the left, a young boy is pictured at his desk, his mouth wrenched open, his arm blurry with movement. On the right, he's sitting calmly. "Diagnosable Disease Entity," the caption reads, implying that this boy's behavior is similar to an infection and should be treated with tablets of CIBA's methylphenidate. But Ritalin isn't like an antibiotic; it doesn't eradicate the root cause of hyperactivity over a ten-day span, and if you stop taking it, the primary behavior returns. As with Laurie's therapy, it alleviates certain symptoms, but there's a necessary caveat: sometimes things might actually get worse.

Then, in 1975, amid the rising scrutiny of stimulants, a seventy-six-year-old allergist in Northern California named Ben F. Feingold published *Why Your Child Is Hyperactive*. In his view, ADHD was a phenomenon that hadn't existed prior to World War II. The same was true, he noted, of most artificial flavors and colorings. Based on his experience running the allergy department at San Francisco's Kaiser Permanente Hospital, Feingold postulated that the new additives were "tampering with the brain and nervous system by short-circuiting some functions." He proposed a dietary cure that eliminated foods such as grapes, apples, hot dogs, sausages, and any drinks with flavoring and coloring agents. In his own follow-up articles, he claimed that as many as 50 percent of children on the diet got better. Unfortunately, a series of more rigorous studies published over the next decade proved that additives have very little effect on hyperactive behavior. But Feingold's approach became especially popular. During the second half of the 1970s, parent associations sprouted up all over the country in support of his theories, and California nearly passed a law requiring that all public-school cafeterias leave out food additives. Even my mother was willing to drive twelve hundred miles to Colorado when I was three years old to see if his diet could help me. In the end there was no improvement, but I can understand its appeal. Feingold was offering what the evidence-based treatments could not, despite decades of research and breakthroughs: a cure for ADHD.

Meanwhile, the new laws would affect the treatment of the disorder in practical ways. Prescriptions could no longer be called in to the pharmacy ahead of time, doctors had to approve each refill, and in certain states, an electronic record was maintained of past use. But the flurry of journalistic and legal attention didn't alter the number of children taking stimulants. By 1976, more than 120 studies had been published on the effectiveness of medication therapy; two years later, the psychologist Robert L. Sprague of the University of Illinois estimated that up to 600,000 children were being prescribed drugs like Ritalin and amphetamine, a three-fold increase in less than a decade. In the same year, the NIMH researcher Judith L. Rapoport published an article in *Science* that documented the medication's beneficial effects on the mathematic abilities of *all* children. So Ritalin's effectiveness, like that of a steroid injection, couldn't be used as evidence that there was something wrong to begin with; the drug increased concentration on specific tasks for everyone.

The field of psychiatry was completing its swing to an organic conception of diagnosis—to a system of treatment supported by a new wave of scientific research. For more than thirty years psychopharmacology had been alleviating the symptoms of serious disorders like schizophrenia, and now antidepressants and antianxiety medications were being increasingly prescribed for the milder neurotic conditions that Freud, in 1890s Vienna, had first sought to treat. The 1980 revision of the *Diagnostic and Statistical Manual* (*DSM*) adopted a medical framework for the identification of symptoms, which made it much easier for family doctors and pediatricians to diagnose psychiatric conditions and prescribe medication.

»

Throughout my year in Mrs. Kovalenko's class, Laurie tried adapting her therapy to my new circumstances: How might I best respond to a teacher who reacted so strongly to my hyperactive behavior? But there was only so much she could do. During our weekly sessions, I stopped offering recaps of the playground and classroom; what was the point? Sometimes we went over the breathing exercises or talked about geology and the solar system, which were my favorite academic subjects. We also created a new rewards system for my behavior at home, which, despite everything, was more or less under control.

After the fight on the blacktop with Tim Gallo, my mother called his mother. She wanted to explain how difficult things had been for me. It was time for everyone to take a step back.

"It doesn't matter who started it," my mother said. "They need to stop beating each other up."

Gallo's mother cut her off. "I know all about your son," she replied—and hung up the phone.

A few weeks later, my mother saw Tim Gallo in the hallway at school—I wasn't there, thankfully—and she told him, "I don't like the way you've been picking on Timmy. Cut it out now. You hear me?" He flipped her off. She was too stunned to say anything else.

Spring came, and each day in Mrs. Kovalenko's class felt the same. She kept dragging my desk into the hallway at the first offense. Then, during Easter break, my family took a ski trip to a friend's cabin in Lake Tahoe, and on one of our last runs I sped past my father and hit a jump, breaking my leg. I'd have to wear a cast and use crutches for a month. When the vacation was over, my mother made an appointment with Mrs. Kovalenko to discuss the extra help I'd need in the classroom.

We arrived at St. Lucy's at lunchtime. I waited in the receptionist's office with Sister Vivian, a pleasantly wrinkled woman in her early sixties. The third-grade classroom was down the hall, and my mother propped my crutches against the wall and left me to go meet Kovalenko. The plan was to start with a few half days and work back up to a normal schedule.

Sister Vivian began asking me questions about Bay Area sports teams. I was happy to show off what I knew, despite the pain in my knee. Then the phone rang.

For the next few minutes I sat quietly. My leg was swollen and stiff, my stomach hurting from all the ibuprofen I'd swallowed. The office seemed menacingly adult: the mahogany desk, beige phone, bulletin board, and Catholic calendar, its holidays circled at equidistant dates like red, inhuman eyes. If there was anywhere left for Mrs. Kovalenko to drag my desk, this was it: a place outside the world of children altogether.

After a while someone walked by and stopped. It was Brendan Tanger. He sat down next to me. Even then he was still much taller than everyone else. His lower lip sagged from his mouth, but he didn't say anything; he just stared out the window, slouching and breathing loudly.

I couldn't stop thinking about the room, my leg, how I wanted to scrape the skin away and make it normal-sized again.

"What are you doing here?" I asked.

He shrugged. At the time I didn't understand; he'd stopped by to keep me company. During our last few years together at St. Lucy's he always took my side after the fights with Gallo. On weekends his mother called mine to invite me over. But I was now at the point where I could notice only the people I was constantly fighting.

Suddenly Brendan straightened up. Someone was approaching in loud, shuffling steps. My mother rushed into the office. She was crying, her mascara a mess on her cheeks.

"Come on," she said. "We're going home."

"What about class?" I asked.

She tugged at me.

"Stop it," I said. "My leg!"

"Timmy!"

"Let go! I want to stay here!"

We struggled as if in slow motion; she really was worried about my knee. Sister Vivian watched and said nothing. Brendan slipped away. The hallway filled with children, and finally I gave up; I let my mother help me back to the car.

>>

When Laurie completed her dissertation in 1980, doctors were prescribing stimulants to alleviate hyperactivity's primary symptoms, regardless of a child's specific circumstances. She was alarmed by the chemical strength of these drugs. Should Ritalin and amphetamine really be the first option for all children with ADHD? And what about the side effects? As the popularity of stimulants increased, how would doctors and psychiatrists address the parallel rise of adverse reactions?

A number of new studies evaluated the drug- and psychotherapy options against each other in terms of how well each treatment alleviated primary symptoms. Ritalin and amphetamine were found to be more effective than Laurie's approach, which was mostly recommended for cases similar to my own—when drugs weren't an option. Her system also had its drawbacks. It was administered only once a week, depended heavily on the skill of the therapist, and could fall apart if one of the adults refused to cooperate.

>>

What exactly did my third-grade teacher say to my mother during their lunchtime meeting? She claimed that I couldn't come back to school until my cast was off—in four weeks. Her reasoning: On crutches, I wouldn't be able to move around fast enough. I'd hold up the rest of the class. I'd cause an even greater distraction.

"Are you kidding me?" my mother shouted.

"No," Mrs. Kovalenko replied. "I am not kidding you."

In retrospect this was discrimination, clear and unlawful; you can't exclude a child from a learning environment because he walks too slowly. But at the time my mother had reached her limit. I was taken out of school. She stayed home from work, relying on our savings for the lost money, and set up daily tutoring sessions with the retired husband of my kindergarten teacher, Mrs. Hartinger. I studied. My leg healed. And I eventually returned to school on a spring morning in April.

I was happy to be back, despite everything—excited to be surrounded by kids my own age again. The first lesson of the day was penmanship. For a while I sat quietly and tried to push letters into the gray, dotted lines, but as I traced the never-ending rows of low *s*'s and tri-humped *m*'s, my hand cramped. I dropped my pencil, picked it up. I opened the desk and took out an eraser, turned in my seat, and tapped my foot, my leg aching. Pamela Kovalenko was watching. I raised my hand and asked to use the bathroom.

"Hurry," she said.

It took forever to limp there and back. I also washed my hands, stopped at the drinking fountain, and peeked in on Sister Vivian, who waved happily. By the time I returned, Mrs. Kovalenko was standing at the door.

"Was there a problem?" she asked in front of everyone.

"I'm going as fast as I can," I said, and limped extra slowly back to my desk.

This was how we tended to interact, first day back or not. The roles had become instinctive. And perhaps we could've made it through the day if Tim Gallo, during my trip to the bathroom, hadn't placed a thumbtack in the center of my chair.

I sat down and pain shot wildly through my butt. I screamed, tried to stand. But I couldn't straighten my leg. The class laughed. Finally I broke free.

"It's not my fault!" I shouted.

Gallo was watching us like everyone else. Tim Shelley was smiling. Mrs. Kovalenko grabbed my desk and began dragging it away.

"No!" I shouted, limping after her.

In the hallway, she turned to me and said, "Sit down."

"Please."

Her eyes were gray and empty. "I'm not going to tell you again."

I climbed into my desk and she shut the door. All alone, my leg on fire, my butt still smarting, I started to sob. I'd been sure, coming back, that things would be better—with her, and with the Tims too. But the classroom was like an eternal complication; sitting inside it, I wanted to escape, and once banished, I could only think about how to get back in again. Being gone so long had made it worse.

I was shaking, crying, struggling to breathe. Then I remembered the techniques that Laurie and I had practiced over the years: soccer players gulping at the air. I tensed my fingers, relaxed them. But I couldn't stop sobbing. Snot and saliva poured across my handwriting lessons. More than anything else I wanted to stand up. Then what? There was still the closed door, and the class beyond, and Kovalenko guarding it. She'd never let me in without a reason. I had to prove that she was wrong. More than anything I needed to be seen as the victim.

I sat up and placed my index finger inside my nose. With my nail, I pressed as hard as I could into the soft central wall of my nostril, and scraped. The pain was overwhelming. Briefly I panicked—what had I done? But as the first crimson drops caught my handwriting lessons, I felt relieved. I was able to stand, and by the time I pushed open the class-room door, blood was streaming down my lips.

"Look!" I shouted.

Pamela Kovalenko looked up and the air went out of her meaty face. As if she'd been hit by wind. Afraid.

》

Perhaps after another hundred years, researchers will find a way to address the causes at the heart of ADHD—without destroying the per-sonality of the child in the process. For now, we're stuck with trying to measure improvement. Do the benefits outweigh the harms? Has the therapy reached its limit? Is there another option? Does success actually mean that things aren't getting worse, and if so, is the ordeal of treatment really worth it?

The problem with ADHD is that what works one day suddenly doesn't the next. You find yourself at a loss. Which is why, in my case, a treatment like Laurie's was always so much better than doing nothing; at the very least, it asked everyone involved to separate the child from his outlandishness, to see past the behavior's coarse mask.

That first day back at St. Lucy's was also my last. I waited with Sister Vivian in the office, a towel against my face, for my mother to pick me up. Summer vacation was still a few weeks away, but my parents decided to take me out of school early.

Mrs. Kovalenko must have been delighted. In June the nuns told her to look elsewhere for work.

That summer, my family decided to register me for our neighborhood public school, Alta Vista, which Laurie thought would offer more flexibility. But the deadline had already passed; we had to file a separate petition.

On a clear July afternoon, I was throwing a tennis ball against our garage door when my mother arrived home from work. The sun was near the coastal mountains, the sprinklers spraying in arcs across the lawn. She stepped out of the car and told me it was official: I'd start fourth grade at Alta Vista in the fall.

"Are you excited?" she asked. I hugged her. With St. Lucy's behind me, I'd be able to turn myself into someone completely new.

»

It's impossible now to look at the Tims from the point of view of my younger self, to judge them under the equation of victim and villain. How can I see these boys as anything except children? A real villain is someone who knows better.

For the next twenty years, Pamela Kovalenko would continue to teach elementary school at locations throughout the Bay Area. As of this writing, she's a faculty member in the outstanding public school system of my hometown of Los Gatos, California. Her classroom is just a few blocks from the house I grew up in.

3

In the Way You'd Watch a
Bird That's Flown in through a Window

The new public school was located in my immediate neighborhood, at the foot of the coastal range that separates San Jose from the ocean towns beyond. There was an upper level of baseball fields bordered by redwoods. Below: classrooms and basketball courts. Everything was on a slope. Each morning before the bell I'd play four square with children dressed in pastel shirts; the girls wore neon leggings, and the scrunchies in their hair were like bright feathers, a contrast to the drab navy uniforms of my previous, Catholic environment.

It was September. I'd just turned ten. Suddenly I wasn't looking over my shoulder at every turn, and on the playground during recess and lunch, surrounded by so many other students, I felt surprisingly anonymous.

Alta Vista was a large elementary school: nearly seventy fourth graders. Unlike St. Lucy's, it had two teachers for every grade. I was assigned to the classroom of Betty Parsons. She was blond, about forty, and her hair was bobbed in the style of Jackie Kennedy. She liked to talk about her favorite movies, food, and sports teams, and while we worked at our desks she'd play songs by the Beach Boys on a portable stereo.

Mrs. Parsons prided herself on her classroom management. She always sat the most active children—usually boys—near her desk. That way she could respond to their added demands and also stay in front of any problems.

It wasn't as if the events from the year before had been erased. I'd be playing basketball or waiting in line at the cafeteria—surrounded by boys and girls who hardly knew me—and suddenly I'd remember: I was the kid who'd stuck a finger up my nose until I started bleeding. But at Alta Vista I wasn't the only ten-year-old with significant behavior problems. Of the others, one stood out immediately: a boy with freckles and matted hair named Jonathan Ashley.

He wasn't in Mrs. Parsons's class. My first memory of him is from a biweekly P.E. session in which all of the fourth-grade students participated together. It was a fall afternoon, the sky beyond the coastal mountains like the surface of a lavish lake. We were playing volleyball while another group was tossing Frisbees in the grass, and at one point I noticed a figure near the grove of redwoods. In both hands he was holding something. I couldn't tell what.

Jonathan was tall for his age: large-boned and at the same time adolescently slim. He had wild eyebrows, red lips, and a broad face. When he began to get upset, his eyes would go skittish and he would press his chin to his chest and bite the front collar of his shirt.

His shirt was in his mouth now. I realized that his hands were filled with small rocks. The other students noticed too and scattered. A girl was calling for the P.E. teacher. It all seemed like some prerehearsed drill.

I heard a *crack*. A stone about the size of my thumb landed nearby. Jonathan was perhaps fifty feet away. His target was clear enough—the participants of our volleyball game—but the arc was unnecessarily steep, and he didn't actually seem to be trying to hit any of us. Finally one of the P.E. teachers ran over to him; he emptied his hands and followed her toward the office.

»

In the fall of 1989 my parents were both thirty-six years old. One of their favorite pictures of themselves is from that time. It was taken at a 1950s-themed church fundraiser. My father is wearing a tight white T-shirt, the sleeves turned under. His jeans are black and greasy. His hair is slicked, his mustache trimmed. In the slim outfit he looks beefed up; it's been nearly a decade since he quit professional baseball, and the adult in the photograph is a long way from the skinny-limbed young man who once traveled on buses to minor-league stadiums across the South and Midwest.

My mother is a head shorter. Her arm is around my father's waist. It's her favorite type of event: the costumes, music, and campy dancing. She's wearing a poodle skirt and a ruffled white blouse, and her black hair is wrapped in a scarf. Her cheeks are smooth with foundation, her posture perfect: alongside my father she looks slim and eager. Together they're smiling.

That year my father left his job at the health club to join a commercial real estate firm. His first big deal was to broker the sale of a winery in the Santa Cruz Mountains, and the resulting commission was more money than we'd seen, enough for a down payment on a new house.

As a family we were entering one of our last great transitions. My father would always be a baseball player at heart—it's still the most salient aspect of his identity—but now he'd found success as a salesman. I remember a fall morning we spent together after he closed the winery deal: we went to the electronics department at Sears and he told me I could buy any video game I wanted. I took forever to decide. Finally I chose a fighter-jet simulator over an alien adventure. But when it was time to pay, he opened his wallet as if he didn't have any money. I panicked. Then he pulled out a $100 bill. "Well, Timmo," he said, winking, "looks like we have enough for *two* games." And to the clerk: "We'll just go ahead and take them both, if it's not too much trouble."

That September my mother supervised the move into our new three-bedroom home. It was only a few blocks away from Alta Vista. She quit her job at the retail store, took up biking and jogging, and volunteered at the local church in Los Gatos.

A month later my parents sat my sister and me down and told us that they'd decided to have another baby: my mother was pregnant. I can't recall the details of the conversation, perhaps because it was followed the next day by a more memorable event.

We were running errands at a shopping center in Los Gatos, my mother, sister, and me—that night the San Francisco Giants were playing the Oakland A's in the World Series, and friends and family would be coming over for dinner to watch the game—when I heard what sounded like someone running toward me. The lights sparked, the shelves swayed, and objects from the aisles showered down. I'd been in an earthquake before but nothing like this.

The shaking lasted fifteen seconds. Then stillness. Car alarms. Feet over broken glass. In the corner of my vision trees and buildings seemed charged with motion, freezing into place only when I looked at them. My mother grabbed my sister and me and together we headed for our crimson minivan, which was parked nearby.

It was the Loma Prieta earthquake—7.1 on the Richter scale—a wave that passed through the residents of my hometown on its way to millions of others. The epicenter had been almost directly below us.

In the car my sister was sobbing. My mother spoke softly to her: "You're safe," she said. "You're with me." I sat in the backseat. I was scared, yes, but not in a recognizable way; suddenly the stakes had changed.

Our house was only a mile down the road. The traffic lights were all off. When we pulled up my father was waiting outside, and my sister got out of her seat and ran to him. My mother and I followed. As we all stood in the driveway my father said, "I'd just turned the game on when boom!" He clapped his hands. "The pictures on the wall were falling everywhere. I was sure the whole house was about to come down." He reached out his arms as if to steady himself.

My mother laughed. My father was smiling. Alongside them both I understood, again, where I was, and I already felt better. In the next instant they glanced at each other, a childlike exchange, as if they were whispering, *Did that really just happen?*

>>

The earthquake killed more than sixty people. Buildings caught fire in the Marina District of San Francisco, the roof of a mall buckled in Santa Cruz, a double-decker section of the 880 Interstate came down in Oakland, and part of the Bay Bridge collapsed. When our power returned I watched footage of the disaster endlessly on television. A number of homes in Los Gatos had been thrown from their foundations. Ours was fine, though in the plaster alongside the garage there now appeared a ten-foot crack, its path like the coastline of some recently emerged continent. Nobody we knew had been hurt.

What scared me the most was the shaking, and it wasn't over. For a week the aftershocks continued. Often they'd arrive in the middle of the night. I remember waking up in my room, our house immobilized in darkness, as the shadows on the walls trembled to life. Afterward I walked down the lightless hallway and stood directly in front of my pregnant mother. "Honey," she said, "there's a blanket for you by the closet." We kept up this arrangement for a while; I slept on the floor at the foot of their bed, the fear lessened by a sense of proximity, and by a steady decline in the aftershocks' frequency and strength.

School was canceled for the rest of the week, and when it finally resumed, the first thing Mrs. Parsons did was tell us her own story from the quake. That afternoon she'd had a ticket to the World Series game in San Francisco. "I looked up and saw the light towers swaying and I thought, *Oh my gosh, the bleachers are collapsing!* I started running down the aisle like a chicken with its head cut off!"

Some of the other students laughed. I was imagining Candlestick Park—the 60,000-seat stadium where I'd seen my father's friends play baseball—imploding in a fiery heap alongside the bay.

Mrs. Parsons began going over our plans for the day.

"But could the bleachers really have collapsed?" I asked.

"Oh no," she said. "They're made of very strong concrete."

"What if the earthquake was bigger?"

She smiled. "I don't think so." She tried to change the subject.

"How about a 9.0 quake?" I asked. "Could that make the stadium fall down?"

"Tim," she said. "We've got a lot to cover today."

But it was as if I hadn't heard her. "What's the largest earthquake in history? Has there ever been a 10.0?"

I was in my usual front-row seat; suddenly I realized that her gaze had frozen completely on me. "Stop interrupting," she said.

This was one of the first times I'd witnessed her tone change so abruptly. I understood why, which of course was upsetting—more than anything I wanted her to like me—and as she went on to talk about all the catching up we'd need to do after missing so much school, I sulked at my desk.

In her fourth-grade class, academics suddenly seemed more important than ever. That morning she introduced our science-fair assignment. "This is serious stuff," she said. She told us a story about a previous student's experiment that had involved a washing machine and too much soap.

When it was time for recess Mrs. Parsons called me to her desk. "I spoke harshly earlier," she explained, "because I didn't think you'd heard what I had to say. There are more than thirty children in this class. I can only answer so many of your questions."

I nodded. All of a sudden I was on the verge of tears, which made me even more upset; ten-year-olds weren't supposed to cry so easily.

"Listen," she said. "Why don't you do your science fair project on earthquakes? That way you can find the answers to all these questions yourself!"

»

Throughout my childhood, each school year tended to cast its distinct shadow over the next. This was especially true when I started fourth grade. At St. Lucy's Pamela Kovalenko had conflated all of my classroom decisions into a matter of willpower—my lack thereof. But Betty Parsons was able to separate behavioral issues from academic ones, so that a slower progress with the former didn't necessarily relate to the latter.

This difference might seem obvious enough, but up until the twentieth century, willpower and intelligence were often considered indistinguishable. One of the first doctors to question their relationship in children happened to be our favorite cape-wearing Victorian: Sir George Frederic Still.

In the same 1902 lecture in which he identified many of the symptoms of what we now call ADHD, he asked: "Is a morbid defect of moral control compatible with a perfectly normal state of the intellect?"

Still defined "moral control" as something similar to willpower: "the control of action in the conformity with the idea of the good of all," including "the good of self." He provided the case histories of behaviorally "defective" boys and girls who nevertheless showed no signs of intellectual impairment. A five-year-old boy threw outrageous tantrums and couldn't play well with others but "was a very pleasing child to talk to and the teacher said that he was 'perfectly intelligent.'" Another five-year-old was "extremely passionate" and "impulsive"; "for instance, in saying 'Good-night' he went round the family five times one night, apparently not noticing that he said it before." This same boy would often walk outside with his boots on the wrong feet. But Still went on to note that the child was "very quick at school. He read small words well, knew his 'twice-times' perfectly, and seemed to be quite up to average in normal intellectual attainments."

Still's lecture was filled with such examples. He eventually claimed that just because these boys and girls couldn't pay attention in certain settings didn't mean that they weren't as "intelligent as any child could be." In fact, he saw this discrepancy as a way to better identify and categorize the unique subset of children with ADHD-esque symptoms.

But Still showed no interest in using this insight to improve his subjects' functionality. In fact, he saw them as the proverbial bad apples: "The pernicious influence which some of these morally defective children may exert on other children is appalling to think of."

At the end of his lecture he speculated on possible educational approaches. Should these children all be confined in "special institutions"? Was there another way to meet their needs? And to what extent should they "be held responsible for their misdoings"?

At the time, the British government was in the process of implementing widespread educational reforms. In 1876, the Education Act made attendance at public schools mandatory for all elementary-aged children. The rapid increase in enrollment posed a new question: What about the subset of this population who, because of mental and behavioral problems, couldn't function in a normal classroom environment? In 1904, the English Royal Commission on the Care and Control of the Feeble Minded was formed to reevaluate the current certification practices. Doctors across the country conducted prevalence studies, determining that at least 4–6 percent of all children could be classified as unfit for normal schooling. The commission's report led to the Mental Deficiency Act of 1913, which established a compulsory system of state-funded specialized education along three grades of impairment: Idiocy ("unable to guard themselves against common physical dangers"); Imbecility ("incapable of managing themselves . . . or . . . of being taught to do so"); and Feeble-Mindedness ("involves disability of mind of such a nature and extent as to make them . . . incapable of receiving education at school"). The last grade was the vaguest and also the largest; it included the borderline category of children who, like those studied by George Frederic Still, possessed standard enough academic ability but couldn't pay attention or behave in the classroom.

One of the Royal Commission's senior medical investigators was a doctor named Alfred Frank Tredgold. Born in 1870, the son of a builder's foreman, Tredgold studied medicine at London Hospital before choosing to specialize in "mental disease." In 1908 he published his first edition of *Mental Deficiency (Amentia),* which over the course of his life would be reissued eight times. In one of the later editions there's a picture of him posing outdoors. He's in his early thirties: a preposterously thin man with a wet-looking mustache and elfin ears. His thick hair has been tousled by the wind, and for this briefest moment he appears to have grown a pair of dark, fledgling horns.

Mental Deficiency expanded upon the commission's findings. In his chapter on "feeble-mindedness," Tredgold offered his own solution to Still's questions about children who lacked "educability" but nevertheless possessed "sufficient intelligence": segregation in day and residential programs. One way Tredgold identified "feeble-mindedness" was through deficits in willpower and attention. "Their behaviour is more often the result of sudden desires and impulses than of deliberate purpose," he wrote; and: "the most trifling thing serves to distract these children from their occupation."

His suggested curriculum included occasional academic material, such as *Aesop's Fables* and "lessons in animal and vegetable life." But the majority of the day was occupied with manual tasks. "Defective children learn more through their hands than their books," he wrote. He cited the example of Goodrich Road Special School in London, where hours were spent practicing how to "cut out and make simple artificial flowers, knit rugs and weave baskets." The children worked on "dressing, feeding, personal cleanliness and tidiness," skills that he deemed to be of "the utmost educational value."

For Tredgold, the intellectual capacity that Still had earlier observed was in fact nothing more than "parrot knowledge." Even if intelligence and behavior could be considered separate entities, a deficit of willpower meant that these children lacked self-awareness—and thus "had really very little understanding of the answers they had put down." In his opinion, the behavioral issues were so damning as to blot out any hope for improvement in other areas.

In the end his version of special education had nothing to do with helping children reach their academic potential. The goal was to convert the hyperactive boy or girl "from a useless, and often dangerous, member of society into one capable of some amount of useful work."

»

During that first fall at my new school, I continued to meet semiregularly with Laurie Hamilton. We'd walk together along the softball fields, the shadows of the redwoods like deep pools in the grass. She'd ask how things were going with my classmates and Mrs. Parsons, who was happy to fill out regular reports on my behavior. Sometimes we'd review the relaxation techniques she'd introduced back at St. Lucy's, or we'd talk about the earthquake and its aftershocks, which had decreased dramatically, along with my fear of them. Already the quake was becoming an object of fascination: something thrilling and vaguely dangerous that had been relegated, safely enough, to the past.

Laurie's therapy was originally structured to be the most intense at its inception, when she first imparted the management strategies to the parents and self-control techniques to the child; by our fifth year together—and without the extenuating circumstances of someone like Pamela Kovalenko—the schedule had naturally tapered to a series of monthly checkups.

Which was a welcome development. At Alta Vista I worried that other children would see us and know immediately that something was wrong with me. And while I still enjoyed the sessions—Laurie could always ask just the right questions to get me talking—I made sure never to mention anything about Jonathan Ashley, even though I found myself thinking about him more often. It was as if just saying his name could conjure up everything that had happened during the previous year; I was convinced that he somehow had the power to expose who I really was.

Jonathan had landed in the class of the other fourth-grade teacher, Mr. Rader: a balding, egg-colored man with bad teeth whose path I crossed only once that year, when I was waiting to use the phone in the office at recess. I'd forgotten my lunch and was calling my mother to have her bring it. Mr. Rader needed the phone too. When the person in front of us finished I stepped forward and started dialing.

"Hold on a minute," he said.

I turned and replied matter-of-factly, "It's my turn, not yours." I felt his ensuing stare, but really I didn't think anything of it—until that night, when he called my house. Did I always talk to adults this way? Were there any boundaries in our home? "What do you intend to do about this?" he demanded.

"Listen," my mother finally said, "he knows he's not supposed to act like that." I was grounded for a few days, and afterward my mother added: "Stay away from that guy."

At lunch and recess, Jonathan liked to join in our basketball games— he was a ferocious rebounder—but sometimes he'd just circle the borders of the playground, dragging his hand along the fence. I began to realize that the other children weren't nearly as interested in him as I was. Alta Vista was a surprisingly accepting environment: for Jonathan, nobody seemed too appalled by his actions; and as for me, I was having a great year, even outside of Mrs. Parsons's class.

That fall I began spending time with a group of boys who were in the other fourth-grade class. There was Raymond, his arms and legs covered with mosquito bites. And Lucas, fair-haired and quiet. And another ten-year-old, Josh, an excellent baseball player.

When school ended they'd gather near the bike rack and ride off to one another's empty houses. One afternoon during the month following the earthquake I happened to be unhitching my bike as well, and when I asked where they were headed, Raymond motioned for me to follow.

"You're saying I can come too?"

"Sure," he replied.

Together we headed for Raymond's house. His mother didn't get off work until six, and with the help of the backyard fence we climbed up onto his roof. On the lawn below was a hand-me-down trampoline. He turned to Lucas and said, "Jump."

"I'm not going first," Lucas replied.

Before I knew it I was stepping forward. I'd been looking for a way to impress these other boys, and now as I searched for a reason not to jump I could only think, *Why not?*

Like that I was plummeting the eight or so feet toward the target. Then I slammed into the trampoline and was thrown forward feet-over-head. My body cleared the metal railing by inches. I crashed in a heap on the grass, the air knocked clean out of me.

I was sure that something vital was broken. The regret! More than anything I wanted my mother; I might have cried out for her if I could've formed the words.

The other boys clambered down from the roof. They were standing over me. At first their faces seemed to confirm it: I was ruined. But eventually I stood up. In fact everything was fine. Even the pain was gone. I laughed, my eyes blurry.

When I arrived home my mother asked me if I'd gotten some good exercise after school.

"What are you talking about?"

"You said you were staying late to play basketball."

We stared at each other. For an instant I wanted to tell her everything. But I didn't; I understood enough about what had just happened to know that a few wrong words could keep it from happening again.

"I'm gonna stay late tomorrow too," I finally replied.

»

Growing up, I'd never been much of a liar, especially with my mother. She could always detect the slightest alteration in my tone or body language. And she *hated* lying. For her, telling the truth was a way of living correctly, and while countless suggestions and reinforcements hadn't made much of a dent in my general behavior, she'd managed from the very beginning to keep me honest.

But when I started spending time with Raymond, Lucas, and Josh, I had no problem telling my mother I was staying late to play basketball. On one of these afternoons I hid with them in the bushes near a busy road. Lucas had gathered a handful of small apples and passed them to us. A station wagon approached and I stood up and let loose: a direct hit on the back windshield. Then we ran together to the fence near the power lines where we'd left our bikes.

I arrived home that afternoon to find my mother sitting in the kitchen with my sister; they were doing a puzzle together. Suddenly I was sure she knew exactly what I'd been up to. I stood in front of the refrigerator and looked sadly at the floor.

"We're having chicken-fried steak," she said. "You should work on your science project before dinner."

I walked quietly to my room. I wondered if she knew that I was lying and simply didn't care, which seemed worse than being caught.

At the time she was already four months pregnant—tired by the end of each day. Besides having to deal with the details of moving our family into the new house, she also had more to do in the evenings now that my father was working later with his new job. A few days later, I walked up to her in the kitchen and told her, "I want to go over to Raymond's house on Monday."

She was cooking spaghetti sauce, stirring an enormous red pot with a wooden spoon. "Who's Raymond?"

"One of my friends."

"Okay. Get me his phone number and I'll talk to his mother."

"His mother won't be home."

She snorted. "Then you can't go."

"Yes I can!" And before she could react, I fled to my room and slammed the door. I was angry, sure, but really I was hoping she'd come upstairs so we could argue about it. She didn't. So I waited until it was time for dinner—for my father to get home from work—and then I sat quietly at the table, hardly eating, hoping that someone would eventually ask me what was wrong. But no one did, and for the rest of the night I was overcome with loneliness, as if I were lost in a crowd.

»

I didn't interact much with Jonathan Ashley during my first year at Alta Vista. Once, when I was returning from a meeting on the playground with Laurie, I watched him run out of his classroom before the recess bell, his eyes wild and his collar wet. The ugly-mouthed Mr. Rader stood in the doorway and shouted, "Get back here!" But Jonathan was already on his way to the grove of redwoods.

I don't know if there were people at Alta Vista looking out for him in the way the nuns had for me at St. Lucy's. Or if his parents were in constant contact with his teacher. Or if he was in the sort of therapy that I received. Or if he took medication. I'm not even sure if it's fair, now, to evaluate his behavior through my own experience with ADHD.

But that's exactly what I did; I took one look at Jonathan and wanted to sling my past around his neck. I didn't care why he got upset—what horrified me was the overreaction. Jonathan was so sensitive that instead of striking back at a logical target, he'd thrust himself against the suddenly-too-close world until his emotion emptied out, and I felt like it was only a matter of time before he directed it all at me.

But for the most part, the first few months at Alta Vista passed quickly. I hadn't gotten in a fistfight yet, one of the longest stretches of my life, and in such a stable environment, I found it much easier to focus on academics.

My science-fair project on earthquakes attempted to explain their geological causes. I made a large orange cardboard display that folded into three panes, each of which documented a different type of tectonic fault: horizontal, oblique, and vertical. In a bottom corner I included a list of the largest earthquakes in history. I drew the illustrations myself, complete with squiggly lines and arrows to represent the earth's wandering crust. On the first draft I also wrote out the explanations. But my handwriting was so bad that for the final product, my mother copied the paragraphs again in pencil and had me trace over the words with a marker.

At the time my family had a set of World Book Encyclopedias from the 1970s, and in the quiet of my upstairs room, I sprawled out on my carpeted floor and went over the section on earthquakes repeatedly. I discovered that the worst earthquakes occurred when one plate drove beneath another, like in Japan and Alaska. The San Andreas Fault, which my hometown sat along, had been created by the North American plate's steady horizontal grind against the southern-moving Pacific. The highest-magnitude events were listed in descending order, beginning with Chile in 1960 (9.5) and Alaska in 1964 (9.2).

I discussed all of this with Betty Parsons. She would let me stay in the classroom at recess, and I remember her eyes widening when I told her about the 1960 Chilean earthquake—"I can't even imagine eleven minutes of shaking!" she said.

That December I turned in my completed display. A few weeks later Mrs. Parsons asked me to stay after class. I thought it was about my behavior; that morning she'd raised her voice after I kept leaving my seat in the minutes before P.E.

"I sent in your project to represent Alta Vista at the district-wide competition," she said. "And guess what! It won!"

I squinted. "Won what?"

"The award for best fourth-grade display in the entire school district. There were hundreds of entries." She was watching me. "Tim," she said. "You worked so hard!"

Instead of meeting up with Raymond, Lucas, and Josh, I pedaled home on my bike. My mother was upstairs. "What's wrong?" she asked when she saw me.

"Mrs. Parsons says I won the science fair."

She screeched. Then she was hugging me and crying. I was crying too. I'd never won anything in my life. The way I felt made no sense.

I *had* worked hard, and now that I'd been rewarded I should've been happy. But the actual emotion was more like a farewell—being cast from one moment to the next without reference—and afterward I worried that my life was about to take some drastic, irreversible turn.

On a night just before winter break, my parents and I went to a ceremony for nominees and winners at the Union School District headquarters. We walked through the maze of other children's exhibits. "This is some really cool stuff," my father said. "Look—I think that one's about how plants work. Photosynthesis!"

We searched for my orange trifold. There were two categories of exhibits, Experiment and Exposition, and I'd won the latter. We finally arrived at my display. The lines of the faults looked as if they'd been drawn by a toddler.

Eventually a thin bookish-looking woman from the school district stopped by. My father shook hands with her. My mother bragged about all the hours I'd spent reading. The woman nodded. "A lot of the time, we can tell that the parents did the majority of the work," she told us. "That wasn't the case here." She had pale eyes, her blouse hanging loosely off her shoulders. "And I mean that in a good way."

»

Betty Parsons never questioned whether someone with my behavioral issues should be educated alongside thirty other children, or if the extra effort I demanded was fair; her approach was to help maximize the potential of all her students, which was something that she had a talent for discerning.

But for much of the twentieth century, the American educational system resembled the British: children deemed unfit for the mainstream were segregated from the rest, if they received any schooling at all. In 1918 Mississippi became the final state to pass a compulsory attendance law, and while implementation and funding varied widely on a case-by-case basis, most US public schools began to offer special programs;

there were classes for "idiots" and "imbeciles," as well as for the broad category of borderline children.

An early American proponent of these classes was the Yale-educated clinical psychologist J. E. W. Wallin. In his 1914 book *The Mental Health of the School Child,* he advocated for the segregation of troubled students. "In the regular grades these children are almost always irritated, disheartened, depressed, or embittered," he wrote, noting how they struggled "against the attempts to force them to apply themselves to subject-matter." Segregating such "ne'er-do-wells" would "free the regular grades of driftwood and dead weights" and "improve the working conditions for the normals."

As in Britain, the special-ed curriculums in America emphasized manual training over academic preparation. Wallin noted that children without any clear intellectual impairments should still be educated with the same kind of physical and social program that was "provided for the morons."

The first person to reevaluate this approach in the context of hyperactive children was Alfred Strauss, the doctor who'd coined the diagnostic term "minimal brain damage."

Strauss believed that all cases of ADHD were the result of previous physical trauma—that symptoms such as severe hyperactivity and inattention were in fact proof that past damage had occurred, even if no record existed. In their 1947 book, he and his colleague Laura E. Lehtinën offered their now-outdated theories on the causes of ADHD-like behavior. However, they also addressed the question of harnessing "the peculiar mental organization" of a child who was "neither crippled nor intellectually retarded" but exhibited serious "behavior abnormalities."

Unlike the British doctors Still and Tredgold, Strauss wasn't obsessed with the future of civilization. He reminded the reader that his subject was "a human being born with the inherited characteristics of his parents . . . and experiencing the environment and its influences." He tried to see the situation through the eyes of his subject: "From the child's point of view, however, his seeming inattentiveness is the expression of an abnormally attentive condition." Almost seventy years later, this description still feels accurate: ADHD as a series of hyperfocused tunnels that are constantly broken and reformed by the intrusion of the outside world.

He eventually concluded that the symptoms were the result of an "exaggerated responsiveness to stimuli." Since he couldn't do anything about the ultimate cause—the assumed damage to the brain—he sought to modify the child's environment, and at a private elementary school in Racine he set up a series of minimal-stimulus classes. The rooms were large, the windows covered with translucent paper, and the seating spread out. The number of students was capped at twelve. All visual stimulation was removed, including "pictures, murals, bulletin boards." Even the teacher's appearance was tightly controlled; Strauss wanted to avoid "the distracting influence of ornamentation such as bracelets, earrings, dangling necklaces, and flowers in the hair." If during a lesson a child began to act out, his desk was moved to the wall and he sat with his back to the class, though the teacher was supposed to explain that this was meant to increase concentration and not as a punishment. "For a very hyperactive and disinhibited child," he wrote, "we have even resorted to the expedient of isolation behind a clinic screen."

In this modified environment the students were taught the same academic curriculum as in mainstream classes, but with the help of physical aids. For math, they used number wheels, abacuses, and blocks that fit onto wooden pegs. For reading: alphabet cards, letter puzzles, and sheets that isolated individual book passages. And to help with writing they carved letters into clay pans, traced parallel lines on onionskin, and enlarged the grips on their pencils. These aids were supposed to strengthen the relationship between symbols such as numbers and letters and what they represented, while also slowing down a process that, in a normal class, a hyperactive child would rush through and fail to learn from.

Strauss was proposing the same solution as his contemporaries to the issue of children with behavior problems—segregation—but with a new twist: he believed that the confines of the right specialized environment could help a child "for the first time experience adequacy in meeting intellectual requirements."

>>

Screens and wall-facing aside, a minimal-stimulus approach like Dr. Alfred Strauss's does hold a certain allure. I remember an early-spring afternoon in my upstairs room. My closet door was covered in a body-length mirror, which reflected the window above my bed just as the sun was setting over the coastal mountains. Suddenly the light in the room doubled and the shadows cleared; I held out my fingers, their tips like glass.

I'd been researching my latest project for Mrs. Parsons: we had to write a five-page narrative on any subject we liked. Once again I chose earthquakes—specifically, the 1906 earthquake that devastated San Francisco. I'd come across a book at the school library that recounted the event from the perspective of survivors. In one story, a policeman stopped and listened as all the dogs along the street began howling at once. Moments later the shaking started. In another, a bellhop escaped his hotel just before it crumbled to the ground. Against the now-empty sky he watched the remaining buildings sway together as if in a waltz. And a woman tried to cook eggs for her family after the quake ended, but the gas lines were ruptured, and her apartment caught fire.

The narratives were alarming but at the time I wasn't afraid; I found myself imagining the events from a safely cinematic perch, and I can still remember the sensation as I finished the chapter about the woman igniting her house: I came awake to my solitary room, the sunset beating the air.

In Mrs. Parsons's classroom I never fell so deeply into our material, and even if I did manage to focus I would struggle when we transitioned to another subject. I always made careless mistakes on math problems, and I'd rush through spelling quizzes without double-checking my answers. On book reports my handwriting was barely legible.

But my fourth-grade teacher was interested in efforts and results equally. That spring I finished my narrative on the 1906 earthquake, and Mrs. Parsons chose it for display at our school-wide writing fair. On my report card I received top grades for academics and just-below-average ones for behavior. When school finally let out for the summer, she pulled me aside and said, "I want you to know that I really enjoyed having you in my classroom." She was looking right at me: a sincere, thoughtful gesture.

But for whatever reason her words reminded me of Laurie's therapy: something I needed, as opposed to something that was true. Also, the other children had already begun shouting in the courtyard, celebrating the arrival of vacation. I could picture Raymond, Lucas, and Josh gathering at the bike rack.

I shrugged, said thank you, and walked off.

»

My brother was born in June of 1990. My mother decided at the last minute to name him Michael Angelo, but a nurse pulled her aside and explained that he'd be teased mercilessly for it down the road—didn't she know about the popular cartoon *Teenage Mutant Ninja Turtles,* in which the characters were eponymous with Renaissance painters?—so my mother settled on the middle name Jonangelo, and my father bought cigars, including a bubble-gum one for me: "It's got powder in there and when you puff it fake smoke comes out!"

For the next week my mother spent most of her time in the bedroom with the baby. She and my father were exhausted. At first I tried to be helpful; I made sure not to bring up the question I'd been asking for months: When could I go out with my friends?

That spring, my mother and I had come to an uneasy truce. I wanted to do what Lucas, Raymond, and Josh got to do without having to lie about it, but she had a rule against houses with no parents at home, so I came up with my own solution: once or twice a week I rode around the neighborhood with the three boys, going down to the creek, playing basketball in the park, or jumping our bikes in the dirt behind the middle school. The other afternoons I had baseball, and Raymond's mother was there on the weekend.

But now it was vacation, and none of us were in summer school. Just as my mother started getting back on her feet—she always hated being cooped up—we were returning from the grocery store with my sister and baby brother when I said, "I want to be able to ride my bike to the video game shop at the mall down by the freeway."

She had deep shadows in her face. "Let's talk about this later," she told me.

I began to argue: it was only a few miles; there were crosswalks; children younger than me got to do it; and how could she trust me to mow the lawn but not this? "Lawnmowers are more dangerous than bikes!" I shouted.

"Stop talking," she said as we pulled up to our house.

"Why? Because you're wrong and you know it?"

She switched off the ignition. My sister unbuckled herself and climbed out. My brother was sleeping in his car seat. I got out too and came around to my mother's side, where she was sitting with the door open. "You're so *illogical*," I said.

But my mother was staring at the steering wheel, her arms draped over its sides. There were tears in her eyes.

"What are you doing?" I asked. By now my sister was beside me.

"I can't get up," she told us. "My hands are on fire."

"What do you mean?"

"Mom!" my sister said.

My mother waved at the air between us. She tried pulling herself up on the steering wheel but fell back into the seat. Finally I helped her from the car, her weight coming down on me. My sister and I walked her into the living room, where she sat in a chair and called my father from the portable phone.

Afterward—after I got my brother out of his car seat, placed him in my mother's arms, and took in the groceries—I could only think about how I was stuck in our kitchen, trusted enough to hold a baby but not to ride my bike a few miles to the mall.

>>

Later that week I watched my mother lift and then drop a full pot of spaghetti on the linoleum floor. She could barely pull down hard enough to open the venetian blinds in the living room. Her joints ached and she felt exhausted all the time. Was I worried about her health? Yes, but I figured that it had to do with her pregnancy. I didn't know that our family doctor had ordered blood and other diagnostic tests; he'd initially suggested postpartum depression, but her symptoms didn't match up.

In August of that summer, my mother sat us all down and explained that she needed more help around the house. She made a list of chores: carrying the laundry upstairs, taking out the garbage, emptying the dishwasher, picking up after the dog, etc. She'd always expected us to pitch in, but in the past I'd found that if I shirked these chores long enough she'd usually end up doing them for me.

I remember an evening a few days after that. We'd already eaten dinner, the light receding; I was outside throwing a tennis ball against our garage when my father pulled up. "Timmo!" he said. "Working on your breaking pitches?" I handed him the ball and he tossed it loosely against our house, the rebound coming perfectly to me. With his two front fingers he made a cutting motion—the sign for a curveball—and I looped one forward. "Stah-rike three!" he said.

My father had gotten home a few hours later than usual. We'd probably been tossing the ball for ten minutes when I heard a high, boiling shout. I looked up to find my mother in the doorway. I figured it was about me, but my father started up the front steps. I followed.

My mother was in sweatpants and a baggy shirt. "I told you how much pain I was in today," she said to him. "I asked you just this once to come home early." She squinted. "Are you drunk?"

"Hey," he told her, "you knew I was playing in a golf tournament." He glanced at me and added, "A *work* golf tournament. With clients."

I winced. He probably did too. But when I looked up she was gone from the doorway.

After a moment my father stepped tentatively into the house. My mother reappeared. She was holding my brother, my sister trailing behind, and as she flew past us I felt my arm yanked forward; before I knew it I was in the backseat. We were leaving. From the half light of our porch my father called, "Patty?"

That night we drove through the marine darkness of the coastal mountains to Monterey, a famous resort town. We checked in at an expensive hotel. As we entered our room my mother said, "It's a vacation!"

"What about our clothes?" I asked.

"We'll buy new ones!"

"Can we order room service?" my sister wondered.

"Yes!" My mother was smiling, but her cheeks looked bloodless and thin. I slunk to the couch near the TV and fell asleep.

That night my two-month-old brother screamed for hours; he had a terrible ear infection. In the morning my mother could barely walk, but she dragged us through a thick summer fog to the town's aquarium. Later we went to a wax museum of 1950s celebrities; Marilyn Monroe looked as if she'd been frozen for centuries and only now, at room temperature, was coming back to life. "Can't I just hang out in the hotel room?" I asked.

"Timmy," she said. "I'll get you anything you want. How about lobster for dinner?"

I loved lobster; I got to eat it only once every few years. "Isn't that too expensive?"

"Who cares!" And off we went to the hotel restaurant, my brother in his stroller, my sister wearing a shirt with the town's name on it. The lobster cost $50, but I barely touched it, staring instead at the green heave of the bay. Each bite felt like taking sides—choosing one parent over the other—when really the only thing I wanted was to be left alone.

For my mother, escaping with us to Monterey wasn't just about punishing my father, or acting impulsively in the face of illness; she was desperate to understand what was happening to her, and for that she needed some emotional—or at the very least physical—distance.

The next day, when we finally got back home, my father was waiting in the doorway. "We saw real sea otters!" my sister shouted. My mother stepped forward. He reached out to hug her. But they didn't immediately embrace; she approached him in a way I'd never seen—sheepishly.

》

That fall I started my last year of elementary school. At Alta Vista, the fifth grade was separated into two thirty-five-children classrooms with a movable wall down the middle, and a few afternoons a week, this partition would recede and our pair of instructors would team-teach, all seventy of us moving through a network of group-work stations.

Jonathan Ashley was in the other class. Raymond, Lucas, and Josh were in mine. For the first time I had a male teacher, Mr. Ellis. He was short and thin-armed with black glasses and a cropped flattop that made him look older than his actual age, which was perhaps forty. "Soon enough you'll be in middle school," he said during an introductory lecture that first week. "It's my job to prepare you for it."

My seat was along the movable wall, and as this short-haired man droned on I found myself listening to the world beyond the partition. Countless children were in there, studying with the other fifth-grade teacher, Ms. Lenz: a small woman in her sixties who liked baseball and spoke in a smoker's voice that made everything she said sound both wry and sincere. I was imagining her class as a flock of small bright birds—each one standing obediently on its desk—when Mr. Ellis said by way of some analogy, "The blues is the only musical form ever invented in America."

"What about rap?" I blurted.

After a moment he dipped his chin and said, "Tim?" But he knew who I was. He'd already met with my mother and declined to fill out Laurie's notes home, explaining that such a system would be unsustainable in a middle-school environment, which he was trying to replicate.

"Well," he finally said, "to answer your question: no. I would suspect that rap music originated somewhere in the tribal regions of Africa."

What could I do? I laughed, a single contemptuous bark. Even then I knew his answer was ridiculous.

Later, during the deluge that was our group-work session, I could feel Mr. Ellis watching me. At one point I stopped what I was doing and caught his small earnest glance; we stared at each other for seconds until he finally looked away.

»

I remember something Laurie Hamilton said during the first month of fifth grade: "Do you know how rare your situation is? A lot of parents of children with ADD fight endlessly over homework."

We were walking along the perimeter of Alta Vista. I'd been arguing with her about why I still had to come to these sessions; hadn't the previous year gone well? Wasn't I smart enough to succeed in school without all the extra attention?

She was complimenting me—"Your mom and dad have never had that problem. You just go up to your room and poof!"—but I could hear only the letters, an *A* and two quick *D*s. After six years Laurie saw my situation clearly: if I could just get along with my teacher and fellow students I'd do fine academically and keep moving forward.

Dr. Alfred Strauss had the same goal in mind when he came up with his low-stimulus education: eliminate the source of conflict, which was rooted in the dynamic environment of the classroom. He thought that "with few notable exceptions," hyperactive children wouldn't reach their academic potential among normal students, even in the presence of "an understanding teacher."

But while I obviously enjoyed working on projects in my quiet up-stairs bedroom, how could a fifth grader interpret Strauss's suggested isolation as anything but a punishment?

Which is one of the problems with segregated learning practices: they tend to create a system-wide sense of inequality. By the middle of the twentieth century, special-ed curriculums remained underdeveloped, the teachers poorly prepared, and the facilities underfunded. Children who found themselves there rarely made it back into the mainstream, and the placement procedures themselves were suspect, targeting minority students in a disproportionate manner. What's more, the proponents of specialized classrooms had failed to offer clear proof that children actually performed better in them.

In the 1950s and '60s, the number of students in special education increased by almost two million. By this point it was illegal to expel children completely from the public school system. For borderline cases there were two options: keep up with everyone else or enter a growing system of segregated learning.

Eventually, advocates for children with disabilities began challenging the existing framework through a series of lawsuits. In the 1972 case *The Pennsylvania Association for Retarded Children v. Pennsylvania,* the parents of thirteen mentally handicapped students contested the current practice in which a school psychologist could declare a child with disabilities "uneducable" and assign them to a classroom with inferior resources. "Stigmatization is a major concern," Judge Thomas A. Masterson wrote in the majority opinion. "Some parents liken it to a sentence of death." He and two other judges ruled that all students had the right to "a meaningful program of education and training." A year later, in *Mills v. the Board of Education of the District of Columbia,* a Washington, DC, court found that ungraded special-ed classrooms were discriminatory: just because certain children had "been labeled as behavioral problems, mentally retarded, emotionally disturbed or hyperactive" didn't mean they forfeited the right to an education "in regular classrooms with supportive services."

There were similar cases in more than twenty states, and in 1973,

Congress began holding hearings on possible federal legislation. Two years later Gerald Ford signed Public Law 94-142: the Education for All Handicapped Children Act (EHA). It granted Americans with disabilities between the ages of three and eighteen the right to "a free appropriate public education" in "the least restrictive environment"—a setting in which they could still interact with non-disabled students. This integration was promoted through Individualized Education Programs (IEPs), which included academic goals for that specific child along with provisions for the extra help necessary to achieving them.

The EHA also banned racial and cultural bias in placement procedures, offered parents the opportunity to challenge a school's decisions, and prohibited segregation except in cases where the disability was so severe, "supplementary aids and services" couldn't help achieve integration in a normal classroom.

The law allowed for the use of tutors, personal attendants, extra time, and other special services. These accommodations were seen as necessary for children with disabilities to succeed in mainstream education, a setting that in its initial design had ignored those who functioned differently than the majority.

»

A morning English lesson in Mr. Ellis's class: I was sitting near the movable wall as he diagrammed sentences on the whiteboard when, from the class next door, I heard a warbled exclamation. It was near and then far off, a sound similar to laughter. But the wall hid the true meaning, and as my own class quieted for a few minutes to identify verbs and nouns on a handout—the kind of pop quiz that Mr. Ellis said we'd see in middle school—I imagined that the inhabitants of Ms. Lenz's room had transformed into a flock of quarreling sparrows.

Later that week I got my quiz back. It had only ten questions and didn't mean much toward our grade. But Mr. Ellis had drawn an enormous *D* at the header.

I raised my hand and pointed out that on one of the questions I'd obviously identified the noun, even though my circle included half of an adjacent adjective.

"You can't give the wrong answer and then claim you meant something else," he said. The other students were already packing up for recess.

"You think I was trying to circle two words?"

"Am I supposed to grade you on your intentions, Tim, or your work?"

"But what about when you get things wrong?" I said. "Who judges *your* work?"

This was how things had been going; we bickered until one of us gained an advantage. At my disposal was public disruption. He'd found that after my success in Mrs. Parsons's class nothing upset me quite like a *D* or an *F*.

"I can regrade the quiz," he finally said. "Though there's a chance your score will be even lower, should I look at it more carefully."

I nodded. "So you admit you didn't grade it 'carefully' enough the first time?"

After everyone filed out for recess, he called me to his desk. "Listen to me," he said. He took off his glasses and, squinting, pinched the small pale fin of his nose. "In middle school all that matters is the work you do. It determines your standing in high school. Which leads to what college you get into. This starts now. Do you understand?"

"Yeah," I said. "You think I'm stupid."

"Do you want to know what I really think?" When he put his glasses back on it was as if his eyes had grown two sizes. "Eventually you're going to run out of excuses."

》

That fall, as my mother continued to suffer from fatigue, general pain, and swelling in her joints, her family doctor sent her to additional specialists for more tests. In the meantime, she was prescribed an extremely high dosage of aspirin: up to eighteen pills a day.

On an afternoon in early December I came home later than usual after riding around the neighborhood. It was nearly dark. From her room my mother asked loudly, "Where were you?" My baby brother was sleeping alongside her.

"Jeez," I replied. "Keep your voice down."

She sat up. "What did you say to me?"

It was a genuine question; she couldn't seem to hear me. I'd find out later that the aspirin treatment was causing her ears to ring continuously. For an entire week she'd felt dizzy and lost within her own body.

"You're gonna wake up Mikey!" I shouted. Then I turned and walked downstairs, ignoring her calls for me to come back.

My father and sister were in the TV room watching basketball together.

"We're playing a game!" my sister shouted. "Daddy, show him."

My father was sunk in a recliner, the footrest kicked out, a couple of empty beers on the table alongside. He glanced up at me through the half light. "Watch this," he said. He snapped his fingers. My sister shot from the room, and when she came back she was holding a fresh beer.

"Fifteen seconds," he told her. "Your best time yet!"

She sat down on the floor and they settled into a silence that was broken every so often by an excitable sports announcer.

Up in my room I turned on all the lights and opened the windows to the darkness, its late-autumn chill. But soon my mother was calling me down for dinner. I imagined my family hunkered together at the table. I didn't want anything to do with them, but at the same time I couldn't stand that they were all down there without me. She shouted louder. Finally I heard her footsteps.

I closed the door and said, "You can't come in my room!"

"What?" She tried the knob. "This is ridiculous. Do I need to get your dad?"

I didn't respond. Soon enough: the heavy, quick steps. "What the hell's the matter with you?" my father demanded. "We're having a family dinner."

I opened the door. They stood together, their faces darkened in astonishment.

I looked at them both and was overcome with anger. Why? Remembering it now is like sinking in water; all that remains is my unrelenting need to move through the two of them.

"I hate you," I told my mother.

She laughed. "You're grounded."

"You can't make me do anything," I said.

My brother was crying downstairs. Behind them I could see my sister, watching. My mother leaned on the doorway and said to my father, "Slap him."

He and I glanced at each other. But before she could say anything else I shouted, "See? You're too weak to hit me yourself!"

She bolted forward. I curled into a ball as her fists came down on my head and neck. It didn't hurt—my mother's wrists were like loose strings—and after a moment I was free; my father had lifted her up. She struggled in his arms. When he finally set her down she collapsed on the floor. "Timmy!" she cried.

I responded in a voice that sounded nothing like my own: "If you touch me again I'm gonna bend your fingers back until they break."

》

In his memoir *An Only Child,* the Irish author Frank O'Connor writes that children can be "abominably cruel" since they "see only one side of any question and because of their powerlessness see it with hysterical clarity."

How did I feel, threatening my mother? Laurie asked me that very question a week later during our therapy session at Alta Vista.

We were walking near the basketball courts. It was a blue winter morning and the sunlight had a beleaguered quality to it, as if its heat wouldn't reach us for days. On my left I could see the dried fringe of the redwoods, their shadows cast solidly in the dirt.

"Like she couldn't tell me what to do," I answered.

Of course I loved my mother. I knew she was suffering. I didn't want to hurt her any more than I wanted to be hurt myself. But in the midst of our fights, words and gestures became a means to an end.

"How are things going with the other children at school?" Laurie asked now.

"Fine." In fact I was mad at Raymond, Lucas, and Josh. A few days before the fight with my mother, I'd gathered alongside them at the bike rack just as Jonathan Ashley drifted over, which was something that had never happened before. But they'd known him for years. And like it was the most natural thing in the world he grabbed his own bike and rode alongside us to the dirt jumps behind the middle school, where he pedaled through them so recklessly even I was impressed. Afterward I was desperate to humiliate him. But I didn't know how. "Your shirt's all chewed up," I finally said.

Jonathan cocked his head. He was smiling. And with a sense of humor I hadn't counted on he bit at his shirt and started panting overdramatically, like a dog.

"Tim," Laurie finally said to me on the playground. Her chin was still sharp, her dark hair streaked with highlights. "Do you think things are getting a bit out of control at home?"

"It was just an argument," I told her.

She stopped. "It's a very difficult time for your parents. And for you."

"You're gonna blame me for making everything worse, right?"

In the cool dome of the morning she placed her hand on my shoulder. "I hardly ever see a patient as long as I've seen you. There's an excellent psychiatrist in San Jose who I think you'd like. He's my cousin. His name is Joe Epstein."

"Wait," I said. The sun, the coastal mountains, the distant shore of the redwoods. Suddenly the playground was like the deck of an enormous ship that she and I had been riding for years. "I'm sorry about what I said to my mom. And to you. And for arguing with everyone lately. And for not listening at school to Mr. Ellis!"

I realized that she was kneeling, reaching out; we were hugging. "Everything's going to work out," she said. "I mean that. But right now it's time to try something new."

»

Laurie Hamilton had insisted from the beginning that her therapy sessions weren't meant to go on forever; her multifaceted approach to ADHD had long since been introduced and reinforced and there weren't any new lessons to implement. During my struggle with Pamela Kovalenko, our meetings had worked well as triage, but now I was much more resistant, and Laurie recognized that my parents weren't in the best position to respond calmly. She also knew the danger of so much conflict. I was getting better at fighting with other people, to the point where it was becoming my first response to the world. And since the goal of any effective therapy is to help a child continue forward in a normal manner—to keep the problems that the behavior causes from interfering with social and academic development—she was finally willing to consider new options, which demanded the expertise of someone like her cousin, Dr. Joe Epstein.

My first meeting with him was scheduled for January, at the end of winter break. Around that time the results finally came back on my mother's health. A doctor at the Stanford University Medical Center told her that she had rheumatoid arthritis, a disease in which the immune system mistakenly attacks the body's healthy tissue around the joints. There's no cure, but the symptoms can be managed with strong steroids like prednisone, which can lead to a severe immune deficiency.

I found out later that when my mother was told the diagnosis she walked out into the brilliant winter parking lot of the university hospital and sobbed. She was relieved. For months she'd been unable to go jogging or have a drink with friends or even carry the laundry downstairs, and at least now she'd learned why; she could start doing something about it.

A few days later my mother sat me down and explained the disease. She emphasized that it wasn't as bad as similar immune disorders like lupus and multiple sclerosis, and on a certain level I understood: this would change our family. But as a child how do you conceive of a chronic illness, something that can last for many more years than the lifetime you've already lived?

We met with Dr. Epstein on a weekday afternoon. He was plump, soft-skinned, and covered everywhere with hair—except for his head. His focus was in child and adolescent psychiatry; he worked in the special-treatment ward of San Jose hospital and had a practice nearby.

The first thing I noticed in his office was a large, surrealistic painting of a teepee. It was black and white with swirling lines, as if the whole thing had been smoked into existence from some underground fire, and as I sat down on his couch I couldn't help but stare.

"You like it?" he asked, following my gaze.

"Why? Did you paint it or something?"

"Ha," he said. "I did not." He wanted to know if I understood why I was here. Could I tell him about how things were going at school? At home? It was similar enough to my sessions with Laurie, and his voice lacked accusation, but I gave short answers, afraid that my words might be used against me.

After a while he called in my parents; for this first session they'd left my sister and brother with a babysitter. He asked my mother to explain the recent difficulties in our family. With a flat, clinical voice she summarized our recent fights. "He's just so angry all the time," she said. "I'm like: how do I get through to that sweet loving boy I know is in there?"

Afterward my father was prompted to weigh in, but he glanced suspiciously at the painting and said, "Yeah, things aren't so good right now."

"Tim?" Dr. Epstein said. "Does this sound accurate?"

I laughed. "They're the crazy ones."

"Watch your tone," my mother said.

"Or what? You'll hit me? You can't even make a fist!"

Dr. Epstein held up his hand. To all of us he said, "It might be time to think about trying medication."

"For who?" I asked.

"He had a terrible reaction to Ritalin when he was younger," my mother said.

"Don't talk about me like I'm not here!" I suddenly felt like I was on a stage, being evaluated by people I couldn't see—and with one more wrong word I'd lose the competition altogether. "That's it." I pointed at my parents. "I'm declaring war on both of you."

This was during the run-up to the first Gulf War; I'd been watching news footage on it constantly over winter break.

My father sighed.

"See?" my mother said. "Do you see what it's like?"

When Dr. Epstein spoke his voice was quiet. "There's no need to make a decision right at this moment," he finally told us.

»

The psychiatrist Edward M. Hallowell, in the 1995 edition of his popular book *Driven to Distraction,* talks about how the primary impulsivity of younger children can result as time goes by in what he calls a "rage re-action"; the lack of inhibition keeps an adolescent from backing down in upsetting situations. He also points out that "repeated failures, misunder-standings, mislabelings, and all manner of other emotional mishaps" can make a child seem "stubborn, willful, or obnoxious," too.

In school I still felt something similar to what I'd experienced back at St. Lucy's, confinement in the daylong sentence of my desk. When we returned from winter break Mr. Ellis assigned our major academic project for the year: a fifteen-page state report. He asked us to put down our top three preferences. I listed the places my father had played mi-nor-league baseball, Florida and Nebraska, along with California.

Secretly I was excited about the assignment. I loved geography. But later that week the selections were announced; I was assigned Ohio. I stood up and shouted, "I didn't even put that down as one of my choices!"

Suddenly the classroom was gray and still; everyone was looking at me, including my teacher. "You know what, Tim?" he finally said. "Be quiet. Wait your turn. Show some respect for your fellow students—for me! How about just once you act your age."

I blinked a few times and sat down. It didn't make sense; if he was trying to provoke me, why did he act so surprised at my response?

I didn't know it at the time, but throughout my fifth-grade year, my mother had actually been in contact with Mr. Ellis; unlike Pamela Kovalenko he'd been willing to talk to her about what was happening in class. During phone conversations and the occasional after-school meetings, which he preferred to written communication like Laurie's notes home, he admitted that he should be more patient. Sometimes he couldn't help but overreact, like when he'd write an enormous *D* on one of my assignments. But in other instances it was simple carelessness; with so many children to worry about he couldn't predict everything that might set me off.

In the case of my state report he'd made a mistake—I was supposed to have gotten Nebraska—and my outburst had caught him off guard. But after such an outrageous challenge there was no way he could give in.

During the next month, whenever we worked on the report in class I would announce in a loud singsong voice, "Why-o why-o why-o, did I ever get Ohio?" Then I'd look toward Mr. Ellis, hoping for a reaction and at the same time hating him for trying to hide it.

»

When I attended Alta Vista in the early 1990s, the school didn't have a psychologist or counselor on staff, and individual teachers dealt with attention and hyperactivity issues as they saw fit.

The 1975 Education for All Handicapped Children Act hadn't specifically addressed ADHD. The term itself didn't yet exist, and a clear set of diagnostic procedures wouldn't be codified until the *DSM-III* was released five years later. Instead, according to the law's definition of "handicapped," children with issues like mine could qualify for additional help in two ways: under the label "seriously emotionally disturbed"; or if they possessed "specific learning disabilities" that affected their capacity "to listen, think, speak, read, write, spell, or do mathematical calculations." But these impairments couldn't be the result of environmental factors; they needed to stem from medical conditions such as "brain injury, minimal brain dysfunction, dyslexia, and developmental aphasia."

So Alfred Strauss's initial term for hyperactivity, MBD, had been buried three steps deep in the new federal law; a child could qualify for help only through an assessment of the problems that the symptoms of ADHD caused, as opposed to just receiving a medical diagnosis, which was also required.

As a result, it wasn't clear exactly how someone with ADHD could access the new services, and by the end of the 1980s most boys and girls with the disorder weren't receiving extra help. In 1989 Congress began to consider revising the 1975 law to include better categorical definitions, which would allow students already diagnosed with ADHD, autism, and traumatic brain injury to qualify immediately.

But other disability organizations opposed ADHD's inclusion. During congressional hearings on the subject, representatives from groups like the National Association of School Psychologists claimed that since there wasn't definitive proof of ADHD's biological origins, a disproportionate number of children could qualify, which would overwhelm the current special-ed framework and draw services away from children with more dire handicaps. Their argument favored the existing setup; students with ADHD would still be eligible under the previous categories.

The result was a compromise. In 1990, when the revised version of the EHA passed both houses of Congress and was renamed the Individuals with Disabilities Education Act (IDEA), autism and traumatic brain injury were included; ADHD was left out. But Congress also mandated that the Office of Special Education Programs (OSEP) clarify that children with the disorder could still qualify for the law's provisions under the categories of severe emotional disturbance and learning disabled, as well as "other health impairment." In October of 1991 OSEP issued a memorandum to all US school districts. Parents and educators across the country were told that ADHD was a legitimate disorder and that students suffering from it were eligible for extra help in the classroom. Over the next decade enrollment in the three qualifying categories would skyrocket, especially under "other health impairment."

So after nearly a century of compulsory schooling our educational system had adopted a legal concept of integration: ideally, children with ADHD would receive extra help and function like everyone else within the mainstream. Not that it always worked out this way.

When IDEA was signed into law I was still in Mr. Ellis's class. He knew about my diagnosis and that I was in therapy. How might I have benefited from an independent education plan? It would have helped with one of our main sources of conflict, his stated objective of preparing us for a middle school environment. That's what an IEP provides: a separate set of goals and milestones that the teacher and student can work toward. It also would've emphasized the importance of treatment; like Laurie's therapy, an IEP draws attention to behavior that is often mistaken for laziness.

But the official memorandum clarifying how I could qualify wouldn't come out for another year. Besides, things had gone so well in Mrs. Parsons's class. In the end my mother, teacher, psychologist, and new psychiatrist never considered applying for an IEP.

》

That spring Mr. Ellis talked about our state report as if it would shine through the ages: "From now on, all your major academic projects will be like this one."

I hated everything about the assignment. In fact I'd come to despise Ohio's very existence. After a month of homework and in-class exercises I still hadn't started many of the requirements—color-coded maps; drawings of the state seal, motto, and bird—and my historical section was filled with sentences like "Ohio is a place where people have lived." I finished most of it the night before.

For grading Mr. Ellis relied on a rubric that kept track of grammar and layout mistakes. When he passed back my report a sheet was stapled to the front, and at the bottom, beneath a cascade of subtractions, the number *60* was circled beside my name.

I'd known going in that my work was terrible. In a sense I'd done it on purpose, as if a bad enough report would make everyone else despise Ohio in the way I did. But a D-minus? On our biggest project of the year? I flipped through the pages. The maps looked threadbare. My crayon marks streaked outside the lines. And my handwriting: the letters were crowded together like debris from a recent storm. I jumped up, threw the report on the ground, and ran from the classroom.

The morning was dull and wet. I sat down on a bench near the basketball courts and tried to squint away tears. The redwoods loomed over me. The sky was an overcast roof. In the distance, the blue slope of the coastal range rose up like an amphitheatre, enormous and steep.

Mr. Ellis was standing in the doorway. He watched me in the way you'd watch a bird that's flown in through a window: there was still a space between us and the exit was the same as the entrance but who could tell the difference now?

»

Over the next few weeks I didn't bother to argue with my fifth-grade teacher. I sat quietly against the movable partition and let the things it kept hidden wash over me, as if I could inhabit both classrooms without being anywhere. After school I was grounded for my low grades, and during my sessions with Dr. Epstein I responded to each of his questions with a yes or a no. Sometimes we'd spend minutes in silence, his surrealistic painting like a mist between us.

The truth was, I still wanted to be seen as good and successful and hardworking by the people around me. I'd rationalized my recent failures in terms of obstacles—my crazy mother and ignorant teacher—but the state report was like the flash in the window of a passing car: it reflected the impediment I wasn't capable of seeing.

Then on a Monday at the end of April I arrived at school and Mr. Ellis told me that for the final month I'd switch to Ms. Lenz's room. He and my mother had been worried about my deteriorating behavior; in my six years of education I'd never really run out of a classroom like that. She believed that a change of environment had always helped in the past, he was more than happy to agree, and Ms. Lenz didn't object. So I gathered up my things and moved one door down.

Mr. Ellis didn't say much about it. He and I had spent nearly a year together. Since my comment on rap music, nothing had gone right. I'm still not sure about his motivation: Did he genuinely believe in the necessity of my failure—that there was no other way to prepare someone like me for everything that was to come—or had he not actually meant for it to go that way at all?

On that first day, Ms. Lenz sat me in the front row, right next to Jonathan Ashley. I tried my best to ignore him, but I'd never been so close to him for so long. His hair was caked and sweaty. He smelled sour. Not to mention the holes at his collar. During a morning lesson he kept banging around in his desk, and just before lunch he aced a peer-graded spelling quiz; he passed it to me, we listened for the correct letters, and I was forced to write *10/10* on the top.

Ms. Lenz reminded me of my Irish grandmothers: she interacted with us as if she'd already gotten a few cocktails under her belt. It took a rather serious infraction on our part to rouse her. By the afternoon I found myself wondering why I hadn't been in her class from the beginning. And then it hit me. Jonathan and I must have been divided on purpose: I'd drawn Mr. Ellis and Jonathan had spent the last eight months with this placid woman. I felt something more startling than jealousy; it was like finding yourself alone in a room long after everyone else has been allowed to leave.

As we filed out of class at the end of the day, I knocked Jonathan into the frame of the door and said, "Watch it! God."

He kept walking. I followed him to the bike rack. "Why'd you run into me like that?" He bent down to undo his chain.

"So you're saying it was on purpose?" I asked.

Jonathan hunched his shoulders and curled his head down to his chest.

I tried to look smug. "You're not gonna start throwing rocks again, are you?"

Other kids were gathering, including Raymond, Lucas, and Josh. I hadn't spent much time with them lately. For the last few months I'd been grounded more often than not, and when we did hang out I could be moody and indignant. Still, they tolerated me; they were generous enough to accept my presence as a given.

I nodded toward them now as if everything I was doing made perfect sense. But they were looking past me. Jonathan had stopped fiddling with his bike. He stood at full height. His shoulders were huge. His shirt was in his mouth, the ratty cotton tensed above his chest, and from somewhere in his throat came a fleshy sound I'd never heard.

In the next instant he rushed at me. I backpedaled. He gave chase for a few steps, I kept fleeing, and after a moment the collar dropped from his teeth; he parted his wet lips as if to say something.

But then he turned and walked back to the bike rack, joining Raymond, Lucas, Josh, and a handful of other boys from our class who'd watched my retreat.

»

Despite her previous experiences with older male doctors, my mother liked Joe Epstein. He listened to everything she had to say, wasn't arrogant, and seemed to understand that my situation couldn't be solved with a cookie-cutter approach.

She and my father weren't eager to put me on a medication, especially considering the way things had gone the first time. Dr. Epstein told them about an older drug: nortriptyline. It was a tricyclic antidepressant, part of the class first discovered in the mid-1950s. Nortriptyline had once been used to treat depression in adults, but by the late 1980s it was occasionally prescribed to adolescents with ADHD when stimulants weren't an option.

Unlike Ritalin, nortriptyline needed to build up in a patient's system, which meant that its effects would take a few weeks to manifest. Dr. Epstein had prescribed it for years and noted that its side effects were minimal. He told my parents that this sort of treatment wouldn't miraculously fix my problems; environmental adjustments, like responding more patiently to my behavior, were necessary.

During the last week of May, we were about halfway through one of our regular therapy sessions when Dr. Epstein went out to the lobby and asked my mother and father to join us. I could tell by their stiff movements that something was up. Finally my new psychiatrist turned to me and said, "I'd like to prescribe you a dose of nortriptyline."

"What the hell is that?"

"Language," my father said. "Come on."

"It's a drug that might help with some of the frustration you've been feeling."

"I'm fine," I said. "You can't just force me to take something. I have a choice."

"Then choose to stop acting like this!" my mother cried. "How about that?"

"I'll spit out the pills. I won't take them."

She stood up. Her hand was gaunt, a knuckle rising behind the finger she pointed at me. "You will."

»

For my parents, the decision to try nortriptyline was also an admission that the level of conflict in our family had spun out of control. For me, taking it felt like losing the one argument that mattered: who was right and who was wrong. The drug represented my mother's ultimate power over me, and it was as if I'd been fighting a battle I now understood to be rigged.

Dr. Epstein started me on it just as my fifth-grade year was ending. I was supposed to take it before dinner. In the wake of our recent therapy session I tried everything to convince my mother I shouldn't be on medication. I talked in a measured voice, let her finish what she had to say, and even suggested alternatives; couldn't we employ one of the old star charts to measure my behavior?

It was the most reasonable I'd been in months—the only tactic I had left—and for the first few days I agreed to swallow the pill. Afterward I'd look up at my mother with huge sad eyes. In response she lifted what had felt like a decades-long grounding, and I was able to ride around the neighborhood again with Raymond, Lucas, and Josh. "Oh, Timmy," she told me. "We just need to find a way to get through the year."

On the afternoon I'd shoved Jonathan into the doorway I hadn't been looking for a fight, but that's what everyone thought. And in a way that rarely happened at Alta Vista, the other fifth graders began to gossip about my threats and retreat. In class I'd catch Jonathan's long, unblinking stares, and on the playground *he* was the one keeping track of *my* whereabouts. I must've crossed some sort of line by bringing up his rock throwing; no one else ever mentioned it, I realized afterward.

On the Wednesday of our final week a few boys I hardly knew asked if I was afraid of what Jonathan might do. I shrugged and told them I could take him. "Unless he freaks out and starts biting or something," I said. The longer I talked the more I believed in the power of my own voice. Finally I mentioned that I'd be at the dirt jumps behind the middle school; he could find me there. And even though they went directly to Jonathan and began talking animatedly, I didn't think anything of it.

That afternoon, as Raymond, Lucas, Josh, and I made our usual stops around the neighborhood, I was happy to be back in a routine. For a while I forgot about nortriptyline and my parents and all the other things that had conspired to ruin my school year.

Eventually we arrived at the dirt jumps. I was just about to take my turn when Jonathan stepped through the chain-link fence. He was on foot. He looked around as if he didn't know where he was. Then he saw me and started forward.

I stopped my bike. I never thought he'd actually seek me out. Up until this moment I'd understood him purely in terms of reaction; as long as I didn't corner him again things would be fine. "Jonathan," I said to him.

But his shirt was already in his mouth. He was a few feet away, closing fast. His eyes went skittish. In the cool spring shadows of the afternoon he looked huge. I realized that his hands were clenching and unclenching to the quick rhythm of his breaths.

What could I do? I hadn't been in a fight in two years, but it wasn't as if I lacked experience. This time I didn't think about retreating. I told myself: *Go crazy.*

We crashed together and suddenly everything felt familiar. The dirt was dim and distant, the fence sketched colorlessly. He jabbed me in the stomach. I hit him in the ear. He elbowed me in the chest and I lost my breath. I could feel the strength of his shoulders; I was pinned. But my fingers were in his face. I twisted them just below his eye, and with a curdling scream I dragged my nails in the white flesh of his cheek. He broke off. I'd gouged three deep incisions all the way to his jaw.

I stood up, shaking, unable to swallow. Jonathan kicked at the dust and held his head as if he were still trying to pry off my fingers. Then he curled his knees to his chest and wailed.

Raymond, Lucas, and Josh were still there, flitting in and out of the afternoon. Jonathan didn't get up.

Somehow I climbed onto my bike and pedaled. My house was only a few blocks away. The sun an empty pane, the mountains like a blanched column across the sky. I looked down and saw under my fingernails the clumps of Jonathan's skin. For a moment I understood perfectly what I'd done—I *felt* it. Not that I could've put it into words. And in the next instant panic carried off everything. Still, there are times in our lives when we manage to glimpse the rough shape of our fates—who we are; where we might very well end up—and while not much can be seen besides a sudden path forward, the terror of looking is elemental: what if our outcome has already been decided?

When I arrived home I was sobbing. My mother saw my torn shirt. "Tell me what happened!" she shouted. I couldn't speak. I punched the railing of our staircase, cutting my knuckle. She fought to hold onto me. Finally I was corralled upstairs, snot and spit clinging to my face. She clapped her hands, splashed water on me, and banged a hairbrush on the counter. Nothing worked. I could barely breathe. Finally she opened the medicine cabinet; she was reaching for the nortriptyline vial.

I stopped sobbing and clenched my jaw.

"Timmy," she said. "Please!"

I started swearing, a rapid string of words not directed at anyone. She pushed the pill toward me. I set my teeth. She tried to place it in my mouth and the gelatin cap broke, white powder on my lips and gums. She pleaded with me, sobbing herself, and started again with a new pill, the drug spilling past my lips as I spit out the capsule. This happened three or four times. When one finally made it through and I swallowed it down, my throat felt chalky: the remains of the earlier pills.

And just like that it was over. As if the drug—the act of taking it— was magic: I went limp on the edge of the bathtub and let my mother cradle me. Eventually, in starts and stops, I told her what happened. She held my shoulders and stroked my hair.

A few minutes later the phone rang. It was Jonathan Ashley's mother. She said that after our fight, her son had come home with deep cuts down his face. He could have lost an eye. She must have gotten our number from the Alta Vista directory, but she didn't mention our school or threaten to report the incident. She just wanted my mother to know what I had done.

»

Many hours later I woke up. It was the middle of the night. My stomach was a knot, expanding. I stumbled to the bathroom and vomited for minutes. My mother found me curled up at the toilet. She asked if I'd eaten anything after dinner, and the next morning she cleaned out the leftovers in the fridge, including a batch of egg salad that we both assumed was the culprit.

At the time neither of us understood what had really happened; I'd probably consumed a hundred milligrams of nortriptyline, more than three times Dr. Epstein's initial dosage. That much of a tricyclic antidepressant can lead to overdose symptoms in about six hours. The mildest is nausea.

»

After my fight with Jonathan there were just two days left in school, and I stayed home for both. When summer vacation started my mother went to my classroom and collected my materials. I sat in the car with my baby brother and peered through the window. It was as if I'd been found innocent of a crime that everyone knew I committed.

Over the next few weeks, as we waited for the nortriptyline to build up in my system, I begged my parents to let me switch school districts. I wanted to attend Fisher, the junior high in the heart of Los Gatos. I told them that it was stronger academically and had better sports teams—it was all I talked about during my sessions with Dr. Epstein—and I even said that I'd happily continue to take the medication if they'd just let me change. Finally they agreed. My mother worked through the red tape to secure the transfer, which was no small feat. I'd start at Fisher in the fall.

The truth was I couldn't imagine ever facing Jonathan again, or Raymond, Lucas, and Josh—or anyone else who knew what I'd done.

4

Biggest Talker

During the summer of 1991 I met weekly with Dr. Epstein to discuss the effects of the new medication. Was the nortriptyline working?

Tricyclic antidepressants are named after their molecular structure, which features a nucleus of three fused rings. Like most psychotropic drugs they were discovered accidentally. Following the success of chlorpromazine in the 1950s, pharmaceutical companies began to experiment with different compounds to treat schizophrenia. Geigy Pharmaceuticals created the first tricyclic antidepressant, imipramine (Tofranil), and in 1955 the Swiss psychiatrist Roland Kuhn tested it on schizophrenic patients at the Münsterlingen asylum. But he found that imipramine agitated their symptoms of psychosis, so instead he tried prescribing it for depression, and in a number of cases, the new compound seemed to alleviate severe symptoms.

Imipramine functions by blocking the reuptake of norepinephrine and serotonin, which increases the supply of these neurotransmitters in the brain. It was introduced in 1959 and for the next three decades would be marketed toward adults. But during the 1960s doctors began examining its effectiveness on childhood disorders, and eventually it was tested on children with ADHD. In a pair of studies conducted in 1965 and 1974, the child psychiatrist Judith L. Rapoport examined imipramine's effect on the disorder's primary symptoms—she wanted to know how it compared to Ritalin. Rapoport is the same doctor who would go on to prove that stimulants increase the concentration of *all* children, not just those with ADHD. In her studies on imipramine she concluded that while the drug could help with behavioral issues in the classroom—and produced minimal side effects—it didn't do much to alleviate fidgeting and impulsivity. "Successful drug treatment of these children should improve attention span," she wrote in a 1974 article for the *Archives of General Psychiatry,* "and not simply lessen 'undesirable' behavior."

But in the 1980s, the use of tricyclic antidepressants was reexamined in relation to a very specific group: older children who couldn't tolerate methylphenidate or amphetamine. A 1983 study in the *Journal of the American Academy of Child Psychiatry* reported that tricyclics outperformed Ritalin in three categories: sociability, depression, and self-esteem. A few years later, the American Academy of Pediatrics recommended tricyclics as an alternative treatment option for hyperactive adolescents "who have become withdrawn and depressed after experiencing years of school failure or poor social adjustment."

Nortriptyline was introduced by Eli Lilly to the US market in 1965. Its most common side effects—sedation, nausea, and dry mouth—proved to be less severe than those of other tricyclics. Like imipramine, it works on serotonin and norepinephrine; in fact it has little to no impact on dopamine, the neurotransmitter influenced by stimulants. It also remains in the system much longer than Ritalin, eliminating the chance of a rebound effect in the evening.

I'm not sure how much Dr. Epstein kept up with the research trends in his field, but from his years of experience he understood that nortriptyline could be a decent fit for someone with my history. Like Laurie's therapy, the drug targeted the way I reacted to the problems that the primary symptoms continued to cause, as opposed to working on concentration and impulsivity in the manner a stimulant might.

That summer, I remember asking Dr. Epstein, "How can you tell if the medication is the reason things get better?"

"Sometimes you can't," he said. "We're not working with scalpels here. More like blunt mallets." And as I imagined my brain being pounded by a hammer the color of a pill container he said that at least nortriptyline was an older drug; he knew about its possible side effects as well as the good it could sometimes do. "What do you think?" he asked.

Things *were* better. My mother had recently started taking a large dosage of the steroid prednisone, which immediately knocked out the worst symptoms of her rheumatoid arthritis. It made her more likely to come down with colds and infections, but for the first time in a year there weren't any limits on what she could do, and her outlook improved considerably. Not to mention the extra emotional support and household work she could suddenly offer up to us all.

I was also excited to be starting a new school. And it was summer; I wasn't in class with Mr. Ellis or anyone else. "I don't feel different," I told Dr. Epstein, "except for the side effects." By this point we'd built up the nortriptyline in my system and were at the full dosage. I'd already explained how my mouth felt dry, especially when I was nervous; how I sometimes got drowsy in the evening; and how occasionally before dinner the pill would stick in my throat and I'd spend minutes swallowing reflexively until the gel cap finally dissolved. I still hated the idea of the drug and everything it represented but now I also hated it physically. "Why do I have to keep taking it if we can't tell whether or not it's helping?"

As Dr. Epstein listened to my questions he tended to look past me for a few contemplative seconds. "I do think things are better," he finally said.

»

Just before my first day at Raymond J. Fisher Middle School my mother took me shopping in downtown Los Gatos. My sister and brother stayed home with my father. Together we went to Chrislow's, an expensive clothing store. It was the beginning of the early-1990s economic recession and the commercial real estate market my father navigated had slowed dramatically. Since he worked on commission we had no idea when things would get better.

But this shopping trip was something I'd been pushing for all summer. I played baseball with the kids who'd be attending Fisher, and they were different than my friends from Alta Vista, which was in a San Jose school district. Los Gatos, in contrast, had become one of the richest towns in the region. During my father's childhood it had still contained a large Italian-immigrant community and most of the land was used for orchards or ranching. But this began to change in the 1980s, when lawyers, doctors, and other well-compensated professionals moved in. Their children were the ones I'd be joining, and with the rise of the Bay Area's technology industry the trend was only getting more pronounced.

The latest fashion for the kids at Fisher was to wear T-shirts and shorts with the label of a prominent surfing company, which were three times as expensive as the kind my mother bought us. These labels were small but clearly identifiable, and the boys who wore them affected a beachy, languid coolness, as if responding to other people's questions took the same strenuous effort as paddling down a wave. They were tan and watchful. Their hair was sun-bleached. I figured that if I could just pull off the look, then the desired attitude would follow.

My mother piled up clothes for me outside the dressing room: khaki shorts, powder-blue tees, and hooded sweatshirts with the texture of expensive towels. She compared various outfits to the color of my eyes as she searched for the right combinations. And although we fought briefly over money—I wanted her to buy more than she could possibly afford—I had fun too; I'd forgotten how lavish her attention could be.

She even took me to a ritzy salon. "Let's do something wild," she told the hairdresser, a young woman with feathery bangs who was immediately taken in by my mother's enthusiasm. They decided on blond highlights.

"What a handsome young man!" my mother said afterward.

"The girls will be lining up," the stylist added. I believed her. Why not? She was blue-eyed and slim and her attention on me in that moment was complete: something I was sure I'd earned.

A few days later I walked into Fisher Middle School with lighter hair and soft surfer clothes. I nodded at kids from my baseball team and let them introduce me to their friends. When I passed a group of girls I could hear them whispering. For a moment I managed to believe that I was the very boy I now resembled, which really wasn't all that different from *being* that boy.

In social studies class before lunch—suddenly we had lockers and were switching rooms on the hour—our teacher, Mr. Jefferson, began asking questions about geography. It was just a bit of fun on the first day, he told us, and he offered candy as a reward. I raised my hand and got one right. Then another. And the next.

After my third answer Mr. Jefferson called on someone else. But when he asked about the capital of Iceland no one volunteered. "This guy's got all the facts," he said after I'd mispronounced *Reykjavík*. I kept raising my hand. Just before the bell, on a question about the mountain range that divided Europe and Asia, he glanced at his shoes and said, "I think that's enough."

I dropped my palm and looked around. My mouth went dry.

How had I thought things would go if on the first day I tried to answer every single question the teacher asked? As the candy piled up on my desk there was only the logic of a game—something that I'd failed to realize included an audience.

Now I could feel everyone else's glances. Some looked confused, others disgusted, and a few clearly angry. Suddenly I was sure they all could tell that, at my house outside the district lines, there was a supply of pills I took each night to keep me from acting in the way I just had.

»

Did I know at the time that the main goal of the new drug therapy was to help moderate the moodiness that the year before had swamped me at home and at school? Probably. That's how Dr. Epstein tried to explain it. As he and I continued to discuss the effects of the new medication, I recounted moments like the one in Mr. Jefferson's class. We also talked about my mother's health and the fight with Jonathan Ashley, what it was like to lose control when the consequences could be so violent.

Unlike Laurie, Dr. Epstein didn't offer specific behavioral strategies. I liked how calm he always appeared, and for the most part our sessions together felt judgment free.

"You don't actually think strangers know you're taking medication," he told me one afternoon. "Right?"

I shrugged. I couldn't explain what I meant: how there were instances in my life when I would meet an adult or child and for a while we'd interact normally, and then something like my hand-raising in Mr. Jefferson's class would occur and I'd be forced to see my actions from the other person's perspective. Taking the medication had reinforced this; rightly or wrongly it represented my lack of power over the way others perceived me.

It's a matter of personal point of view, sure, but the larger question affects everyone: When people look at a child with ADHD, what do they *really* see?

A century ago the answer was simple enough: a threat. When George Frederic Still identified many of the symptoms of ADHD at London's Royal College, he told his audience, "The serious danger which these children constitute both to themselves and to society calls, I think, for more active recognition."

He was worried about violence. Toward the end of his lecture he described a ten-year-old boy's physical abuse of siblings, other children, and animals. He also provided the story of a fourteen-year-old American child who, "when not allowed to have breakfast with the rest of the family and threatened with punishment by his grandfather for stealing some money, deliberately shot himself, with very serious, but not fatal, result."

But for Still, the most pressing threat was sexual. "I shall not go into details, for they would serve no useful purpose," he said—and went on to describe how these children were known "to expose themselves indecently" and could act so lustily they shouldn't be left alone with members of the opposite sex. He even lighted on the topic of masturbation, though only in passing, since in his own admission such a thing was also "common in children who show no morbid defect of moral control."

Still believed that it was his duty to warn parents about these children, but he didn't go so far as to offer possible solutions. "My object in these lectures has been simply to investigate," he assured us in his last paragraph.

One of his contemporaries, however, was more than willing to take the next step. Alfred Frank Tredgold, the doctor with horn-looking hair who'd advised the 1904 Royal Commission on "mentally deficient" school children and had afterward advocated for their educational segregation, saw the supposed sexual deviance of Still's subjects as nothing less than apocalyptic.

Tredgold subscribed to a faulty theory of evolutionary genetics that had been championed by the nineteenth-century English scientist and eugenics advocate Francis Galton; he believed that mental illness was caused by a yet-to-be-identified "germinal impairment" that became more severe each time it was passed down to a new generation.

This fact, coupled with what he perceived as the increased fertility of feeble-minded individuals, threatened to destroy everything that he and other social Darwinists held dear. "The result is to bring about an increasing ratio of the mentally, physically, and socially unfit," he wrote in his 1922 edition of *Mental Deficiency,* "which, if unchecked, must not only handicap social progress, but which may hurl the State into the abyss of degeneracy." In his opinion the recent directives in specialized education were well founded but inadequate; something more needed to be done.

At the end of his book Tredgold broached the possibility of "a lethal chamber": the mass execution of those who fell into his categories of mental illness. But even though he saw the merits of such a proposal—"I do not say that society, in self-defence, would be unjustified in adopting such a method of ridding itself of its anti-social constituents"—he admitted that it was too impractical "in the present state of public opinion."

Dr. Alfred Tredgold wasn't some conspiracist writing in anonymity. He was one of the most prominent experts on mental illness in the early twentieth century: a popular author and lecturer, president of the psychological wing of the Royal Society of Medicine, and advisor to the Board of Education and Ministry of Health. By the 1920s his theories on "germinal impairment" had already fallen out of favor—replaced by a more modern conception of genetics—but he continued to believe that without the intercession of healthy individuals like himself, "disease of the mind" would multiply exponentially to threaten "the future welfare of the nation."

So instead of genocide he settled on a long-term proposal. In a chapter titled "Sociology," Tredgold advocated a three-step solution to the problem posed by everyone with mental illness, including those "feeble-minded" children with attention and hyperactivity issues: "(1) Sterilization; (2) compulsory segregation during the reproductive age; and (3) the regulation of marriage."

»

On an overcast fall morning at Fisher I was walking back to class after using the bathroom when I realized someone was following me. I stopped and turned around.

A large young man was standing a few feet away. He had a shaved head, and his jeans were torn at the knees. With tight black eyes he glared at me as if we'd known each other for years. I figured from his bulk that he was an eighth grader, probably one of the skateboarders who loitered at the nearby convenience store after school, but I couldn't place him.

He wet his lips with his tongue and said, "What the fuck?"

It was an excellent question, one I should have broached myself. At the very least I could've asked what he wanted, but on a certain level I understood—he was intimidating me—and for that there was only one response.

I glared back. He stepped forward. Before I realized it we were circling each other. "Look away," he said.

I shook my head. When he came nearer I made a fist. But all of a sudden he walked past me, continuing on to wherever he'd been headed.

I stood there for a while and tried to remember how I knew him. What I didn't yet realize was that a good number of people at the school already knew *me*. Following my difficult year at Alta Vista I'd let my guard down. Now, among so many strangers, I felt comfortable again to say and do whatever popped into my head. Out of all the students at Fisher I probably had the loudest voice. When I told stories I waved my hands and bounced around in place. I laughed at jokes people hadn't meant to make, and I asked questions to which the answers were obvious. Standing in the quad during recess or lunch and talking quickly to anyone close by, I was nothing like the laid-back surfer my clothes suggested.

Later that day I saw the big eighth grader in P.E. class. He was standing with a lanky kid whom I'd recently taunted during a pickup basketball game. I hadn't thought anything of it, and who knows if that was the reason I'd been followed, but the truth was I'd developed the traits of the worst sort of athlete—an indignant loser and a boastful winner—even though I hated these traits and wanted, more than anything, to be seen as steely and determined.

That afternoon the activity was dodgeball. All of the grades were mixed together in Fisher's gym, a hangar-sized structure with lacquered hardwood. The P.E. coach, Mr. Lowe, walked to the middle of the court. He'd been a college baseball star and had the air of someone who was tired of teaching us the things we should already know. He emptied out a dozen volleyballs, blew his whistle to start the game, and disappeared.

The volleyballs were freshly pumped. Thrown hard enough they could knock you off your feet. The smaller children huddled out-of-range near the bleachers, but I scrambled across the middle. I loved this game, its kinetic confusion. I caught other people's tosses and fired my own. Soon enough the rest of my team had been hit, and I was the last one left. But instead of retreating I preened near the middle line.

Then suddenly I was pinned. Hands through my armpits. Chest and neck exposed. Someone had snuck up from behind. I struggled and twisted, but whoever it was held on. In the next instant the lanky eighth grader appeared. From a few feet away he fired multiple volleyballs into my gut. When I was finally released I spun around to find the big skateboarder; he'd been strong enough to hold me in place. Now he rejoined the crowd. Mr. Lowe was walking over. I was sobbing. "Do something!" I screamed at my teacher.

"You should probably go to the locker room," he said.

Outside, the sky was low and overcast. It had rained recently, and in the distance the dirt of the school's baseball field had darkened to the color of silt. Instead of heading for the locker room I waited in the fold of the gym door for the skateboarder and his friend.

I didn't think about what would happen when they eventually came out. Or why Mr. Lowe had taken so long to break it up. Or for what educational reason we were playing dodgeball, and with volleyballs ripe enough to burst.

As I crouched in the doorway I recognized what was happening. But how do you learn from repetition if the event that repeats itself is a colorless corridor, if the only way out of it is through the destination you're trying to avoid?

The game ended and children streamed between the doors. When the lanky kid emerged I clocked him in the nose. He squawked and held his face. The huge skateboarder appeared and I tried to hit him. My fist landed somewhere in his bulk. He wrapped his arms around me, and I was lifted up, a wrestling move, but I wiggled free. My one chance: we were face-to-face. I threw an uppercut at his jaw. At the last moment he ducked his head, and my left thumb caught the back of his skull. The force of the punch compacted at the lowest knuckle, and when I looked down, my thumb slacked from my hand like an afterthought. Then it was on me: the hard blue clarity of pain.

After that I mostly remember movement. People closed in, Mr. Lowe broke through, and I was ordered to report to the vice principal. I walked to his office: a room with a dusty desk lamp that cast everything in shades of green, where I was told to wait, my thumb no longer fitting my hand.

Eventually the vice principal arrived. Mr. Powell: I'd never met him before. He was nearly fifty, bald and thin-limbed, and I realized that over his left eye he was wearing a deep-black patch, exactly like a pirate might. He asked for details and I tried to explain.

"So you hurt your hand punching the other boy?" he said.

As we were still talking my mother appeared. At the sight of her I started sobbing breathlessly. She saw my thumb and shouted, "He needs to go to the emergency room!"

Mr. Powell explained the fight and told my mother that I would be suspended for two days.

"No," she said to him. "Nah-ah. He was being bullied."

He looked at her with his one placid eye.

"I want to talk to the principal!" she cried.

He shrugged and called in Mr. Baumgartner, a red-cheeked man whose head seemed too large for his neck; he glanced at all of us with a helpless, half-cocked expression. After listening to both sides he swallowed and said, "I'll have to go with Mr. Powell on this one."

At the hospital I arranged my hand in a series of excruciating X-rays: my thumb was broken clean through at its base. In my room that night, on painkillers and half awake, I could hear my parents arguing. My father thought I'd hit the other boy with my thumb tucked inside my fist. "You see what happens when you coddle him?" he was telling my mother. "All your shopping and haircuts!" But he wasn't angry. "Poor guy," he finally said. "Everyone's gonna think he punches like a girl."

»

I wasn't the only person suspended. Mr. Powell had doled out the same punishment to the bulky skateboarder. When I came back to school I didn't expect things to be settled, and in a sense they weren't. As I walked down the corridors older boys would sometimes shout threats at me; they wore black jeans and white Vans shoes that they'd purchased from a boutique skate shop downtown. I found out later that the skateboarder's parents were successful lawyers, and at the time I hated him in the way you might expect—I was desperate to get even—but to this day I can't remember his name.

In fact, we wouldn't really cross paths again at Fisher. In P.E. he and his skinny friend left me alone. They probably figured it wasn't worth it. Who knew how I'd react if they came at me again? And besides, with what new humiliation could they possibly top the scene I'd already made?

In a therapy session after the fight I shouted, "I thought the nortriptyline was supposed to keep things like this from happening!"

Dr. Epstein laughed.

"You think it's funny? Why do I have to take a pill and come see you if everything is gonna stay the way it was?"

I thought he'd point out that my hand wouldn't be in a cast if I'd chosen to walk away when I had the chance, or gone to someone at the school after the first encounter, or kept my mouth shut on the basketball court to begin with. By now I'd already considered these options, but none of them seemed to matter. I was attacked because of what these older children saw in me. And even though I couldn't stand the idea of taking medication I'd also secretly hoped that it might change the very thing that kept forcing me to play the role of aggressor or victim in these conflicts I couldn't avoid.

"Junior high is a fairly terrible place," Dr. Epstein finally said. The smile from his earlier laughter lingered. "The good news is that you won't be stuck in it forever." He asked about the specifics of the break, and for the next few minutes he talked about the different ways bones can set. I was lucky; such intense trauma to the base of my thumb could have very easily required surgery.

»

I had to wear my forearm-to-fingers cast for a month and a half. That November, just as I was about to get it off, I received a summons to the vice principal's office.

I thought it was a follow-up to my suspension. On the walk there I replayed the fight in my head, and by the time I arrived at his door I was sure he'd agree: I'd been punished unjustly, and on top of that confined to six weeks of itchy plaster!

Mr. Powell was sitting behind the green shade of his desk lamp. He was still wearing the eye patch, and its strap bit into the crown of his bald head. "I finally received your records from your previous school," he said. There was a folder on his desk. "I have to tell you, these marks are just terrible."

Behind him the walls were the color of seawater. He tapped the folder. "Well?"

I told him things were going fine academically. Which was true: I liked the structure of middle school, how we switched between subject-specific classrooms, and while I didn't get along with some of my teachers, we spent only one hour a day together. Of course there were new challenges like bringing the right book to class, keeping track of homework assignments, and adjusting to different sets of expectations. Needless to say, I'd never be a perfect student, but I wanted to get good grades—to be *seen* by my teachers in that light—and the academic material was more interesting than ever. We dissected fetal pigs in science. In social studies we learned about famous Supreme Court cases. In English we were reading *To Kill a Mockingbird.*

"I'm not talking about that," Mr. Powell said.

Without thinking I leaned forward to see what was in front of him. He closed the file. When he finally spoke his voice was very formal: "We can't have any more incidents like your altercation in physical education."

"They threw volleyballs at me!"

For a moment Mr. Powell's office felt like the hull of a boat, rough and mildewed. And an actual eye patch! "All right," he finally said. He placed the file at the top of a large stack.

"All right what?" I couldn't help but wonder if he'd finally taken my side.

He put a palm over the seeing half of his face and sighed. "Our conversation is over, Mr. Denevi. You can go."

I hurried out of the office. For the rest of the semester I did my best to avoid his piercing gaze, but once in a while I'd come around a corner too quickly and he'd be there, or during an assembly everyone else would quiet and as I babbled on I'd glimpse him off to the side, staring.

Then in December his black pirate patch was gone. In its place was a real eye that moved with the other in the fleshy bust of his head. The fact that the patch disappeared so suddenly made me wonder if perhaps I'd imagined it all along.

》

One of the difficulties with ADHD is that, often enough, questions of blame and questions of causality can feel indistinguishable. In the first half of the twentieth century, following the crude biological reasoning of social Darwinists like Sir George F. Still and Alfred Tredgold, the explanation for aberrant behavior shifted from "germinal impairments" to one based in experience.

Sigmund Freud believed that many of the perceived childhood traumas later manifesting as mental illness were the result of parental influence. A father had competed with his son for the mother's love, or vice versa, or both parents had suppressed their child's natural sexual awareness, or certain elemental needs had been denied. At first Freud applied his reasoning to cases of adult hysteria or neurosis, but eventually his followers adapted it to explain a vast constellation of disorders.

In 1948, the emigrant German analyst Frieda Fromm-Reichmann, who'd spent the previous decade working at the Chestnut Lodge institution in Maryland, claimed in an article for *Psychiatry* that schizophrenia was the result of "initial traumatic warp and thwarting experiences at a very early period of life"—at a stage before a child had a chance to develop "a marked and stable degree of relatedness to other people."

But what kind of experience could be severe enough to bring about the onset of psychosis two decades later? According to Dr. Fromm-Reichmann, the disorder stemmed from the rejection a schizophrenic must have encountered "in important people of his infancy and childhood, as a rule, mainly in a schizophrenogenic mother."

The meaning of this maternal adjective was never actually explained. In fact, Dr. Fromm-Reichmann avoided elaborating on said mother's transgressions except to point to a dearth of "benevolent contact." Her larger argument was that parental harm could cause the child to transgress "the threshold of endurance" because, at his core, a schizophrenic was "motivated by his fear of repetitional rejection."

The implication: schizophrenia is an unconscious *decision* to withdraw from the world; a patient chooses to behave this way because he can't bear being hurt again like he once was by a parent. All of this dovetails nicely with Dr. Fromm-Reichmann's proposed treatment: an analyst must offer "insight into the nature of the early trauma" by establishing the "type of doctor-patient relationship" that speaks to both "the rejected child in the schizophrenic" and "the grown-up person." As in, all you need to do is admit that your mother was a monster and like a fever your psychosis will lift.

Dr. Fromm-Reichmann didn't offer any evidence to support this treatment. And while much of her article comes across as vaguely spiritual—"Sullivan teaches that there is no developmental period when the human exists outside the realm of interpersonal relatedness"—it had a significant impact and would go on to influence psychiatry's explanation of mania, depression, and paranoia.

Similar interpretations of Freudian theory would also determine the treatment of childhood mental disorders. For the most part Freud had avoided psychoanalyzing children—his case study into the horse-penis phobia of poor Little Hans was an exception—but by the middle of the twentieth century his youngest daughter had become a leading expert on the matter.

Anna Freud began applying her father's version of psychiatric treatment to children in the 1920s in the form of play therapy. At the start of World War II she fled with her family to London, where she and fellow Austrian analyst Melanie Klein began to battle over who should be crowned the true heir to psychoanalysis. Both women believed that trauma and repression could manifest at young ages in the form of behavioral problems—and that something like ADHD was a response to the unconscious apprehension that children felt when they failed to meet certain natural developmental stages. In her 1932 book *The Psychoanalysis of Children,* Klein argued that behaviors like "fidgetiness" and "excessive mobility" were caused by feelings of anxiety about being kept in the dark over the stage of sexual development first encountered around the age of five—a time when the child, according to Freudian thinking, begins to realize that he or she is fully equipped with the necessary reproductive organs.

This point of view was further popularized by the famous postwar pediatrician and bestselling author Benjamin Spock. His book *Baby and Child Care,* first published in 1947, would be reissued seven times over the next fifty years. The front cover of the 1968 version boasts, "Over 22,000,000 copies sold." On its back is a picture of the author. He's sitting on a plaid couch surrounded by no less than eight children, most of them wearing yellow. In his lap is a young girl: together they're reading a book. He's almost seventy, his bald head made lumpy by the light, and with his eyes downcast and chin against his chest it's as if he's managed to nod off for a few precious seconds.

Dr. Spock's book included section titles like "The One Year Old: What Makes Him Tick," "Fears around Three, Four and Five," and "Problems of Feeding and Development: Fat Children." But for the most part his tone was surprisingly disarming. In his preface to the fourth edition he wrote, "The most important thing I have to say is that you should not take too literally what is said in this book." He was quick to admit that different situations and people call for unique approaches. Still, he was offering advice based on a very specific conception of why things happen. In the chapter "Managing Young Children: Discipline," he claimed that "too harsh a repression of aggressive feelings and sexual interest may lead to neurosis." "These ideas are commonplace today," he assured us—including the fact that "unconscious thoughts are as influential as conscious ones."

In a sense Freud's worldview had come full circle: a mother or father who interfered with a child's basic impulses to feed or defecate or comprehend sexual mechanics could do such extensive damage, the subsequent disorder would now manifest immediately, as opposed to decades later in the form of neurosis.

Thus a healthy child represented thoughtful, conscientious parents. While one who fidgeted and threw tantrums had been repressed by his mother, or lacked the right amount of discipline, or was engaged in an epic sexual struggle with his father. Which is exactly how many people tended to see a hyperactive boy or girl during a large segment of the twentieth century: as the product of shitty parenting.

>>

By the time I was in sixth grade, how did my mother and father *really* feel about my behavior—the way it must have looked through the eyes of other parents?

My mother, bless her, has always displayed an enormous capacity to disregard embarrassment. But in my father's case the prospect was a bit more complicated. That winter we started my final season in Little League. He was the head coach, and our team, the Expos, was the best in Los Gatos. For as long as I could remember he'd attended my baseball games. Over the years he'd drawn on his experience to teach me the physical motions of the sport, and by now I was one of our league's more accomplished players.

He'd also spent the last half decade hammering home proper on-field etiquette. Much of this had to do with decisions like what base to throw to, whether or not to advance as a runner, and when to lay off a pitch instead of swinging. "Tell yourself what you're going to do before the ball is hit," he always said. And: "You'll make physical errors. Fine. It's the mental ones that are inexcusable."

Included in this instruction was the implicit ideal of how a ballplayer should carry himself. Run hard on everything; keep your head up when you make an error; and leave arguments with the umpire to your coaches.

Along with a few other twelve-year-olds I'd been on our team for three seasons. In each of the last two we'd lost the championship game. My father had drafted our players from a general tryout, trained them, and added new boys here and there. He understood that it was just Little League baseball—on Sundays he still played in his own competitive adult league—but after so many hours hitting groundballs and working on bunt defense he wanted what I wanted: to win. And this year I felt the pressure more than the rest. Now the kids in the league went to my school.

Early in the season I was up to bat with runners on first and second base. From the coach's box my father tapped his hat and swiped his belt, the sign for a bunt play, but I thought it was a perfect chance for a double steal. So I gave him my own sign in return.

"Time-out!" he shouted. He rushed down the baseline. "What the hell's the matter with you?"

Recently I'd seen a movie in which the wily old catcher, at a crucial moment in the game, stepped out of the batter's box and signed a play to his coach. At the time I'd thought it was brilliant, and since then I'd been looking for a chance to try it out myself.

"You don't tell the coach what play to call!" my father shouted.

We ended up winning the game by a landslide, but on the car ride home he kept shaking his head. "I don't care what you *thought* you were doing," he finally said.

》

Throughout that Little League season, as I kept interrupting my father's pregame pep talks, and taunting the other team's pitcher, and throwing my bat against the screen when I struck out, our car rides from the field became shouting matches. He was incredulous. During his professional playing days he was never bigger or stronger than the other players, but one of his main advantages had always been his on-field instinct.

Near the end of the season we played the Padres, a team with an equally outstanding record. The week before, I kept imagining moments of grace: a winning hit, a diving catch to save us from a loss, a bold base-running decision that in retrospect made perfect sense. These images were not hard to come by; each night my father and I liked to watch the San Francisco Giants, and once in a while these grown men would find themselves celebrating a surprise victory like a bunch of giddy twelve-year-olds.

The game was on a Friday, a leafy spring afternoon, the shadow of the coastal mountains in the outfield. Even the name of the park was evocative: *Blossom Hill.* I was playing shortstop, and in one of the early innings a boy hit a sharp groundball to me. There were two outs, a runner on third. The score was 0–0. I fielded it smoothly. I had time to set my feet and throw, and I started to think about it all: the arm angle, pace, and grip I might choose. Now I was almost out of time. I fired to first, the throw sailed high, and their runner on third scored.

For the next few pitches I stood where I was and wanted to scream— at myself, the players, and the opposing batter, whose fault it had been for hitting that grounder in the first place. After the inning my father patted me on the back and said, "Think about the next play."

Toward the end of the game I came up to bat with the tying run in scoring position. There were two outs. On a curveball I hit a drive down the right field line. It was hooking, and when the ball finally landed there was a sickening space of inches between its impact and the chalk. I saw this as clearly as everyone else, and the umpire called it correctly—foul.

"What?" I screamed. "You're blind!"

He was a high-school kid with a ribbon of pimples where his mask touched his forehead, and he looked down at me blankly.

"Fair!" I said. "Make the right call!"

From the coach's box my father shouted, "Get back in there and swing the bat!" But I couldn't, not until I was awarded the hit that would make up for my error, and the longer I refused to let the game continue the more righteous I felt.

Finally my father had to come over and push me into the batter's box. I struck out on the next pitch. We lost 1–0. During his postgame speech my father talked to the team about mental preparation and coming back strong. But I could sense everyone's disappointment.

"Sometimes the breaks just don't go your way and you gotta go out and get 'em next time," he said.

I threw my hands in the air. "The ball was fair! That's not a break. Why didn't you argue about it anyway? You're *my* dad."

"It was foul," he said. "Let it go."

I told him he was wrong. I had a better angle. He should trust me. We went back and forth like this while the other parents, waiting to take their children home, crowded around the dugout. I could tell by the way my father's lips disappeared into his mouth that he was about to snap, which just made me press harder.

Then he started screaming at me. Spittle clung to his mustache. His dark forehead was blushed through. "Get out of here! Now! Right now! Get out of my sight! Go to the car and wait for me there!"

I stood where I was. "No," I said. I glanced dramatically at him, but now he looked as if he might actually hit me, something he'd never done. So with perhaps twenty people watching, I walked out of the dugout—stopping at the exit to announce, "I quit! I'm off the team forever!"

>>

That afternoon the car ride home lasted about ten minutes. Our shouting match was epic, a riot of past offenses—*You've never done this for me! You only think about what's best for you!*—until finally he looked close to tears. "Don't you understand?" he said. "They're all talking about us right now: 'Those crazy fucking Denevis.' Doesn't that make you feel ashamed?"

One of the most dangerous weapons in my family can be a sudden shift to reason. But at that moment his words had the opposite effect; they only reinforced the fact that he'd acted so wildly—something that for once made us equal. And the more upset he appeared the closer to him I felt.

In the end I didn't quit the team. I actually forgot I'd said that until my father brought it up awkwardly the next day. For the championship game we faced the Padres again, and I played well enough, but we lost by a run.

>>

To this day I don't know all that much about Dr. Joe Epstein's background, but his outlook never felt excessively biological, especially compared to my first psychiatrist, Dr. Smythe, who'd set out to treat ADHD like a bacterial infection.

With Dr. Epstein I had the feeling that if the nortriptyline proved a poor fit, a new option could be to take nothing at all. Like his cousin Laurie Hamilton he was a pragmatist: biology has its limits and so does the influence of our environment. Which makes sense, considering the complex interaction of factors involved in any psychological disorder. But this type of approach wasn't necessarily common.

When I started seeing Dr. Epstein in the early 1990s, psychiatry was still reeling from its recent ideological battles. The last hundred years had seen the rise and fall of theories that, in their heyday, explained much more than the origin of mental illness; they were meant to illuminate the mystery of human existence. There'd been social Darwinism and Freudian theory, and also the biological determinism that came out of the psychopharmacological revolution. In the 1960s a new ideology surfaced: the antipsychiatry movement.

As Edward Shorter notes, "The movement's basic argument was that psychiatric illness is not medical in nature but social, political, and legal: Society defines what schizophrenia or depression is, and not nature." The correct approach, then, is to recognize and break down the societal factors responsible for a disorder like ADHD, thus enlightening the individual sufferers to the fact that they aren't really suffering: their normal mode of functioning has been pathologized by larger forces—capitalism, science, religion, etc.—and the discipline of psychiatry is simply an enforcer of cultural norms.

One of the movement's most prominent voices was the French philosopher Michel Foucault. In 1961 he published *Madness and Civilization*—claiming, among other things, that the concept of mental illness was invented during the Enlightenment as a means to marginalize the creative, freethinking individuals who threatened the status quo. There was also Thomas S. Szasz, a former psychoanalyst who wrote in 1960, "It is customary to define psychiatry as a medical specialty concerned with the study, diagnosis, and treatment of mental illness. This is a worthless and misleading definition. Mental illness is a myth. Psychi-atrists are not concerned with mental illnesses and their treatments." Another former Freudian, the British doctor R. D. Laing, applied this line of thinking directly to schizophrenia. He chronicled his experi-ences at London's Tavistock Hospital in his 1960 *The Divided Self*. For the most part the book reads like bad counterculture poetry—"To be a potentially seeable object is to be constantly exposed to danger"; and, "The self tries to destroy the world by reducing it to dust and ashes, without assimilating it"—but his central argument was an extension of Foucault and Szasz's. "The schizophrenic is often making a fool of himself and the doctor," Laing wrote. "He is playing at being mad to avoid at all costs the possibility of being held *responsible* for a single coherent idea, or intention."

These three writers were well-known in academic circles, but in the 1960s the novelist Ken Kesey helped introduce their ideology to a much larger audience. His famous *One Flew over the Cuckoo's Nest* featured the character Randle McMurphy, a gambler claiming insanity to escape a prison term. Kesey described McMurphy as "just a wanderer and log-ging bum" that "society persecutes," and the plot of the book follows the character's struggle against Nurse Ratched, the administrator of the ward who uses electroshock therapy to silence dissent. The 1975 film adaptation won the Oscar for Best Picture, and in the role of McMurphy the actor Jack Nicholson came to embody a key argument of the move-ment: the people we perceive as mentally ill are just more sensitive to the oppressive forces of society—which actually makes them saner than the rest of us.

That same year the sociologist Peter Conrad published "The Discov-ery of Hyperkinesis: Notes on the Medicalization of Deviant Behavior" in the journal *Social Problems*. Conrad, then a young professor at Drake University, applied Foucault and Szasz's thinking to ADHD. He argued that psychiatry and public health had "traditionally functioned as agents of social control," and that before World War II, the symptoms of the disorder had never been grouped together. Thus, diagnosing children as hyperactive was actually a means of medicalizing deviance. So like schizophrenia or depression, ADHD didn't exist: larger societal institutions were forcing us to recognize behavioral problems that only registered as a "mental illness" because we were being told to see them as such.

Who were these larger institutions? The Association for Children with Learning Disabilities—a nonprofit organization for disadvantaged children—along with the drug companies who'd tricked them into denying the sociological basis for the disorder. He also compared the work of American mental health professionals to the Soviet Union's treatment of dissidents: by attempting to define "the overactive, restless, and disruptive child as hyperkinetic," someone like Laurie Hamilton or Joe Epstein "depoliticizes deviance in the same manner." He claimed that stimulants were just another "social control mechanism."

Peter Conrad cited ADHD as an example of his broader sociological argument about mental illness; he didn't humanize the symptoms or provide real-life cases, and his article lacked a familiarity with childhood behavior in general. In fact, his adherence to doctrine can seem just as heartless as the moralism of doctors like Still and Tredgold, especially to someone with firsthand experience of the disorder.

The antipsychiatry movement's belief system was based on repudiation—of the biological, the experiential, of authority in general. It wasn't necessarily more extreme than the other psychiatric ideologies of the twentieth century, but like Freudian theory, it refused to incorporate the rational aspects of an opposing viewpoint, or to acknowledge the messy, real-life contradictions that often accompany mental illness. The only solution was to replace the wrong ideology with a better one, which meant that, among other things, the rhetoric could get fast and loose at a moment's notice, to the point where someone always seemed to be calling someone else Hitler, or a Nazi, or at the very least a Soviet.

Conrad's 1975 article influenced an entire generation of sociologists. But he wasn't the only person applying the antipsychiatry movement's premise to ADHD. In that same year the journalists Peter Schrag and

regardless of what "cool" might actually mean, the behavior associated with ADHD represents the opposite: immaturity, oversensitivity, and distractibility—inattention to the trends and cues that determine teenage social life. Were the most popular children at Fisher simply the best at perceiving and mimicking these trends, or did they possess something inherent in their personalities that lined up well with the most valued traits? In my case it didn't matter. I was fundamentally uncool, people eventually figured it out, and there was nothing I could do. And while no one outside my family knew I was seeing a psychiatrist and taking medication—such factors hadn't in themselves made me unpopular—I took them as signs, and I couldn't imagine becoming well-liked and sought-after while both were still in place. Not that I stopped trying.

After our initial shopping trip to Chrislow's my mother refused to buy me another run of expensive clothes, and for the start of seventh grade she purchased a four-pack of white tees from Target. At the time the economy was so bad, we were struggling to make our mortgage payment, but I only knew I couldn't wear last year's surfer outfits—they were ratty and dated—and the new, logo-less clothes defeated the purpose. My solution? I got my brother's markers and drew the surf company's design on one of the blank shirts. It looked like you might expect. So instead, for reasons that have long since been lost to memory, I tried writing my last name in the company's stylish font. I held it up to the light. Not bad, I thought. I began to wonder what the big deal was: why pay so much for a few letters stenciled at the chest when you could do it yourself? Really it was a crime. And the more shirts I made the grander my ideas became: eventually I found myself thinking of possible names for my new clothing line. This was when my mother came downstairs. She looked at the shirts and asked what I thought I was doing.

"Would you buy one if it were from a real company?" I said to her. "Something with a catchy title, like 'Denevi Wear.' Or maybe 'Denevi Style'?"

In a surprisingly gentle manner she explained that it looked as if my little brother had made the shirts, and that I'd ruined an entire pack of them in the process. I now saw the childish color scheme and off-center letters and how the cheap felt markers had bled through the cotton. But a few days later I still proceeded to tell the boys from my baseball team exactly what I'd tried to do—"Denevi Gear," I said. "It just sounds right, you know?"

That fall these same boys were playing together on an elite soccer team, and at school they liked to wear their blue-and-white Adidas warm-up jackets. I didn't play soccer anymore—I'd tried out for goalie a few years back and had crashed into the post, twice, trying to block the ball—but for months I pestered my mother until, at Christmas, she bought me this very jacket. I showed up after the break wearing it and tried to stand naturally alongside these boys. They kept quiet. "Soccer's such a beautiful game," I finally said. "You gotta respect it or it won't respect you."

Then in the winter I took the money an aunt had given me for the holidays and decided to buy the most popular kids in my grade presents. As I browsed a dollar store that was within walking distance of my house I kept thinking, *Who can say no to free stuff?* I purchased cheap things—a book, a rubber baseball, a headband for the best-looking girl in our class—and in bursts of sincerity I handed these trinkets over to their recipients, explaining, "Just because."

To look back on that world! You wake up each morning and walk the bright corridors: the sound of voices, of lockers rattling shut. Everyone is in motion, and you think that maybe this is the day things will turn around. Then they notice you. The tone drops. You hear whispers, feel the glances; you're *meant* to feel them. It's like the plunge in humidity after a thunderstorm. This is their weapon, not fistfights or taunts; the other teenagers let you know you've offended them simply by showing just how much your presence disrupts their own. And you're forced to see yourself from only one perspective: theirs.

Another person would've kept walking. But I dealt with being unpopular like anything else; I headed down the corridor each day as if for the first time. And I always stopped and talked to the girl who was glaring at me, or the boy who'd pretended not to hear my heavy-footed approach. Because it genuinely seemed like the only option, especially compared to not doing anything at all.

》

That spring I did experience one lasting social achievement: a girlfriend. She was an eighth grader, a year older. How did it happen? A friend of hers with wild red hair cornered me one afternoon and said that I should guess who might be interested. When I couldn't she came out with it—Christina Teplov, a girl in my drama class. Christina was very tall and had the sturdy limbs of a basketball forward. With her high cheekbones and dark hair she affected a pale, Russian prettiness. Not that I could've articulated such a thing then.

To Christina and her friends I was a slim, fast-talking boy with long eyelashes and the audacity to say what was on his mind, or something like that. Maybe they were just bored and fourteen years old and I seemed interesting. It didn't make much sense, considering how annoying the girls in my grade found me, but at the time I'd been waiting for someone to notice what I was sure everyone else had missed.

On our big date we went to see the movie *Groundhog Day* in downtown Los Gatos. It was February, raining. She was wearing a bright-purple sweater, and as we walked down the shallow aisle to our seats she asked, "Have you ever seen mothballs?"

I shrugged. "Sure."

"How'd you get their little legs open?"

I realized it was a joke—she was smiling expectantly—but I didn't understand: I kept imagining fluffs of cotton being divided into smaller pieces. Then we sat down, the lights dimmed and the film started, and she leaned against the armrest. When I tilted my head to see if she wanted more licorice her mouth locked onto mine and she began plying her tongue, diligently, against my own. After a few seconds I responded. And for the next half hour we went on like this: a make-out session in which only our mouths touched. It was as if we were both working very hard to masticate the same piece of beef. When we finally broke apart there was suddenly the theater, its screen bright with the antics of Bill Murray, who'd found himself waking up over and over again in the same morning of his life. A few minutes later Christina cast her hot breath in my direction and we did the whole thing a second time.

During the next couple of weeks we met on the benches near the cafeteria, or on the bleachers along the baseball field, or at the tables just off the quad; we'd sit down and throw ourselves into long, digestive kisses, livened by the risk of being discovered—Mr. Powell was known to be roaming the halls.

One day at lunch Christina's redheaded friend appeared again and smiled sadly. I've forgotten her name, but she was childishly plump, smelled like body odor, and had enormous breasts; they were hard and obtrusive and behind them she held her shoulders stiffly. "Christina wants to break up with you," she said. I could tell by the way she was watching me that something was expected. So I tried to think on everything I'd lost. At first the tears were intermittent. The redhead rubbed my arm. Then I was sobbing. She withdrew. When I finally calmed down she bent close and whispered something in my ear that I didn't catch. But a few days later we were a couple. She and Christina then entered into a fierce feud and divided their friends and enemies alike.

Another month of openmouthed kisses, the redhead's body odor smelling like citrus and sweaty gym clothes, her recent breasts perched awkwardly between us. It was spring. Each night she'd call me on the phone to complain about Christina. I joined in by criticizing the boys in my grade. Every once in a while my mother would pick up and start dialing, and as I shrieked and pleaded with her to get off the line she'd say, "Hi, who's this?"

The redhead and I dated for a while and then, on a day I was home sick, she called at lunch from a school pay phone and broke up with me. I was devastated. But the actual blow came when she and Christina went off to high school and I was left where I'd started. Deep down I'd hoped that they would somehow manage to take me along. But I saw these two girls only a couple of more times. In fact, a few years later I attended a play at our local theater and was surprised to find Christina, having slimmed into the classical elegance of her body, in the starring role.

It was a noir production. She was the damsel in distress, her eyes smoky and dark, and as I watched her run between suitors of dubious intent I found myself recalling the way she'd been in middle school. It felt like a memory from another person's life, something made permanent by its refusal to be part of the larger narrative, the one with psychiatrists and medication and ADHD that, even now, threatens to subsume all those things continuing to arrive without a clear explanation from the past.

》

By the spring of 1993 I'd been taking the nortriptyline for two years. Dr. Epstein and I were talking about this fact when I told him point-blank that I wanted to go off it.

"Okay," he said.

Even though we met regularly—and I don't remember him lying to me—I hesitated. "That's not what my parents are gonna say." Wasn't it always their decision?

"It's not as if you'll be on this medication the rest of your life," he replied. The offer stood between us, I realized it was genuine, and I knew I should say something. But I could only watch him watching me. "It's something to think about," he finally said.

I was almost fourteen years old. Over the previous two years I'd cultivated an opinion on behavior-modifying drugs that was strikingly similar to the one advocated, decades earlier, by the antipsychiatry movement: everything came down to power, perspective, and the machinations of larger forces.

This makes sense to a teenager. But sitting in Dr. Epstein's office and faced with a clear choice, could I say without a doubt that a drug like nortriptyline was fundamentally incapable of improving my life?

According to thinkers like Michel Foucault and Thomas Szasz, personal improvement comes only from insight, and drugs at best can help this process along. But they rejected modern psychiatry's assumption that certain states of mind could exist beyond the reach of self-awareness—and could only be influenced by psychotropic medications such as stimulants and antidepressants. Taken to its logical extreme, their argument is startling: there's no biological basis to mental illness since biology itself can be influenced by insight. Why do people still suffer from a range of physical ailments? They simply haven't learned the correct way to perceive themselves and others.

This position was best articulated by the founder of the Church of Scientology, L. Ron Hubbard. In 1950 Hubbard, a science-fiction writer who'd worked in Hollywood, was laid up in an Oakland military hospital with life-threatening injuries. Modern medicine wasn't helping, and he decided to heal himself; he supposedly discovered a set of fundamental truths about human nature, which unlocked an avenue of perception that allowed him to overcome his organic limitations. These truths became the foundation for his new religion.

By following his guidelines, practitioners of Scientology could heal their bodies and increase their intelligence. "Our most spectacular feat was raising a boy from 83 IQ to 212," Hubbard told the *Saturday Evening Post* in 1964. It was the same with mental illness. Hubbard believed that the cause of all self-destructive behavior had to do with our reactions to "engrams": memories of traumatic events that had been buried deep within our consciousness. Sufferers could drain these engrams by following Hubbard's steps to self-awareness—first revealed in his book *Dianetics*—and also by undergoing a series of psychotherapeutic sessions called "auditing." The goal was to turn the "reactive" mind "clear." It was strikingly similar to Sigmund Freud's approach: repression, trauma, and transference. Not that Scientology sees it this way.

In their view, other forms of treatment are not just incorrect; they're heretical. And psychiatrists are the biggest heretics of all. In 1969 Hubbard teamed up with Thomas Szasz to create the Citizens Commission on Human Rights (CCHR). On its website the CCHR describes itself as "a mental health watchdog" that's "taken a stance against the biological/drug model of 'disease' that is continually promoted by the psychiatric/pharmaceutical industry as a way to sell drugs." They offer a wide catalog of publications, including *Behind Terrorism: Psychiatry Manipulating Minds,* which seeks to expose "hidden key players in the alarming and explosive upsurge in terrorism today—psychiatrists and psychologists." They've also established a museum in Los Angeles called Psychiatry: An Industry of Death.

But the CCHR's most effective mode of attack has been conducted through the American legal system. In the 1970s, it petitioned state legislators to outlaw electroshock therapy, which Hubbard believed increased the amount of engrams in the body. And in the 1980s it used its ample resources to address the issue of ADHD.

Scientologists believe that children are seriously hyperactive or inattentive because they haven't yet cast out their engrams—and that the only way to do so is follow Hubbard's path to self-realization. Psychotropic drugs mask this realization, impeding the engram-removal process, which means that stimulants push children in the wrong direction, away from the knowledge that, once acquired, will grant them a fuller dominion over the physical world. Thus the act of taking a medication such as Ritalin is similar to a transgression that, in another religion, would start you down the road to brimstone and hellfire.

In the second half of the 1980s, the CCHR filed more than a dozen lawsuits over the use of stimulant medications, including a $125 million suit against the American Psychiatric Association. These cases were all thrown out of court, but they generated an enormous amount of attention: newspapers, magazines, television programs such as *Nightline,* and talk-show hosts such as Geraldo Rivera and Phil Donahue publicized Scientology's view of ADHD to millions. The result was measurable:

between 1988 and 1990, the number of Ritalin prescriptions decreased by as much as 39 percent.

So by the beginning of the 1990s, a religion with an estimated 25,000 followers had managed to influence our perception of the disorder more effectively than any other group. For the Church of Scientology, the dispute wasn't about methodology or effectiveness; stimulants represented a threat to a hyperactive child's eternal soul.

»

On the last day of seventh grade I got into an argument with another boy in my class. It was over something trivial, but after a brief back and forth we began shouting at each other in the quad. His name was Ronnie Cain. He had spectacularly blue eyes, and after one of my insults these eyes went livid and his grin said: *I am going to punch you in your stupid face.*

Ronnie had spent the last few years in and out of foster homes—I knew this, somehow. At school he wore a leather jacket and a nickel-colored chain that might've been plastic, and mostly he kept to himself.

Other children had gathered. I still could've walked away, but the whole thing had caught me off guard. Besides, school was finally out. Seventh grade had been a moderate success: my grades were fine, my teachers had tolerated me, and this last day didn't bring with it the usual stress that had accompanied the end of previous years.

I wanted to explain to Ronnie that I was sorry I'd offended him, but I could tell by his tight smile that he wouldn't listen. So for one of the few times in a situation like this I just stood where I was and waited to see what would happen.

Ronnie shoved me hard. I stumbled back. He shoved me again. But at least I was in motion; I walked through the corridor with the heavy steps of someone trying not to run. Ronnie followed. So did a handful of boys who weren't really friends with either of us. Eventually I made it out of Fisher's open-air halls and into the hot June light.

It was noon. For the final day of school we'd been released early, and I was supposed to walk to my grandmother Jo Ann's house, where my mother would pick me up. With Ronnie a few steps behind I continued down the street. Every so often I'd hear a rush of steps and he'd shove me, a blow that bent my spine and snapped back my head to reveal, briefly, the uninterrupted light of the sky.

But I knew if I turned around something terrible would happen, so I kept moving forward. We came to the traffic light at a busy intersection, and suddenly there was nothing to do but wait for it to change; my grandmother's house was located a few more blocks down, in a leafy neighborhood everyone called the Manor.

Ronnie circled around. "You think you're hot shit?" he shouted. Together we were spinning. He was trying to face me, I kept turning, and I didn't really hear what he was saying—I was about to finally lose it and attack—when I realized he was calling me "rich." As in: "rich kid." He'd been yelling it the whole time.

I looked at him. Eyes and crazed smile—something else. Exasperation? The light changed, I hurried forward, and he didn't follow. Halfway across the asphalt I glanced back. Ronnie stood at the sidewalk: a thirteen-year-old boy wearing a leather jacket, which was ridiculous, considering the time of year.

»

I have no idea what I must have said to offend Ronnie. Something about his silver chain? Or could I have been dumb enough to mention his living situation? I'm sure I've said worse. But when I told my parents and Dr. Epstein what had happened I left out the backstory. In the new version Ronnie came after me for no reason and then shouted the stuff about money. Didn't he know that I lived outside of the school district in a house worth hundreds of thousands of dollars less than everyone else's? And hadn't I done the right thing by not fighting back?

My mother agreed. My father asked why another kid would follow me for an entire block if I hadn't said *something*. My psychiatrist wanted to know what I planned to do about it.

"Weren't you listening?" I told him. "I *avoided* a fight."

"Nobody responds well to humiliation," he eventually said.

»

Around that time I had begun listening exclusively to rap music. I'd been a fan of the Beastie Boys and Digital Underground, but now Dr. Dre and Snoop Dogg were releasing a series of songs with harmonies taken from 1970s funk. During the summer after seventh grade I memorized every lyric from their album *The Chronic*—a record-store clerk who looked exactly like Rod Stewart had ignored the Parental Advisory label when he sold it to me—and by August the worldview of these musicians had become my own: everyone else was *inauthentic*.

This applied first and foremost to the wealthy children at Fisher. The economy was still terrible and my father's commissions were down—and here were these rich families who had everything and didn't even realize it. What's more privileged than that?

It was an easy enough blind spot to inhabit. Just replace jealousy with blame and a sense of superiority, not to mention a few catchy rap lyrics. Should it matter if your family still has more money than most? Or if, with the brown hair and hazel eyes of a nineteenth-century Protestant banker, you're appropriating aspects of a culture that you're not in a position to claim? Or that one of your clearest advantages is a set of parents who are involved in every aspect of your childhood, whose love you've never doubted, and who genuinely care as much about the outcome of your life as their own?

No. You are fourteen and ignorant of race and class. Listen to the lyrics. They make sense. You've also been punished for crimes you didn't commit. Of course you should boast about it to everyone who'll listen. Especially if for as long as you can remember the people at school and on the playground have treated you like the most culpable person in their midst.

A few weeks before eighth grade started I asked my mother to buy me baggy jeans for school. When we went to the mall I tried on the pair I wanted—many sizes too big—and she laughed. "I'm not paying for something that fits two of you," she said. So the next day I went into my parents' shared closet and grabbed one of her old maternity pairs. In the mirror they looked baggy enough, if a bit flared at the hips. That afternoon I was wearing them in our living room—rapping along loudly to a song on MTV—when my father burst through the door.

"I heard shouting," he said.

I told him it was just me.

He glanced at my jeans.

"How do I sound?" I asked.

"What?"

"Do I sound like they do?"

He looked at the screen, then at me, the denim bunching and sagging like a pair of riding pants, and after a moment he backed out of the room.

At the time I had no idea that the record companies had marketed these songs specifically to suburban teenagers with every gesture in mind, that the baggy fashion trends emulated prison jumpsuits—and that people were making millions of dollars off it all. I was happy to wear my flannel shirt in the heat. To plod along in my big basketball shoes. At the mall I bought less-terrible-looking jeans with birthday money from my grandmother. I purposely used words like "ain't" in normal conversation. I was sure that I'd finally discovered a way to turn my personality into an advantage, and if it hadn't been Snoop Dogg that summer I might've found something else, but his videos played every few hours on MTV, and I could listen to my portable CD player all day long.

»

At the end of August I broke my wrist playing touch football, and when I started eighth grade I was wearing a cast, again, on my left hand.

It fit perfectly with my new appearance. For the first week I dragged myself around in my enormous clothes hoping that everyone would notice. That Friday I was waiting in the grass along the school's parking lot for my mother to pick me up when Ronnie Cain walked over.

I hadn't seen him in months. He was still wearing the leather jacket and chain. He shouted, I said something tough back, and he shoved me. I went down hard on my broken wrist, the pain blaring through everything. When I stood up I saw Ronnie's smile and I wanted to knock it from his face in the way you would a mask. I swung at him with my natural hand, my left, and the cast cracked into his temple. By now I was five-feet-eight-inches tall, a hundred and thirty pounds, and with the added plaster my wrist weighed as much as a small club.

The impact knocked Ronnie out. You could see it in the sag of his shoulders, how his knees shed their tension; he fell in a heap and I was suddenly unable to recognize what he'd become, the grass beneath him like the bed of some long-extinct sea.

Eventually Ronnie stirred. I sat down next to him. People were gathering, children and parents blocking off the sun. Ronnie lifted himself up and we waited silently together, his right eye swollen shut. The parking lot was surrounded by cars, one of which must have contained my mother.

Soon enough I was led into Mr. Powell's empty office. The blinds were drawn. When he finally arrived I noticed that the eye patch was back. He sat down across from me and said, "Well?"

I tried to explain myself, but I kept seeing the violence of what I'd done, the repeating image of Ronnie's fall.

Then my mother arrived. She blinked at the dimness. Mr. Powell started to explain that I'd gotten into a fight, but when he mentioned the other boy's name she shouted, "He's the one who followed Timmy home last year!" To my surprise she began to accuse my vice principal of being too lax on bullying. Wasn't it his job to protect kids like me?

Mr. Powell waited until she was finished and then said that, legally, I could be charged with assault for using a cast in a fight.

My mother's face went calm. "Listen," she said to him. "It takes two to tango." Then she explained that I was currently seeing a psychiatrist and on an antidepressant for my behavioral problems. "I'm not saying Timmy didn't do anything wrong," she told him. "But he's really been working hard to avoid situations like these—we all have."

Mr. Powell heard her out, and afterward he and my mother went to see Principal Baumgartner, who must have offered his opinion. My punishment was the same as last time, a two-day suspension, and there wasn't any more talk of legal ramifications.

I didn't understand. Why hadn't Mr. Powell seen through her excuses? Didn't he already know about Dr. Epstein and the nortriptyline? I'd assumed he was out to get me since the first moment I'd met him, and I couldn't imagine a better opportunity than the one that had just presented itself.

During all of this Ronnie Cain must have been waiting with an ice pack in the nurse's office. I don't remember if he was suspended for the same amount of time. Or how long it took his face to heal. Or if someone eventually arrived to pick him up.

»

If for over a century children with ADHD have been perceived as a threat, the products of bad parenting, the victims of our authoritarian society, and as souls in need of saving, how did these perceptions influence the way *my family* approached the disorder?

I remember an afternoon during that terrible third-grade year with Mrs. Kovalenko. I was home with a broken leg—banned for a month from the classroom—and my mother decided to rent a wheelchair and drive us both across the mountains toward Santa Cruz. She wouldn't say where we were going.

For weeks I'd been stuck inside the house, attending tutoring sessions, playing video games, and watching television, and she'd been talking about doing something outdoors for a while.

During the car ride she hummed along to an Amy Grant album and pointed out the signs of towns—"Capitola! Your dad and I once spent a summer there. It has the best margaritas." When we arrived at the coast the fog had receded. My mother stopped in a parking lot and unfolded the wheelchair, its spokes gleaming in the sun, but I wouldn't get in. I was horrified that people might see me in it and think I was handicapped. "Timmy," she said. "How are crutches any different?"

Finally I relented. She had no problem pushing me up the steep path. We were climbing a seaside cliff that was lined densely with trees. Their trunks reached right up to the canopy, the branches grown together like the scaffolding of an impossibly intricate roof. From a distance everything appeared in motion, but the day wasn't windy, and as my mother directed me into the cool, salt-smelling grove, I realized that the things I'd mistaken for leaves were actually thousands of butterflies—monarchs—their wings flaring like enormous copper coins. They were in the middle of their northward migration; every year they rested in this same place before moving on.

"What do you think?" my mother asked. I realized she was watching me. She must have seen my amazement—as well as my attempt, now, to cover it up.

"Butterflies," I said.

For the next hour she pushed me along the path. We crossed in and out of the canopy's shadow. Now and then she said something about God and connectedness but it was generally quiet going.

Whenever we passed other visitors, their eyes raised to the trees, I squirmed. I wanted to tell each of them it was just a broken leg—that I'd gotten it skiing—and by the time we made it back to the parking lot I was sullen and fidgety. But on the way home I must've fallen asleep, because when I woke up it was dark, and I wasn't sure where I was, but the light in the car went on and my mother was talking softly to my father, who'd come down the steps to carry me inside.

How does my family perceive something like ADHD? For their part, my parents have always understood that a child doesn't deserve to be at a disadvantage, and from the beginning they were willing to offer whatever help they deemed necessary.

Can the reliance on such help eventually lead to new complications? Of course. But that's a question you only get to ask once you're making progress.

»

After my second suspension from school my parents told me that under no circumstances was I to get in another fight. "You're gonna get hurt," my father said. "Or hurt someone else," my mother added. I didn't have the heart to point out that both these things had already happened.

At the time I was applying to high schools. We'd known for a while that I wouldn't be able to attend the one in Fisher's district. This didn't have anything to do with my behavior; Los Gatos High was one of the richest in the country and it wasn't accepting transfers. My parents thought that the public high school near our house was too rough-and-tumble, so I began to apply to the private Catholic schools in the area: St. Francis, Archbishop Mitty, and Bellarmine College Preparatory.

When I came back from my suspension there was a noticeable change in the way the other children saw me. After all, I'd knocked out cold one of the tougher kids in the school.

For the most part the rest of the year was uneventful. I turned in my applications on time, talked to Dr. Epstein about the far-off prospect of college—"The preparation begins now," he said—and found myself engaged in an awkward truce with most of the other eighth graders. Even the popular girls seemed hesitant to judge me in the way they once had.

That spring I did get into one more fistfight. It was in P.E. We'd just finished a session of moon ball: baseball played with the overly ripe volleyballs Mr. Lowe seemed so fond of. I'd hit the game-winning home run, and I was bragging about it in the locker room to a few sixth graders when a kid in my class scoffed.

His name was Jason Hammad. He was sitting next to me: a small-mouthed boy with opaque glasses and a nasal voice that made everything he said sound contemptuous.

"Hey motherfucker," I told him. "You got an opinion?"

He shook his head fiercely. And that was that. But when I turned back around the sixth graders were gazing at me. One of them—a blond kid who played baseball with my cousin—said, "Doesn't he know you fuck people up?"

I glanced at them and then at Jason. "Yeah," I finally said. "Don't you?"

In a tone that could've been an elderly librarian's, Jason replied, "Just shut up."

For a moment I didn't move. Since my fight with Ronnie nobody had challenged me. Now the sixth graders were watching both of us. I stood over Jason and said that, in fact, he was the one who should shut up. He told me to get out of his face. I asked him how exactly he planned on making me do that. And as he started to move away I landed a quick jab at his nose.

Jason sat back down. His eyes went tight. Then he cocked his mouth and began to wail.

I hadn't hit him hard, and there wasn't any blood. His glasses weren't even broken. But his crying was jagged and hysterical and kept getting louder. More than anything I wanted it to stop. Finally I heard myself shout, "I'm so sorry!"

The sixth graders looked confusedly at each other. Jason kept wailing. Snot blubbered down his face, which he finally placed in his hands, his whole body shaking.

Mr. Lowe arrived and asked Jason why he was crying, and when there was no answer, our P.E. coach told him he better go find the nurse.

I changed out of my gym clothes quickly. The sixth graders were sneaking bewildered glances in my direction, but I didn't care; I needed to catch up with Jason before he got to the nurse's.

I found him in an empty hall. When he saw me he shrunk back.

"You can't tell them I hit you," I said. "You gotta say you fell."

He was still sniffing. I realized that this was probably the first time he'd ever been punched in the face.

"Please," I said.

After a moment he nodded.

The open-air hallway smelled like concrete and banana peels and wet paper bags; the garbage cans were still packed full from lunch. "Are you okay?" I finally asked.

He let out that long piercing wail all over again. Which was how I left him—barely making it to my next class on time.

About thirty minutes later, Mr. Powell appeared in the doorway. His one eye met mine and I followed him to his office without a word. Inside: the same ocean-green lamp, his blinds like cords of dark wood. I waited for him to dig into me. Instead he explained that Jason, sobbing, had told the nurse he fell down—and only later revealed what really happened. "I've never thought of you as a liar," he said. "Or a bully."

I was speechless; neither had I. After a while he said, "Do I think you're a good kid, Mr. Denevi? Sure. That's not the issue." He talked about how over the years he'd seen too many children arrive at worse ends than I'd care to imagine. And most of them didn't come from families who were working so hard in their favor. "You're entering dangerous territory," he finally told me.

The moment that followed was one of the eeriest of my childhood; as I was getting ready to leave I realized that Mr. Powell's pirate patch had somehow migrated, during the past three years, from his left eye to his right. For seconds I stood and stared. Once again he had to tell me to exit his office; my mother was on her way.

»

I was suspended two days, again, for hitting Jason. When my mother arrived she grabbed my arm and dragged me down the hallway in what must have seemed a dangerous manner. Even before we got to the car she was screaming. Who did I think I was? What kind of monster punches an innocent kid in the face? And after all the times she'd stuck up for me! My life was *over*—did I realize it? Did I have any idea how much trouble I was in? What high school would accept a boy who'd been suspended *three* times!

She was sobbing and screaming—swerving in her lane—and by the time we got home her wrath had taken the place of the thing I'd done. I had two choices: be consumed or fight back.

We arrived in our driveway and for the next few minutes, as the sun slanted in through the windows, we sat in the parked car and screamed at each other. Finally I told her it was all her fault because she was the one who'd made me go on the nortriptyline in the first place.

"What the fuck are you talking about?" she replied.

"Dr. Epstein said I could stop taking it if I wanted to!"

For three years I'd been on a psychotropic drug. I still couldn't really *feel* its benefits, but things hadn't gotten any worse than they'd been; and while I've never subscribed to the idea that the act of undergoing this specific treatment was somehow more harmful than the behavior it was meant to improve, at the time I couldn't help but think that the longer I took it the more likely I was to keep doing the things I'd already done. Which is one of the problems with a medication meant to address that point where personality and biology meet: if the drug really does work, its benefit can feel unmerited; and if it fails, well, your fate is confirmed— there's something so deep and irreversible at the heart of you that even a pill can't reach it. Either way you find yourself struggling to distinguish the things you can change from all those you can't.

"I'm going off it," I shouted at my mother in our rapidly heating car. "And there's nothing you can do about it."

»

Toward the end of eighth grade, Mr. Powell came to my science class. I thought he was there to make an announcement, but he proceeded to tell the full story behind his wandering eye patch.

About three years earlier a blurry curtain had spread across his vision, and when he went to the doctor he learned that his left retina had detached. There hadn't been any physical trauma; it'd simply happened. He underwent emergency surgery and his eye was saved. But this year the same thing had occurred again with his right eye; as soon as the vivid half of the world went gray he was rushed to the hospital.

The worst part, he said, was the recovery. Both times he had to sit blindfolded in a chair with his forehead flush against a table—in twelve-hour sessions—so that the surgery could set. He spent the days listening to audiobooks, but after a while he felt like he was going crazy. "It was the hardest thing I've ever done," he said. When his vision had filmed over that second time he'd experienced a moment of hesitation; he wasn't sure he could stand going through the process all over again. "What would *you* do to save your sight?" he asked us.

I understood the reason for his visit. Recently we'd dissected cows' eyes and had talked about retinas and pupils. But I always believed that things like this were really about me, even if I knew they couldn't be. What would *I* have done? As I imagined myself in Mr. Powell's shoes, I suddenly felt elated by the prospect of a choice that could affect everything—a moment in which I was the only one who got to decide what might happen next.

》

At the end of the year I received word on my high-school applications. I'd been accepted at Bellarmine and St. Francis. But Archbishop Mitty—the easiest to get into—had rejected me; they'd called about my behavior marks during my suspension for punching Jason, and Mr. Powell had answered their questions honestly.

Bellarmine was an all-boys institution known for its strict discipline, but it was more exclusive than St. Francis—respected for its success in academics and athletics—and the commute would be much shorter. Looking back, I don't think it was ever a question. As soon as I got into

Bellarmine it felt like I was already on my way there, leaving behind all the people I'd spent the previous three years with. Most of them I wouldn't see again.

Which was fine by me. On the last day the yearbook came out. It included a supplement with categories like Most Likely to Succeed. I opened it to find that, out of the entire school, I'd been voted Biggest Talker.

5

Dead and in Jail for Life

The summer before I started high school, my parents and I sat down with Dr. Epstein to talk about discontinuing my antidepressant medication.

My mother claimed she was concerned about the upcoming transition to Bellarmine. I argued that I was old enough to make my own decisions on the subject. My father didn't take sides. At the end of the session Dr. Epstein suggested a compromise: I could taper down the nortriptyline and then spend a month off of it. "Think of it as a trial run," he said.

Over the next few weeks I tried to observe everything from a point of remove. My mouth wasn't so dry, and I didn't feel drowsy in the evening. But was I moody, or depressed, or more impulsive and less focused? As I spent the weeks in the usual manner—playing Nintendo, listening to music, and hitting Wiffle Balls with a friend—the only thing I really noticed was that I felt pretty much the same.

My mother was watching, too. At night she'd stop by my room and demand then and there that I fold the laundry or empty the dishwasher.

If I argued it was a mark against me, but I couldn't stand the fact that she *expected* an argument, so I called her on it—"You're doing this on purpose"—and then we'd be fighting for real, each claiming that the other was wrong, until out of nowhere she'd say, "That's it! Not another word!" Which would just make me all the more sullen.

After a month we returned to Dr. Epstein's office. It was August, the heat sinking across the valley for a few heavy hours each afternoon. I'd recently turned fifteen. My mother and I went together; my sister and brother stayed home with my father. As we traveled through off-ramps and overpasses toward downtown San Jose, neither of us spoke.

The session started and Dr. Epstein asked my mother to go first. She mentioned the fights I was sure she'd instigated. But then she told him I wasn't eating as much; my body language appeared more languid; and most of all, I was less active—sitting in my room all day listening to my CD player. "He's just not *himself*," she finally said. Such claims were easy enough to refute, and when it was my turn to speak I did, but I was beginning to understand that the question wasn't as simple as who was right and who was wrong.

My psychiatrist was quiet as he heard us out. I knew my mother trusted him. I did too. He held the type of power over us that you earn after years of listening carefully. "I do think that the situation has continued to improve," he eventually said. He pointed out my recent acceptance to a prestigious school. In his opinion, I understood the stakes; now the consequences for fighting would be much more dire. But more importantly, in only three years I'd legally become an adult, and a conversation like this would be irrelevant. "I think it's Tim's choice," he told us.

My mother didn't throw her hands in the air, or swear, or rip the surrealistic painting of the teepee from the wall. But her eyes narrowed. Her shoulders were hunched. Sitting in her chair and not looking at either of us she was burning.

What had I expected? That she'd suddenly see the issue from my perspective? When had I ever known her to relent, especially when it came to her child's welfare? She had always been able to make reality fit a particular perspective—hers. Usually this worked in my favor. She believed I was a decent, loving boy and it didn't matter how many other people saw things differently; they were wrong. But she was also terrified that something awful was going to happen to me: I'd be expelled, or get beaten to a pulp in a fight, or fall off a roof and crack my head open. In her view, treating my behavior really was a matter of life and death.

I realized that even Dr. Epstein's opinion wouldn't change her mind. Although she might eventually give in on the issue of medication, I'd never be able to convince her of what such a decision represented: that I no longer needed drugs to help me function like everyone else. In fact, it was starting to dawn on me that the only way to show her I was a rational and mature young man would be to consider going back on the nortriptyline under my own free will.

I'd taken it for three years. Nobody knew. The pills didn't stick in my throat like they used to, and I'd grown accustomed to having a dry mouth. Say I went off the drug; wouldn't we just be back here in a few months debating her latest version of the truth? Wasn't it entirely within her grasp to force my behavior into the direction she expected it to go? And didn't she still hold the trump card: the power to decide the things I could and couldn't do?

"Fine," I told my psychiatrist. "I'll keep taking it." As I said this I felt further apart from my mother than ever. I was angry, yes, but it was more like heartache: I'd been forced to confront the limits of what she was capable of seeing.

》

Bellarmine College Preparatory was located in downtown San Jose. A Jesuit institution, it was founded in 1851 as part of the Santa Clara mission complex, but by the time I arrived it had moved to a sprawling campus near the airport. Some of the buildings were modern—blue and glassy with open-air corridors—while others resembled the midcentury architecture of my first grammar school. The quad was set with oak trees and rolling tracts of manicured grass. But Bellarmine wasn't like an East Coast boarding school; the tuition was reasonable enough, the students were commuters, there was a dress code but no uniform requirement, and the education had a Catholic slant.

It was about a twenty-minute drive from my house, and at the end of our first car ride there my mother told me, "I can't believe my firstborn son is so big that now he's going off to high school. Timmy! I'm proud of you."

Then I was alone at Bellarmine. The light filtered down through the trees. The concrete walkways were still wet from the morning fog. I began to notice the crush of students; I had on new jeans and a big Chicago White Sox hat and was sure I was about to make a number of friends.

But these other kids all seemed to be wearing workout clothes. Their hair was uncombed, they spoke dispassionately, and even when the bell rang for first period they hardly moved.

As I hurried to my classroom it hit me: out of the twelve hundred students on this campus there wasn't a single girl. In fact, nearly all the teachers were men. I'd known this coming in, of course. For the most part I bought into the school's talking points: an all-male education makes it easier to concentrate on academics and diminishes bullying and faddishness, and besides, there was always our sister school, Presentation, which was located on the other side of town.

But by this point I liked almost everything about girls—their gestures, voices, even the brightness of their skirts and blouses. Most of all I enjoyed talking to them; I'd try and flirt in the only way I knew how, by offering overly sincere comments. Without them Bellarmine felt shapeless. How on earth would I manage to navigate such a place for the next *four years*?

That wasn't the only surprise on my first day. As I went from class to class, my new instructors explained the school's disciplinary system. It was known as JUG—Justice Under God. You could receive a JUG for almost anything: a forgotten book, a missed homework assignment, insubordination, talking too loudly, wearing the wrong shoes, not raising your hand, daydreaming, tardiness, etc. Their enforcement depended on the teacher; a few handed them out indiscriminately, others as a form of crowd control, and some not at all. You served your JUGs after school in a designated detention hall, where you were ordered to copy passages from the Bible or write five hundred times *I Will Not Be Late.* Occasionally you'd be sent out into the quad to pick up trash, and for more severe infractions there were Saturday JUGs, during which you spent four hours raking leaves and shoveling dirt.

At my previous school, something like forgetting a book had been an academic issue; you lost participation points. But at Bellarmine it became moral, a failure of willpower. On my first day I watched every move I made, barely escaping a JUG in science class for talking out of turn.

When I arrived home that afternoon I fell asleep on our couch. My mother had to wake me up for dinner, the nortriptyline in her hand like the promise of something I'd long since given up trying to imagine.

»

That year I began hanging out with two boys who'd grown up in the town next to mine, Steven Kelley and Isaac Stipe. We were in the same debate class, and at lunch we tended to gather under an oak tree in the grassy quad.

Steven Kelley was slim, wore flannel shirts, and had an angular nose and short hair. Usually he moved in jolts, but during a conversation he'd freeze and tilt his head to take in each word. Talking to him was like losing an argument you didn't know you'd started.

Ike Stipe was taller and thinner than both of us. He had a shaved scalp. His earlobes were loose and perforated from the jewelry he wasn't allowed to wear at school. With his bony jaw, socketed eyes, and enormous boots, he was just as smart as Steven but his logic was edgier; he seemed more willing to make and accept ridiculous statements.

On a bright winter afternoon we were complaining about our debate teacher, Mr. Ballard—I wasn't really paying attention—when one of them said "ADD."

I froze. Overhead the oak caught the breeze, its branches straining. I realized that Steven must've been the one who said it; he liked to employ terminology in his arguments.

But now Stipe was talking and Steven was looking down and smiling thinly. The conversation had moved on to the subject of marijuana—the difficulty of getting it—and Stipe was bragging about a connection he had, someone older.

"Bullshit," Steven finally said.

Stipe shrugged. "You'll see," he told him. "Just fucking wait."

And that was that. Lunch was over. I'd assumed that Steven had used the term in reference to me. But as the bell sounded and I watched these two boys depart for class, I was suddenly sure that they both shared a history similar to mine—and that they'd actually been talking about it, right here in the quad, while I'd been staring off into space.

»

A few weeks later Steven, Stipe, and I were sitting under the oak tree at lunch when an instructor approached in our direction. He was in his twenties, clean-shaven, and even though the weather had turned cold and rainy he was wearing soccer shorts. A decade earlier he'd been an all-state athlete at Bellarmine, which was common enough. Our faculty was diverse—Jesuits, young Stanford grads, former engineers, and even a few 1960s protest-types who now taught *On the Road* and Beat poetry to seniors—but a good number also coached a sport.

It had been raining all day, the drops like a fine scrim beyond the shelter of our tree. As this young teacher got closer I noticed that his cheeks and forehead were raw. He was probably on his way home with the flu, walking the concrete path between the school and the faculty parking lot.

He stopped in front of us. His eyes were webbed painfully. "What are you looking at?" he said.

I glanced down.

"I asked you a question!"

He was standing in front of Steven Kelley, who stared right back. Neither of them spoke. After a while Steven began to shake his head. He did this slowly, a gesture of pure disapproval. I couldn't believe it; I'd never seen one of my peers judge the behavior of an adult so succinctly.

The teacher spit into the wet grass. His face was ugly with rain, his tiny shorts plastered to his legs. He was miserable! We all knew it. Why hadn't he just kept walking? At the time I was beginning to understand that the instructors who'd once gone here were often the strictest enforcers of the disciplinary system. For them insubordination was more like a reunion, except now they were on the proper side. It was a victim's logic—a survivor's—and even then I sensed the danger.

This teacher told Steven, "You know what your look says to me? It says, 'Go fuck yourself.'"

For the first time Steven glanced away, and when he looked back up I could see the recognition in his eyes. "Why would I need a look to tell you that?"

The teacher grabbed his arm. Together they tensed. I was sure Steven was about to throw a punch—guaranteed expulsion. But he relaxed; his shoulders slumped and his arm sagged. The teacher tugged him violently into the rain, great banners of it coming down now, and after a while they disappeared in the direction of the dean's office.

》

Sometimes I like to think of ADHD—of my experience with it, at least—as a space that exists between desire and reality. This space is largest when you're younger and tends to diminish as the years pass. But does it ever close up entirely? In other words: What's the long-term prognosis for a child who is growing up severely hyperactive?

A hundred years ago, our favorite British doctors approached this question in the way you might expect. Sir George Frederic Still thought that hyperactive children lagged behind their more attentive peers because their brains hadn't properly evolved. His speculation was based on a Darwinian interpretation of causes; he believed that "volitional inhibition"—the control of one's attention, will, and emotions—was a "late development" in the eons-long saga of human evolution. And since the prospect of an evolutionary leap tends to fall outside the general skill-set of doctors—Victorian or otherwise—these children would suffer from their symptoms for the rest of their lives. As evidence he quoted the story of a Maori tribal leader, first reported by Charles Darwin, who "cried like a child because the sailors spoilt his favourite cloak by powdering it with flour." In Still's opinion this chieftain had wept "over causes which in a higher race would fail entirely to produce any such expression of emotion."

So George Frederic Still was arguing that the childhood symptoms of what we now call ADHD were static and irreversible: British boys and girls with clear evolutionary shortcomings would eventually grow up to resemble the empire's least civilized subjects. No wonder he was so worried about existential threats to society. What could be more horrifying to our good doctor than the prospect of a large man sobbing over his ruined cape?

His contemporary Alfred Tredgold saw the issue in the same light. "Feeble-minded" children who struggled with hyperactivity and concentration would pass unchanged into adulthood—eventually joining the class of "defectives" that Tredgold had helped legally define in the Mental Deficiency Act of 1913. And while he admitted that segregated educational environments might help control some of the symptoms, nothing could be done about the real cause: a "germinal impairment" seeded deep within a child's brain. "Now the essence of mental defect is that it is incurable," he wrote in *Mental Deficiency*. Hence his continued calls for forced sterilization, among other things.

Together these doctors were offering conjectural evidence; they believed that biological abnormalities at the root of the symptoms created a hopeless deficiency of willpower. Neither took the time to pursue the next logical step and follow their subjects into adulthood. Why would they? The main reason they paid so much attention to ADHD-esque behavior was because it served their larger argument: children with mental illness—whether it be "imbecility" or a "moral defect" of attention—were an evolutionary dead-end.

About both Still and Tredgold, our present-day ADHD expert Dr. Russell A. Barkley writes, "We should therefore not . . . obscure either the dedication these early scientist/practitioners brought to the children within their professional care or the valuable theoretical insights they provided about this disorder, tainted as the latter may have been with the cultural biases of the time." Needless to say, Dr. Barkley's point of view—that of a medical professional judging previous contributors to his field—is purposely narrow.

Instead let's consider them a final time. Sir G. F. Still in his enormous cape. Tredgold and his devilish hair. For more than a century they've been gazing out at us, a pair of men frozen in their attitudes; and of the many things they must have expected the future to bring—evolutionarily or otherwise—I'll tell you what they never counted on: a day when the subjects of their studies would be in a position to evaluate the authority on which their work was based.

»

Unlike Fisher, Bellarmine's student body was diverse, and as I got to know kids from different backgrounds, I couldn't help but notice that my clothing style of enormous jeans and a sideways hat was offensive . . . and embarrassing. Besides, in an all-boys environment it was frowned upon to put so much effort into your appearance. My musical tastes were also changing; I still listened to rap, but Steven Kelley had a large collection of classic rock records, and I'd begun buying CDs by Led Zeppelin and Jimi Hendrix so I could argue with him over who was better.

In the quad at lunch we talked about movies, albums, and the week-end parties thrown by people they claimed to know. We also recounted the stories behind our most recent JUGs.

They usually went like this: I'd be taking an open-book exam in science and the Buddy Holly–looking instructor would tell me I had two options: I could go to my locker and get the textbook I'd forgotten, which would mean a JUG; or I could stop whining and start the test, which I was now sure to fail. "There *are* such things as stupid questions," he liked to say. "Stupid people ask them."

Or my Latin teacher, an old Jesuit who'd just undergone a series of painful dental procedures, would call on us at random to translate lines from Cicero. If we muddled them it meant we weren't keeping up on our vocabulary homework: JUG.

Ike Stipe got JUGs in the hallway for dress-code violations. Steven was given a whole week of JUGs for his rainy run-in with the soccer coach. I even got one for asking to use the office phone in a rude voice.

During lunch in the quad, as Steven Kelley and Ike Stipe took apart the logic behind our school's rules, I marveled at their articulation. They were far and away the smartest kids I'd ever met and I wanted to be like them: precise and dismissive.

I remember a spring morning in Mr. Ballard's debate class. Steven and Stipe weren't there; that semester they were taking a different section. Along with a partner I was up against two other boys on a policy issue—immigration—and as my teammate delivered a rebuttal, our teacher shambled to the blackboard and wrote in chalk NO BRIEF BARFING!, which was a way of saying you shouldn't read from your notes while speaking.

My classmates erupted in laughter. My teammate couldn't see what our teacher had done, and he assumed that everyone was mocking something he'd said. Mr. Ballard stood chuckling by the blackboard. My partner trailed off and sat down.

I stood up and shouted, "That's not fair!"

The roomful of boys quieted. "Mr. Denevi," my teacher said. "What's fair and unfair is always up for debate, especially in this course." Everyone laughed again.

At the end of the period Mr. Ballard called me up to his desk. On the wall behind him was a picture from perhaps twenty years earlier: in it his hair was long, he was holding what appeared to be a beer, and the look on his face said, *Let's get this party started!* Alongside it were plaques and awards.

Everyone else left. Ballard looked me up and down. Even today I can still hear his voice; he sounded exactly like Rush Limbaugh. "I think we could probably use a lesson in treating others with respect," he told me.

I tried to imagine Steven Kelley standing in my place. *"We?"* I responded.

During my subsequent JUG, I was forced to copy the genealogy at the beginning of Matthew's gospel: *Abraham begat Isaac; and Jacob begat Judah and his brethren; and Judah begat Perez and Zerah and Tamar . . .*

»

One of the perks of Bellarmine was its schedule: every Friday we were released three hours early. I'd been petitioning my mother to let me spend the afternoon with Steven Kelley and Ike Stipe in Saratoga, their hometown.

She and I had been getting along better ever since I'd agreed to go back on my antidepressant medication, and after a while she gave in; I could catch a ride to Saratoga with Steven and his cousin, an upperclassman named Copeland, and later Ike Stipe's mother would drive me home. "Call me if your plans change," she said that morning.

It was May, sunny. I rode in the backseat of Copeland's old Jeep Cherokee to a park in the hills. Steven had gotten some rum, Copeland had his own flask, and Stipe produced a joint. We sat at a wooden picnic table. The view was crowned by enormous pines, their needles in a bed at our feet. I'd never really been drunk, at least like this.

For the next few hours I sipped and smoked, enjoying the buoyancy of my own skin. Steven gave a monologue on the brilliance of Jimmy Page. Stipe tried to climb a tree. At one point I balanced on the edge of the picnic table and jump-kicked the air, a reenactment of the final scene in *The Karate Kid.*

Copeland's hair was blond and glossy, and as he watched us he seemed resigned, but to what I couldn't tell. Every so often he demanded that we drink and I always complied. After one long slug of whiskey he slapped me on the back.

Then Steven and Ike were arguing with him; it was time to go. Copeland was obviously drunk. We'd had family friends who'd been killed because of drinking and driving, and a few years earlier I'd been terrified by a graphic assembly on the subject, but suddenly we were all piling into Copeland's Jeep Cherokee, its windows blanched with dust.

We headed up the road into the coastal mountains. Each corner seemed to arrive faster. At one of them another car appeared. We swerved violently, and I was thrown against the window. But it was just a fishtail. The other car laid into its horn, and briefly I imagined my mother—her voice like this strange, shrill burst of sound. Then I looked at Stipe and at Steven Kelley and began to laugh.

We continued up the mountain. The evening was dry and cloudless, coming on early in the blue shadows of the trees. Our destination was a house of multiple levels built into a ridge: my first real party. Inside, the rooms were bright and boisterous. Girls held red cups, their shoulders bare; it seemed like I was speaking to all of them at once. The environment felt loud and unpredictable and short on memory.

I passed between the keg and the packed rooms. Steven was talking animatedly with a group of older boys, then he was downing shots with his cousin. Stipe had disappeared somewhere near the deck.

Later I found myself in the driveway focusing on the black tips of the pines and trying not to throw up. Copeland walked out. His hair was wavy, like something shining in water, and he offered me his flask. "Come on, dude," he said. But before I could reply he was in his car, alone; as if in slow motion he descended the road, his taillights blinking through the trees. It was the last time I'd ever see him. In a few weeks he'd be expelled from Bellarmine, something about drugs in his locker.

Eventually Ike Stipe's mother picked us up. I was driven home—left on the curb out front. When I turned toward the doorway it was already open. My mother was standing in her white robe, its edges struck with light.

I understood clearly enough. I was hours late, hadn't called, could barely stand: this was a new kind of trouble. But for a moment I wanted to run up the stairs and give her an enormous hug. "Look!" I'd tell her, holding up the evidence of the afternoon—its glancing girls and loud boys—something we could both marvel at, our past together like a color that was finally beginning to fade. "You were right!" I'd say.

>>

For as long as I can remember, my family has talked about drinking as a way to relax. "Why don't you have an eggnog and stop sulking around?" my parents would say to each other at the holidays. Or: "Jesus, just take a deep breath and sip your wine." We didn't have any of those dour, violent alcoholics populating the most recent generations. My Italian grandfathers were a bit too controlling to get completely smashed, and while my Irish grandmothers drank daily—religiously, you could say—it tended to wash them in an altogether bemused light, at least from my perspective. I can't recall a moment in childhood when I could actually tell that my mother and father were drunk, but for them alcohol went hand in hand with the excitement of a party.

The summer following eighth grade, my parents had sat me down and explained that it would be okay if I had a few drinks with them one night; that way I could experience what it felt like in a safe environment. It sounded like the most uncool thing I'd ever heard.

But after my Friday night in Saratoga all that kind of talk disap-peared. "You don't fucking get it," my mother shouted the next day. "You'll be expelled! You'll go to jail! You'll end up dead on the side of a road!" She laid it out plainly enough: "You are not allowed to drink." Later my father pulled me aside. "You're just too young," he told me. "Wait till you're in college."

I was grounded, the one recourse my mother had left. At my next session with Dr. Epstein I went on about what hypocrites my parents were. "They're worse than Bellarmine!" I told him. On some level I must have been sensitive to the contradiction: I was taking a drug to help me get along better with people and then there was alcohol, something that seemed to do the trick without all the shame and fuss—and more effectively, for that matter. But the main reason I wanted to drink was the most obvious: the outstanding time I'd had.

"You're still six years away from the legal age," Dr. Epstein said. He talked about the delicate, developing brain of a teenager; alcohol muddled a decision-making process that was already suspect. "It's such a significant gamble."

He sounded logical enough. But for me the choice was simple: a night like the one in Saratoga had never existed before because it could only exist with alcohol.

»

Over the last century, as the long-term prospects of a child with ADHD continued to be revised, a key part of the debate centered on something called "the core deficit": a single behavioral issue through which the oth-ers might be explained.

This deficit is not the same as the disorder's root cause. For example, doctors Still and Tredgold blamed everything on evolutionary factors, but they didn't evaluate the primary symptoms in relation to one an-other, as in, a child can't sit still *because* he's struggling to focus, or vice versa. The same went for Alfred Strauss, the doctor who coined the term "minimal brain damage"; he argued that since the disorder was the result of permanent physical damage, its symptoms would exist throughout a person's life span as they always had.

But researchers eventually began to examine these symptoms in a more cause-and-effect manner. In a 1957 article for *Pediatrics,* Maurice W. Laufer and Eric Denhoff, doctors at the Bradley Hospital in Rhode Island—where stimulants were first used to treat ADHD—outlined the disorder's main symptoms, identified hyperactivity as the most important, and advocated for a new diagnostic label, "Hyperkinetic Impulse Disorder," to better reflect this.

In a bit of a twist, Laufer and Denhoff agreed with the Freudian explanation for ADHD—unmet needs and unconscious conflicts—but they argued that a child with the disorder was *biologically* more sensitive to environmental influences because of previous damage to the "diencephalon," a large region of the brain that includes the hypothalamus. To support this theory they conducted a "photo-Metrozol threshold" experiment. It involved stimulants, strobe lights, and an EEG: the hyperactive children undergoing it supposedly showed more agitation in their brain-pattern readouts, which at the time was seen as evidence for "diencephalic dysfunction."

In retrospect this experiment was inconclusive—and disturbing; it would never hold up to today's ethical standards. But Laufer and Denhoff used it as a way to explain how "stimuli flooding in from both peripheral receptors and viscera" could lead to the core deficit, hyperactivity, which in turn created problems with impulsivity and focus.

At the end of their paper, after describing the action of various stimulants, these doctors offered a new long-term prognosis: "In later years this syndrome tends to wane spontaneously and disappear. We have not seen it persist in those patients whom we have followed to adult life." By "syndrome" they meant hyperactivity, which might diminish "at any age from 8 to 18."

Three years later, the clinical psychologist Stella Chess published "Diagnosis and Treatment of the Hyperactive Child" in the *New York*

State Journal of Medicine. Her goal was to better define the disorder. Like Laufer and Denhoff, she saw hyperactivity as the core deficit and noted that, in most cases, it disappeared by adulthood. These and similar studies would influence the diagnostic criteria for the 1968 *DSM-II,* which called ADHD "Hyperkinetic Reaction of Childhood," cited "over-activity" as its first symptom, and concluded that "the behavior usually diminishes by adolescence."

So by the second half of the twentieth century, ADHD was thought for the most part to be what doctors call developmentally benign: any problems that children with the disorder might experience in high school and beyond had to do with secondary issues—the habits that had been formed after years of conflict, poor academic performance, and unmet expectations—and not the primary symptoms, which would supposedly vanish.

»

It's difficult to remember exactly why I'd once been sure that both Steven Kelley and Ike Stipe had ADHD. I'd felt it since we first met—one of the reasons I liked them immediately—and at the time all the proof I needed was right in front of me: their personalities. I even went so far as to assume that they'd both been on medication, though I never asked them about it.

At the start of sophomore year Steven and I joined Mr. Ballard's debate team. I loved the formal nature of a good policy debate, how I could argue someone to the ground without the threat of physical violence. Steven seemed to enjoy its logical breadth, and he could go anywhere with a rebuttal. I began to look forward to the fear in our opponents' eyes, something between dread and expectation, as they waited to see how my partner might come at them next.

Mr. Ballard was waiting for us to slip up in the same way we were on the lookout for any chance to embarrass him. On an afternoon in October, Steven and I were serving as debate tutors—each week one team skipped practice to provide extra help for freshmen—when a young man with bright-red glasses showed up.

He was fifteen minutes late for his appointment. He wanted us to go through his ten-page advocacy speech, and we could've done so quickly enough, still finishing on time, but we'd been looking forward to leaving early.

"You should come back tomorrow," I said.

The freshman wasn't sure. But Steven got him to sign in the log that he'd had a full session with us—proof we'd stayed—and we headed across the street to a Mexican restaurant for cheap burritos.

The next day our debate teacher grabbed us out of practice. We followed him up to his classroom with the plaques and youthful picture. "In all my years of teaching," he said in his Rush Limbaugh voice, "I've never seen two students act so selfishly." Weren't we ashamed at what we'd done? Taking advantage of a freshman!

Of course he'd asked the student how our session went. We'd been caught falsifying the tutoring log. Steven didn't argue, and neither did I. Finally Ballard got to the details. It was an interesting proposition: How much could he hit us with?

The punishment was a Saturday JUG and an indefinite suspension from the team. His accompanying disciplinary note sounded even more outraged, which worked in my favor with my parents: How could the real-life infraction possibly equal his overblown version of it?

That Saturday Steven and I shoveled dirt for hours. But there were ten other boys alongside us, and the work wasn't hard. The young Jesuit in charge seemed uncomfortable with the idea of using physical labor as a form of punishment; he let us slack off all we wanted. Afterward he even brought us doughnuts. Steven and I sat in the autumn light and talked about our plans for the evening. A party in Willow Glen. Perhaps a dance at our sister school, Presentation. By now Ike Stipe had his license and the valley was suddenly small and bright.

》

My first two years at Bellarmine weren't all JUGs and angry teachers. For sophomore religion I had Father Ray Allender. He was older and would always stop and talk to anyone who approached him, and in his class he taught us to examine the gospels from a historical perspective; we analyzed their themes, intended audiences, and possible authors. At the end of each period we discussed topics like abortion and the death penalty. Sometimes I'd stay after to argue my position further and he'd listen patiently.

I also had a health class titled Drugs, Alcohol, and Human Sexuality with Mike Amundsen, one of the school's college counselors. He was a slim former hippie who enjoyed classic rock music and liked to talk about race and economics in terms of privilege. On drinking he was pragmatic. Sure we were going to do it—some of us, at least—but we needed to be safe and never drive. We also discussed substance abuse, premarital sex, masturbation, and homosexuality—nothing was off-limits. Which was probably the point.

I didn't know it at the time, but my mother was friends with Mr. Amundsen through Santa Clara University, and she'd asked him to look out for me at Bellarmine. That year she also had Father Allender over to dinner—along with his brother, a Jesuit too—and I remember that together we discussed the story of Lazarus in John's gospel: What must it have been like to return to life after being dead in a tomb for nearly a week?

The spring of my sophomore year I made the baseball team, and my grades were the highest they'd been; it was as if my best teachers had decided to sit back and let me knock my brain against whatever fresh obstacle I could find.

At home my mother and I had reached one of our truces: a few week-ends a month she let me spend the night at Steven Kelley or Ike Stipe's house. They had later curfews and their mothers weren't as rigid, and when I came back home the next day I lied about where I'd been and what I'd done.

It wasn't hard. I was still convinced that my mother was wrong about my antidepressant medication. The issue was one of credibility: I hated that she saw me as a child in need of protection, and she assumed that, when it came to alcohol, I no longer *wanted* to make the right choices.

Dr. Epstein had helped bridge this gap. That spring, however, he moved his practice to a town out past Santa Cruz. For a while we kept up the sessions, but the distance wasn't feasible.

I remember our last visit. My mother and father took me out of school early and we drove through the scattered afternoon light of the coastal mountains. My psychiatrist's new office was down a leafy road. When we arrived he greeted us warmly.

A few months earlier Dr. Epstein had suggested cutting my medication's dosage in half; in his opinion things were better. My mother, to my surprise, had agreed.

His new office had redwood walls and a colorful carpet. The surrealistic painting of the teepee hadn't made the trip. My parents both said that the lower dosage didn't seem to be influencing my behavior in a negative way. I talked about the improved side effects: my mouth no longer dried out at the first sign of nervousness, and at night I wasn't so drowsy. In the end we agreed to remain at the lower dosage.

By this point I'd been seeing Dr. Epstein regularly for half a decade. Throughout it all he'd never really talked about my situation in medical terms, with the diagnostic labels that can feel inseparable from the behavior itself. In his office the most important patterns had always been the ones that linked the past and the present.

"You've come a long way," he said. He was gazing right at me. I realized that his hair was almost gone, the soft skin of his head in fetters beneath his ears. I was older too; sixty pounds heavier and nearly a foot taller than when we'd first met. In fact, we were about the same height. And for once I felt like I understood what he was really saying—the part he'd chosen to leave out—an act of subtlety that made me wonder, with a sense of gratitude and regret, about everything else during our years of regular conversations I might've overlooked.

»

At the end of sophomore year there was a dance in Bellarmine's enormous gym. I'd been looking forward to it for months: only students from my school were allowed to attend, but any girl in the valley could go.

That evening Ike Stipe, Steven Kelley, and I split a bottle of gin beneath the awning of a nearby train station. Then like everyone else we stood in line to get inside. Beyond the entrance I could already see the tumult of bodies, lights strobing their movement. My baseball coach, Mr. Dinero, was checking IDs. He was in his forties; wore his black hair in a ponytail; and had a meaty chest, muscled neck, and skinny little legs. At one time he'd been a college football player. That winter, when I found out I'd made the baseball team—about ninety boys had competed for only eighteen spots—I'd rushed up to him and said, "Thank you so much for choosing me!"

"Thank someone else," he'd replied. "I wanted to cut you."

Ike Stipe approached Mr. Dinero first and showed his student ID. Dinero mumbled something—probably about the skull at the center of Stipe's shirt—but he was allowed to pass.

I went next. I breathed through my nose, chewed on my gum, and smiled awkwardly. The ID was loose in my fingers, but Mr. Dinero waved it away. I walked toward the gym.

An instant later he was calling after me—"Denevi!"

I spun around, trying to keep my balance.

"I can hear you from here," he told me.

Had I said something? I figured that if I just stood up straight and looked right at him everything would be fine.

"Pick up your feet when you walk!" It was a familiar complaint; in the dugout I had a tendency to drag my metal cleats in a manner that drove him crazy.

Inside the gym, young women crowded together. A fog machine draped the spaces between us with a sickly, mechanized smell. The strobe lights captured everyone at intervals, and a row of large speakers pounded out electronic-sounding dance songs.

Stipe had complained at the train station that we hadn't brought enough alcohol. I was drunk, yes, but not outlandishly. It seemed just right. Usually—sober and surrounded by so many girls—I felt jittery and insufficient; there was something wrong with me and soon enough they'd figure it out. But now I had a sensation of maturity. After all, who better to navigate this strange, overstimulating landscape than me?

A girl with a purple headband walked by. She glanced in my direction. I followed her, and together we joined her group of friends. One of them leaned in, her breath smelling like licorice. "My name's Cassie," she said. For an instant I wanted to ask her more questions than she could answer, which was how situations like this tended to go; I'd babble on and the expectation in a beautiful face would disappear.

Instead I started dancing. They did too. I waved my hands, singing with a deep, affected voice. Throughout the gym the girls outnumbered the boys three-to-one, a simple enough equation; you just had to be willing to be caught.

A moment later I felt a tap on my shoulder. Stipe was standing behind me. I'd meant to look for him when I got in. But I was surprised; he'd never needed my help to approach a group of girls. At the last dance he'd snuck off into a corner with a very tall senior, her arms snaking hungrily inside his shirt.

He glanced back at the door and motioned for me to follow. I did. At the entrance, Mr. Dinero was standing with his hand on Steven's shoulder. It was an absurd pose: the giant former athlete holding in place a fidgety sixteen-year-old while other students presented their IDs. Steven kept turning to Dinero and shouting. My baseball coach ignored him.

I wanted to go over to find out what was happening. Mr. Dinero had never met Steven, but he and I were familiar enough; there had to be something I could say or do to make things better. But I was terrified he'd clamp one of those hands down on me, and a moment later an elderly Jesuit arrived. Steven was led away.

I don't remember what Ike and I did for the rest of the night, or how I got home, or if I said anything to Mr. Dinero at our next practice. But the punishment for drinking at a dance was a five-day suspension and full academic and social probation for a year. When Steven came back a week later he told us what happened: Dinero had smelled alcohol.

"But you were chewing gum," I said. "We all were." Hadn't he held his breath like the rest of us?

Steven smiled thinly. "When that asshole took my ID he looked at it and said, 'I don't like your face.'"

"So?" Mr. Dinero said pretty much the same thing to me, regularly.

Steven stopped smiling. "So I bet he actually thought I was just gonna take his shit and go on my way like everyone else."

»

By the time someone with ADHD is sixteen years old, how does the hyperactive, inattentive, and impulsive behavior begin to diminish, especially when compared to that of other children?

I remember an afternoon at Bellarmine: an endless lecture by my sophomore history teacher on Oliver Cromwell and the English Civil War. By this point I'd flipped ahead in my textbook, played tic-tac-toe against myself, and used up my one bathroom break. I'd even gone over the lyrics to my favorite Jimi Hendrix songs. Still the bell wouldn't ring. Could I make it? Was it worth a JUG to jump up and free myself?

There are worse things in this world than a history class at a private high school—and I'm sure my fellow students had their own issues with a lengthy lecture on Cromwellian democracy—but even today I can still feel the vise of that room, the cage it made of my arms and legs, and the bargain it demanded. Why? What *really* kept me in there? What was forcing me out? And how did I always seem to find myself stuck between these extremes, willing to barter JUGs for a chance to cross the distance to the door?

Perhaps it's better to rephrase the question altogether. What if ADHD in adolescence and adulthood is less about the diminishment of symptoms and more about their interplay? As in, certain behaviors will persist, others will change, and some might even get worse—but as a whole they'll continue to interact, influencing behavior throughout a person's lifespan. Which brings us back to the concept of the primary deficit: the one factor that might impact all the others.

By the early 1970s, most researchers believed that hyperactivity was the defining symptom of the disorder. But in 1972 a team of psychologists at Montreal's McGill University, directed by Dr. Virginia I. Douglas, offered a new hypothesis. Douglas and her colleagues had spent the previous decade studying hyperactive children through a battery of cognitive and behavioral tests, and she published their findings under the title, "Stop, Look and Listen: The Problem of Sustained Attention and Impulse Control in Hyperactive and Normal Children."

Douglas was seeking to separate measurable, quantifiable data from "the clinical folklore" that influenced previous research. "Our first goal was to define as accurately as possible the specific disabilities that characterize the hyperactive child," she wrote. But to do so she had to adopt new forms of measurement, including something called the Continuous Performance Test (CPT): for fifteen minutes children were asked to identify and respond to stimuli on a screen while Douglas observed variations in their ability to pay attention and sit still. She also streamlined and updated the process of gathering information from parents, schools, and the children themselves, and she placed more rigorous controls on age and socioeconomic status. Her proposition: if she and her team could eliminate the variables that in the past had negatively influenced research, would the facts of the disorder still resemble our previous conceptions of it?

Douglas's data suggested that contrary to what was previously thought, a child's concentration was not affected by physical activity; her subjects scored just as well on tests like the CPT whether they were moving or seated, and "attention problems" tended to persist even if the boy or girl was "working alone in a relatively empty, sound-proof room." These and other results led to a striking observation: hyperactivity wasn't necessarily interfering with a child's capacity to focus. In fact Douglas proposed the opposite: an "inability to sustain attention" was actually the core behavioral issue of the disorder.

On the basis of these findings, she offered a revised prognosis for adolescents and adults. The team at McGill had continued to administer tests as their subjects got older, and they found that, while the level of hyperactivity did decrease, "impulsivity and inability to attend remain[ed] a problem" that often caused academic and social issues in high school. As a result, Dr. Douglas argued that ADHD was *not* developmentally benign: "These first follow-up investigations provide little hope that maturation is restoring these children to normality."

Douglas's paper had its share of shortcomings. Tests like the CPT weren't perfect measurements of attention; they contained their own biases, variables, and limitations, and in the time since, they've fallen out of favor as diagnostic criteria. Also, at the end of her paper, she slipped into the always-perilous realm of morality when she equated a lack of attention to a deficit of personal willpower.

But her work was the most thorough on the disorder at that time. It also evaluated the efficacy of stimulants, the link between hyperactivity and learning disabilities, and the many ways in which her subjects were *similar* to other children. In the end she characterized the problem at the heart of the disorder as "the inability to stop, look and listen." These findings would change the way ADHD was conceptualized; based on Douglas's work, the 1980 *DSM-III* offered a new diagnostic label: "Attention Deficit Disorder." Even today, when most people consider the array of primary and secondary symptoms, they tend to think of *attention* first.

One of the members of Douglas's McGill team, the psychologist Gabrielle Weiss, continued to follow up with the children they'd studied, and in 1986 she and her colleague Lily Hechtman published *Hyperactive Children Grown Up.*

Like Douglas, they found that issues with attention and impulse

control were still prevalent in more than half of the cases. But their subjects also reported something else: while excessive motor activity did
decrease with age, it was often replaced by a feeling of "inappropriate
restlessness" that never diminished—and in some cases got worse.

Weiss and Hechtman also studied addiction: Did a childhood history
of stimulant medications increase the chance of drug and alcohol abuse
in adolescence and adulthood, and could having ADHD lead to addiction
later in life?

"While hyperactive adolescents may consume more alcohol and non-
medical drugs (usually hash or marijuana) more frequently," they wrote,
"there is no evidence of alcoholism or significant drug addiction when
compared to normal controls." The same went for "stimulant-treated
hyperactives"—as they got older they were prone to drink or try drugs
more intensely and consume too much at one time—but "in general,
studies did not indicate that drug addiction or alcoholism in adulthood
was an outcome of the childhood syndrome." Which is to say: it couldn't
be *caused* by the disorder's symptoms, or by its main method of treatment, in the way that ADHD can't be created out of nothing by parenting
practices. And while this is different than the issue of comorbidity—the
simultaneous existence of two chronic diseases—they concluded that the
path toward full-blown addiction was a separate one.

At the end of their book, the doctors took the surprising step of asking one of their original subjects—Ian Murray, in his late twenties and
working as a mental health professional—to reflect on his childhood of
treatment for ADHD. Under the chapter title "Looking Back," Murray
described fights with teachers and other children, his confusion at the
battery of diagnostic tests, and the powerlessness he felt when he took
medication—first chlorpromazine and later Ritalin—which he finally
convinced his parents to let him quit.

"What was the matter with me?" he wrote. "I didn't look different.
I wasn't missing an arm or a leg. I wasn't deaf or blind." As a teenager
he failed most of his classes and nearly dropped out of school. Eventually, with the help of a guidance counselor and tutors, his grades

improved, he applied to college, and he began volunteering at hospital clinics.

Murray confided that as a child he just wanted to "slip by unnoticed," but his behavior made that impossible and the treatment never seemed to help. "My dignity and self-esteem rested on my ability to conceal from anyone that there was something wrong with me," he wrote. "This strange dishonesty has stuck with me since my early years."

》

On a summer night, Steven, Ike, and I were riding in a car when the person driving—a freshman at Santa Clara University who knew Ike from somewhere—passed back a bottle of whiskey.

That weekend my family had gone on vacation to a friend's house in the delta, but I'd been allowed to stay in town with my grandmother Jo Ann.

We were on our way to a college party. Stipe took the bottle first. He'd just shaved his head into a Mohawk, and his scalp looked naked and rough, his hair in a fan. He gulped a few slugs and passed it to me. The driver was wearing a white baseball cap, the collar of his shirt popped upward. He caught my glance in the rearview and said, "You boys ready to get your drink on?"

I'd never been to a college party before, and all day I'd been imagining the lives of the people I'd meet. I opened the back of my throat as if I were slugging a beer and gulped down an enormous amount of whiskey. My nostrils burned. Water through my eyes. The alcohol was like a curtain in my stomach, and when I was finished a third of the bottle was gone.

"This kid is going to die!" the driver said. He sounded ecstatic. I raised the bottle for another swig. It wasn't the first time I'd drunk hard alcohol, and I should've known how much was too much, at least in a ballpark sense, but trying to remember my thoughts in that moment is like describing the shape and density of whatever it is that creates a sense of distance; I was simply in motion. I took another huge gulp.

For the next few minutes everything felt uneven. Steven glanced at me. He was embarrassed. Then he was laughing. Stipe's hair was like an exotic fish, angling darkly. I was trying to hold our destination steady in my thoughts—a college party!—but the ride was endless. There were only the windows of the car, the world and its details setting through them—street lamps and dry avenues, the lights like lanterns in the darkness, as if the coastal mountains had only recently floated in from the ocean, ornamenting this one, unrepeatable moment.

Soon enough I was in a garden. Green tomatoes. A maze of vines. The party was behind me. Leaning, I understood: I still needed to go inside for the first time.

Later I was sitting on a parked car. "Denevi!" people were shouting. But I wasn't ready, and in the meantime they could wait.

Back at the party: suddenly there was water, its ceramic light. Hands reached for my chest. They felt sumptuous, indefinite—my shirt was being pulled open. A mouth descended. I laughed. A palm slapped my face. Again. Then I was in a room with blue, subterranean walls. "What's your name?" they demanded. I didn't answer; to do so would've been an admission, something that might trap me there. Which was the last thing I remember: the night like a beacon, broadcasting.

When I woke up it was morning. The bed beneath me was still made, and my shirt was missing. To my left, towering on a shelf, a row of Hello Kitty dolls stared down at me, their paws like poorly formed question marks. I was in my aunt's childhood room—back at my grandmother's house.

I wandered, bare-chested, into the hall. The carpet felt elastic. So did my steps. I was still drunk.

In a living-room chair, her blanket pulled up to her neck, my grandmother was still asleep. My father's mother: at the time she was in her late sixties.

"What's going on?" I asked.

She sat up. Then she reached for her stylish black glasses and slid them over her eyes. "Your friends brought you home last night and I couldn't wake you up. I had to call the paramedics."

My elegant, Irish grandmother; we'd always gotten along well. She'd never been too upset by my behavior and I liked how slow she was to react. The night before, I'd thought about telling her I was going to a party, but instead I'd made up something about seeing a movie in town.

"Are you doing drugs?" she asked.

"What? Why would you even say that?"

She shrugged. "The paramedics said that the alcohol was mixed with something else. They were about to take you to the emergency room when you finally started to respond." She got to her feet. The light from the morning windows hit her chin and cheeks, masking her throat in a deep, youthful shadow. "Do you want to call your mother or should I?"

»

Years later my sister, Katie, who was twelve at the time, told me that when that phone call came, my mother screamed, "Lord Jesus!" and fell to the floor. My father heard her and assumed that someone had died. And even after our family had packed up and started home, my mother couldn't stop sobbing. The fact that I was alive and well seemed to be beside the point. It was what she'd always feared; left to my own devices I'd drink myself into oblivion.

While a tricyclic like nortriptyline isn't as reactive to alcohol as other antidepressants, especially at lower dosages, so much whiskey could've sent me into a state of shock. A few days later I called Steven and he said that someone had found me passed out over the toilet, my face in the bowl. A girl with lifeguard training had started to give me CPR before they realized I was breathing.

I was grounded indefinitely. During the months that followed I worked on the maintenance staff of a health club and played on a recreational baseball team. Each night I had to be home by eight.

My father tried to talk to me about what had happened. "Why'd you drink *so much*?" he wanted to know. But my mother and I were at an impasse. It didn't matter that she'd been right and I was wrong, or that the whole thing had genuinely scared me, too. She'd taken the freedom that I believed everyone my age was owed, and I can't remember trusting her less than I did then. I'm sure the feeling was mutual.

For their part, Steven and Ike had a fantastic summer. They'd both gotten their licenses, and throughout July and August they attended concerts, went on campouts with girls, and took a road trip down the coast. When school resumed, the three of us gathered at lunch under the oak tree in the quad. I knew my mother would eventually lift the grounding; the alternative—confining a seventeen-year-old to his room for the rest of the year—was not an option.

That September I promised I wouldn't drink. Finally I was allowed to go out again on the weekends, and at the end of the month I went with my two friends to a dance at our sister school, Presentation.

Steven picked up me and Stipe and drove us to his house. His parents weren't home. We had an hour or so to kill, and as we sat in the lawn chairs of Steven's modest backyard, Stipe lit a joint, the flame illuminating his recently shaved head. I sipped from a beer at such a slow pace I was able to convince myself that I'd abstained altogether. Steven was smoking clove cigarettes; he said he wasn't drinking because he was driving. But he seemed listless and distracted, and I was sure that he was angry about the way I'd acted at the college party, which was how I always tended to see the emotions of other people—as a judgment on what I had or hadn't done.

The dance was in Presentation's auditorium. It took fifteen minutes to drive there and we waited in line for just as long. When we finally got to the front, the darkness felt gloomy and masculine; I realized that boys outnumbered the girls by a wide margin. After a while Stipe mentioned a possible party in Sunnyvale, and we decided to leave.

Outside, the night was cool and wet, the fog approaching motionlessly from the coastal mountains. Steven told us to hold on; first he wanted to smoke. Just around the corner from the entrance he lit up a cigarette and we waited alongside. But a moment later a figure approached us from the parking lot, and when I realized it was a cop I straightened up. So did Stipe.

"You gotta put that out," this officer said to Steven. He was beefy and blond, his hair was cut short, and beneath his radio and badge his chest seemed unnaturally puffed.

Legally we were still too young to smoke. I started toward the car. So did Stipe. But Steven stood where he was and took another pull.

The cop stepped forward. "Hey, kid," he said. His voice was loud and tired.

"I'm almost done," Steven said.

This cop glanced around. "You better leave," he said to all of us. I nodded quickly.

"That's exactly what you want," Steven replied. "Right? Then when I get in my car you can pull me over for something I didn't do."

"Get your friend out of my face," the officer said. With his buzz cut and barrel chest he looked terrifying enough, but I didn't move. The truth was I *hated* this cop; my whole life I'd wanted to tell this exact type of authority figure to go fuck himself but had always been too scared or confused to pull it off.

Steven took another drag on his fragrant cigarette, the smoke in his face, and said, "What are you gonna do, shoot me with your gun?"

We were told to line up against the wall. The officer pulled out a pair of handcuffs, and with an air of ceremony, placed them on Steven. Then he radioed in his status. Another police car showed up. We were each asked our age, name, and school affiliation. "Cute chains," he said to Stipe. After a while he turned his smile to me. "You as drunk as your buddy here?"

I didn't answer.

"Lying to a police officer is a crime."

"I had one beer," I said, adding, "just to relax."

"You need alcohol to calm down?" He took out a large cell phone. "What's your number?"

"No!" I shouted. "I didn't do anything!"

"Keep your voice down. You had your chance to leave."

In the next instant I was crying. Wet, adult tears; it didn't matter that

Stipe and Steven could see. "You don't know my mother! If you tell her it's the police she's gonna think I'm dead!"

"I can call her now or she can pick you up later in jail."

I gave him the number.

"This is Officer Mazzaro with the San Jose Police," he said into the receiver. "No, please, listen for a moment—he's fine. I'm at Presentation School. I need you to come pick him up."

Just before my mother arrived, this Officer Mazzaro bent over Steven Kelley, who was sitting with his hands cuffed, and said, "Tomorrow afternoon I'll head over to Bellarmine and drop in on your principal. He and I are good friends. I bet you didn't know that. I'm gonna tell him how you acted tonight, and I have a feeling he'll agree with everything I say. How's that sound?"

Steven looked up. It was the same expression he'd used a few years earlier on that young soccer coach, his eyes like a mirror. But the cop had already turned away.

»

There's a question we still haven't addressed: What, exactly, is "attention"—especially within the context of ADHD?

According to William James, a favorite of the doctors and researchers studying the disorder, the answer has to do with self-control: "Effort of attention is the essential phenomenon of will." Sir George Frederic Still used this quote over a century ago to preface his section on the threats posed by hyperactive children, and in the years since, attention and willpower have often been equated: a deficit in one translated to a lack of the other.

But is there perhaps another explanation for why a subset of the population—people who seem perfectly capable of acting deliberately in certain aspects of life—could possess a genuine desire to stop, look, and listen and still fail to do so?

In the second half of the 1980s, researchers began to reexamine Virginia Douglas's theory that attention was the disorder's primary deficit.

Among them was Dr. Russell A. Barkley, our contemporary expert and the author of the multivolume *ADHD: A Handbook*. After a series of new studies, he and his colleagues concluded that children with ADHD weren't all that different from everyone else when it came to the "perception, filtering, and processing of information"—which was how he defined attention. Was there another way to conceptualize the primary symptoms? Barkley and his colleagues began studying foresight, and eventually he offered a new theory: "a deficit in responding to behavioral consequences, not attention, might be the difficulty in ADHD."

So in his opinion, children with the disorder were struggling to recognize the boundaries around them. These boundaries had been set in place with clear repercussions, but he argued that having ADHD made you less susceptible to "reinforcement, punishment, or both." Which meant that struggles such as arriving somewhere on time, bringing home the proper textbook, sitting still in class, and backing down from a fight could all stem from a deficit of inhibition—restraint.

Dr. Barkley ultimately characterized this as "disinhibition": children with ADHD struggle with rule-governed behavior because, in the moment, they don't perceive the outcomes of their choices and aren't as motivated to act accordingly. He argued that its root cause was organic—related to dopamine transport and brain development—and that the best way to treat it was with stimulants, which raise the levels of this neurotransmitter by blocking its reuptake.

Barkley eventually applied his new theory to the disorder's long-term prognosis. By the second half of the 1990s, additional follow-up studies on adolescent and adult outcomes were available, and he summarized these findings in the 1998 edition of his *Handbook*.

What does the future look like for someone with ADHD? According to Barkley's statistics, up to 65 percent of children with the disorder can expect to experience its primary symptoms in adulthood. Almost 30 percent will exhibit serious antisocial behavior. The risk of comorbid psychiatric disorders will be much more likely, including major depression (28% vs. 12%). The same thing applies to crimes such as theft (85% vs.

66%), breaking and entering (20% vs. 8%), assault with a deadly weapon (22% vs. 7%), and arrest for a felony (22% vs. 3%). Grade-point averages and class rankings in high school are significantly lower, while the rates of suspension (60% vs. 18%), expulsion (13% vs. 5%), and dropout (30% vs. 10%) are higher. The chances of receiving a college degree are slim (5% vs. 40%). There's also an increased risk for car accidents, including hit-and-runs (14% vs. 2%) and crashes in which the vehicle is totaled (49% vs. 16%). And while addiction itself isn't necessarily more prevalent, a lack of moderation is, especially when it comes to legal substances like alcohol and cigarettes.

Dr. Barkley capped his data with a final statistic: people who have ADHD will die, on average, at least 10 percent earlier than their counterparts. He based this claim on the follow-up work to a longitudinal study of gifted children, initiated by the educational psychologist Lewis Madison Terman in 1921, that included a category of boys and girls defined as impulsive and overactive. In fact, Barkley thinks that 10 percent is too low; in his view, "the risk for reduced longevity in those with ADHD" is actually much greater.

Russell A. Barkley first started researching ADHD in the 1970s as a graduate student in psychology at the University of North Carolina Chapel Hill. Since then he's written over 180 papers on the subject and, in his own estimation, received nine thousand scholarly citations. There's a picture of him on the homepage of his personal website. He's in his early sixties and has a trim white beard. His arms are crossed, his shoulders squared, and he's staring seriously at the camera with the air of someone who's grown tired of listening to opinions he doesn't respect. From Dr. Barkley's perspective, the statistics listed above are first and foremost an argument for the necessity of psychiatric intervention: he's trying to convince parents that ADHD is a real, lifelong threat, and that treatment is the initial line of defense. But the same stats look a bit different from the perspective of someone whose future is suggested in them.

What does it mean if, throughout your life, you'll struggle to notice the borders that everyone else can recognize? Isn't this just another way of describing "inattention"? If willpower implies a decision to cross or heed known boundaries, and if foresight is about recognizing them in the first place, then how can you expect to comprehend a wrong turn except through the process of looking back? And while relying on reflection is one way to make better choices in life, it's a process you can only employ after you've gotten far enough along, right?

Dr. Barkley's statistics also communicate that a large number of people with the disorder *aren't* suffering from the aforementioned problems, and when you stop to consider more severe types of environmental and medical disadvantage, his probabilities aren't overwhelming. But if ADHD doesn't determine you, it does tend to limit your second chances—a reality that, at the very least, places a premium on the moments in which you're conscious of deciding what happens next.

》

Officer Mazzaro wasn't bluffing about his connection to my school's principal. I didn't realize it at the time, but he had a son who was a student at Bellarmine, and over the past few years he'd used his status in the San Jose Police Department to work his way through the school's power structure. Later I'd hear a story about how he liked to park near campus and follow his son's friends for a few blocks; he'd turn on his siren, pull them over, run up to their window, and, seeing the terror on their faces, break out in laughter. Eventually he came under investigation and was fired from the police force, or so I heard.

The day after the Presentation dance he recounted how we'd dishonored Bellarmine's standing in the community, an offense that, according to our school's code of conduct, was just as punishable as alcohol and drug use.

Steven Kelley was expelled immediately; he was already on probation for drinking at our spring dance. Stipe and I would have our fates decided by a disciplinary board, and in the meantime we were suspended.

Of course I told my parents that it wasn't my fault. I'd had only one beer! I'd acted respectfully to the police officer and answered all his questions! I'd told the *truth*!

"You're not listening," my father shot back. "I always said that if you kept doing stupid shit something bad was gonna happen, and it sure fucking did!"

The day before the disciplinary hearing, I called Steven Kelley. I asked if he'd decided what school to attend next. Were his parents as pissed as mine? He hardly spoke, and suddenly I began to wonder if he even cared what happened to me or Stipe. It was one of those moments you dread—the realization that someone has always been more important to you than you are to them—and considering all the blows that were in the process of coming down, this was perhaps the hardest. Over the last few years I'd sometimes felt foolish around him, and idiotic, but I never felt *different.* And while it was the same with Stipe, who I liked well enough, Steven's point of view was the one through which I kept trying to see the world. He was the first person my age I respected.

That night, I sat with my parents in their room and we went over what I should say to the disciplinary board.

"You go in there and keep your mouth shut," my mother said. "You understand?"

They made me write out exactly what had happened with Officer Mazzaro. I was supposed to read from it at the hearing. They also thought I should recount my history of mental illness, the medication I took, and the fact that we were currently between psychiatrists. In their opinion, the only chance I had was to prostrate myself before Bellarmine's authority.

"Listen," my father said. "I love you. We both do. But we can't go with you into that room tomorrow."

»

The hearing was held on the top floor of Bellarmine's administrative building. When I arrived a secretary told me to wait in a chair near a door the color of damp wood. Beyond it I could hear voices; Ike Stipe was up first.

I tried to read over the statement I'd written, and eventually the door swung open and Stipe stepped out. I stood up. He was wearing a fat, shiny tie. His head was still shaved, and his eyes looked blank and frightening, enormously round. Before I could say anything he walked past.

Inside, three Jesuits, dressed in the same standard black outfit and white collar, were sitting at a glossy table. I recognized our principal, Father McGuire, who was perhaps sixty; he had curly gray hair and a red, waterlogged face. "Tell me what happened at the Presentation dance," he said to me.

I pulled out my statement and started reading. But when I came to the part about my history of medication and psychiatric treatment my voice went flat. Hadn't the goal of all those years with Laurie and Joe Epstein been to keep me out of a room like this? Did I really expect to use my history as an excuse, now, with these men? I saw myself through their eyes: it was as if I'd chopped off one of my hands, thrown it on the floor between us, and shouted, *Look!*

When I was finished, Father McGuire glanced at the other priests. Then he turned to me and said, "You're spineless."

For a moment I thought I'd misheard.

"It's true," he continued. "When I look at you I see nothing at the center. You don't deserve the honor of calling yourself a Bellarmine student." His jaw began to quiver. His eyes were wet. It didn't make sense. Was this a show, or did he genuinely feel so overcome? "Do you even want to be a part of this community?" he demanded.

"Yes," I finally replied.

"Okay," Father McGuire said.

"Okay what?"

"Get your things and go to class."

"I'm not expelled?"

Something familiar crossed his face: impatience. He told me that I'd be placed on yearlong probation; I wouldn't be allowed to play baseball, rejoin the debate team, or attend extracurricular events.

At lunch that afternoon I looked everywhere for Ike Stipe. But he was gone. He'd been asked the same question as me and had refused to respond.

»

Years later, on an afternoon in my early twenties, I received a phone call from my mother. "It's about Steven Kelley," she said.

After being expelled, he'd gone to Saratoga High, one of the best public schools in the country. I didn't see him again until we were both seniors. It was at a religious retreat that my mother forced me to attend. Steven had gained twenty pounds, and as we talked—he asked about my life and told me about his—he seemed eager. I felt uncharacteristically shy. "We should keep in touch," he said. Later I heard that the weight gain was from a medication cocktail, and that he'd spent time in a psychiatric ward.

"Is he okay?" I asked my mother.

The night earlier, Steven had been released from the hospital because of a problem with his insurance. For the previous three days he'd been on a suicide watch; at home, waiting for the paperwork to clear, his mother stayed up the entire night looking after him. Eventually she fell asleep. Steven went outside, found a saw, and in an instant cut the artery at his neck. He bled to death in his backyard.

I listened as these details arrived over the phone. "Timmy," my mother was saying. "He was very sick."

For the first time in years I thought about contacting Ike Stipe, but that wasn't possible. After he got kicked out of Bellarmine his parents went through a messy divorce. I saw him in Los Gatos one night, his hair spiked menacingly. He was wearing skull earrings, a necklace of chains, and big black boots. We were both eighteen, adults, but before he could recognize me I turned away.

Around then he dropped out of high school and began robbing houses in his affluent neighborhood. He was caught once, twice, and finally a third time; under California's Three Strikes law he was sentenced to life in prison.

On the phone that afternoon, my mother talked about Steven's upcoming funeral mass. She was planning to go. I lived too far away. Even so, I'm not sure I would've had it in me to attend. But a good number of people from Bellarmine did. Afterward I found out that during the final song, Mr. Ballard, our old debate teacher, raised his palms to the ceiling and in his distinct voice sang louder than everyone else.

6

Last Thing You Learn Is That You Always Gotta Wait

My new psychiatrist's office was located in a tree-lined building about a mile from my house. On my first visit I went alone; I'd just gotten my license. A little over a month had passed since the disciplinary hearing at Bellarmine.

The receptionist in the waiting room seemed curt and suspicious, but I answered her questions about my insurance card calmly. In my years of psychiatric treatment I'd never gone to a session by myself, and more than anything I wanted to sound and act like an adult.

I sat down and waited. A large aquarium stood against a nearby wall, and in its sluggish, subaqueous light, a few ragged fish were circling one another. Finally the door to the hallway opened. A woman stepped out, Dr. Sandra Austin: she was dressed in a gray blazer and had straight, dark hair that was parted at the temple. When she greeted me her voice sounded high-pitched—informal—and for a moment she seemed younger than she must've been, which was perhaps forty.

Laurie Hamilton had recommended Dr. Austin, who specialized in adolescent psychiatry. Her office was small. We sat facing each other, and in her lilting voice she asked the reason for my visit. *Because my mother made me!* I wanted to answer. Instead, in short sentences, I described the recent drama.

But like Dr. Epstein—and like Laurie, too—Dr. Austin seemed to understand that the trick was to get me talking, and soon I was filling her in on the various details of the previous decade. I don't think I used the term "ADHD," but she did. She wanted to know why I was taking a low daily dosage of antidepressants for something she'd always treated with stimulants. "You've never been prescribed Ritalin?" she asked.

I tried to tell her what had happened when I was six. "Something to do with the rebound effect," I said. "I kinda went crazy."

She explained that a new generation of time-release stimulants had come onto the market. "It really is different now," she said. "What do you think?"

The offer caught me off guard. Up to this point, the issue of medication had always been a matter of something or nothing.

"It's a possibility to consider," she finally told me.

We probably talked for forty-five minutes. At the end the discussion turned toward college. "Is there a goal that you're trying right now to attain?" she asked.

The answer came out before I had a chance to think: "To graduate from Bellarmine and move as far away from here as possible."

>>

After Steven Kelley and Ike Stipe were expelled, some of my classmates started to say that I'd saved myself by blaming everything on my friends. At lunch I took to eating alone in a corner of the school's library; I'd pass the time catching up on my reading for junior English.

That semester we were doing a poetry unit on writers like Andrew Marvell, Alfred Lord Tennyson, John Keats, and also the modernists

Ezra Pound and T. S. Eliot. I decided to write a paper on Eliot's *The Waste Land.* It was an enormous poem told in numerous voices that all seemed to be talking about the end of the world, among other things. I missed most of what was going on, but I did read it multiple times. Outside, Bellarmine's quad was boisterous and sunlit, a landscape of glances that at any moment could turn mean or aloof. The same was true in the poem. But through the artifice of Eliot's perspective I was blameless and still: an observer.

I found myself focusing on academics, one of the few areas under my control. That year, my chemistry teacher was the school's varsity football coach, Mr. Lasko. Some of the boys in our class also played on his team. He had a hard, round belly and flashing eyes, and when I interrupted one of our first lectures with a question about the noble gases, he stammered, "I don't think this is the time or the place."

I laughed. "To talk about *chemistry?*"

Later someone told me that if I'd been on the football team and spoken to him like that, I'd still be running laps. As the semester progressed, my comments always seemed to throw him off-balance, and by December my participation grade was too low; I'd need to ace the final.

We went to school on a half-day schedule during exams. The rest of the time was for studying. The night before the chemistry final I parked myself at the kitchen table and reread the chapters from our textbook. When I wanted to get up—my arms and legs shifting as if in a current—I pictured Lasko's dismissive eyes. I'd tried motivating myself like this in the past, but now, to my surprise, I was able to stay in place. And the more I worked the less rote the material became.

After dinner I set up extra lamps to help keep me awake, and my mother made sure that my sister and brother left me alone. Around eleven my father came up from the TV room; I heard him stop in the doorway to the kitchen.

"What's with all the lights?" he asked.

"I'm studying."

"You gotta use every bulb in the house?"

"Dad, it helps me stay awake."

He switched off an overhead lamp. "Electricity costs money."

My mother shouted at him to leave me alone. "All right!" he finally said. He clicked the light back on and glanced in my direction: What on earth had compelled me—his oldest son, a person he knew better than anyone—to sit for hours in a grove of our house's tallest lamps, their brightness straining the kitchen?

I stayed up until three in the morning, read the chapters again, took notes, and answered practice problems. For whatever reason it wasn't impossible to stay still. The following afternoon, I knew exactly what the test wanted from me, and I answered each of the two hundred questions correctly. The first and last perfect score of my life: for a few days I'd catch myself thinking about the periodic table, its possibilities; there was, after all, a telling beauty to the way in which its elements might separate and combine.

»

That Christmas, my mother heard a story from one of her college friends: over winter vacation, at a tournament in Los Angeles, the best players on my school's varsity basketball team had been caught smoking marijuana in their hotel room. It was the coach who'd found them. The most lenient punishment—a disciplinary hearing, suspensions, and social and athletic probation—would have decimated the roster. But there never was a hearing. The boys involved were given a few dozen hours of community service and allowed to remain on the team.

My mother made an appointment with Father McGuire. On a winter morning—there were still a few days of vacation left—she walked into his office and said, "I want you to end Timmy's probation." She told him that she knew about what had happened in L.A. Could he explain why certain kids didn't have to play by the same rules as everyone else? Is that the type of justice Bellarmine advocated?

"Okay," he finally said. The probation would be lifted, and I'd be able to play sports, attend social functions, and participate in clubs and after-school activities.

But my mother had an additional demand: she knew that Father McGuire had called me spineless during the discipline hearing, and she wanted him to apologize.

When vacation ended Father McGuire called me into his office. I figured I was in some sort of trouble, but as far as I knew I hadn't done anything wrong. He sat across from me at his desk, and when he looked up his eyes were huge and wet. Then we were shaking hands. He seemed to be overcome by the same intense emotion I'd noticed during the disciplinary hearing. "We think you've done an excellent job turning things around this past semester," he said, "and I want you to know that we've decided to end your punishment early."

My mother hadn't told me she'd been in to see him. I found out much later; it was probably one of the few times she managed to keep a secret like that. Though it wasn't a first. The year before, when my baseball coach Mr. Dinero had said he hadn't wanted me on the team—I'd mentioned it in passing to my parents—my father had called him up and asked just who the hell he thought he was. What kind of adult tells a teenager something like that? "I know you're a football guy and never played a day of competitive baseball in your life," my father said, "but at least you can try and act like you know what you're doing." Later, when Mr. Dinero pulled me aside and explained he'd meant the comment as a joke, I didn't think much of it.

In his office that afternoon, Father McGuire said that he was going to write me a letter. "I've started it," he explained, "but I'd like to look it over a few more times before I give it to you." I was intrigued; what did he have to say that couldn't be expressed in person? But the letter never arrived, and soon enough I forgot all about it—until a few months later, when my principal stopped me as I was changing classes. "Did you get my letter?" he asked.

"Um," I said. "Yes. Thank you for sending it."

He closed his eyes and placed both his hands over mine. His face was bare, childlike. He might have been smiling. Then he walked away, and I was left standing in the middle of my school's crowded quad.

》

That spring, during our semimonthly sessions, Dr. Austin mentioned the new drug therapies again; they could help me get along better with other people, including my teachers, and on tests I could stay focused. Was I willing to see if one might work?

More than a decade had passed since I was prescribed a stimulant. The truth was, the medications themselves hadn't really changed. There was still Ritalin (methylphenidate) and Dexedrine (dextroamphetamine). Another drug, Adderall (amphetamine salts), was approved in 1996 for children with ADHD, but it was actually just a mixture of different types of amphetamine, which in this new combination offered longer-lasting effects at lower dosages.

The real difference, now, was in delivery. By this point the major pharmaceutical companies had begun to use time-release technology. For Ritalin, the mechanism was powered by osmosis: a child swallowed a pill with multiple doses in it, and as water was absorbed through the permeable membrane of a laser-created hole, the medication was pushed out at a controlled rate. For amphetamine, the process was governed by a mixture of beads: some dissolved right away while others, because of their less-soluble shells, took much longer to break down.

Children taking these types of pills didn't need to report to the nurse's office at school for a midday dose, and the controlled-release helped with the up-and-down nature of the medication; the drug remained in the bloodstream at a constant level throughout the day, diminishing the rebound effect.

These technical advances represented a shift in the pharmaceutical industry. For most of the twentieth century, there wasn't much money in marketing psychotropic medications to children; the development process was costly and uncertain, and most of the research into stimulants was conducted by academics or by the National Institute of Mental Health. But in 1984 Congress passed the Hatch-Waxman Act, which made generic prescriptions more readily available. And in 1997, the Food and Drug Administration Modernization Act offered companies a six-month patent extension on any newly approved drug that had included childhood trials during its testing process. This increased profits on popular medications such as Prozac—for Eli Lilly, the extra patent protection ended up being worth nearly $2 billion—while also providing money for research on other pharmaceuticals, such as stimulants.

The result: in the second half of the 1990s, as companies spent more and more on the testing and development of psychotropic medications for children, their earnings skyrocketed. The number of children taking Ritalin had increased fourfold since I was first prescribed it, and the popularity of Adderall helped turn its manufacturer, Shire, into one of the industry's biggest success stories. This trend did not exist within a vacuum—the number of children on stimulants was about half the expected prevalence rate for ADHD—but at the beginning of the twenty-first century, the pharmaceutical industry was one of the most profitable in the world, and part of its success was based on the popularity of drugs like Ritalin.

This parallel rise in prescription rates and profits led to a familiar criticism: normal childhood behavior was being medicalized for financial gain. In the 1990s, the most vocal critic on the subject was Peter Breggin, a psychiatrist who'd been questioning the use of psychotropic drugs for decades.

Dr. Breggin graduated from Harvard during the 1950s and later earned his medical degree at Case Western University, and in the 1970s and '80s he published a series of books with titles such as *Toxic Psychiatry* and *Psychiatric Drugs: Hazards to the Brain.* Eventually he turned his attention to stimulants. In his 1998 *Talking Back to Ritalin,* he wrote, "Diagnosing a child with ADHD is basically harmful and should never be done. Its main purpose is to justify the use of drugs." He argued that the disorder's primary symptoms were caused by bad parenting—that the "Psychopharmaceutical Complex" had conspired with the American Psychiatric Association to profit from something that didn't exist.

There's a picture of Dr. Breggin on his personal website. He's in his early seventies, and his hair is white and sheer, capped thinly against the pink heights of his skull. He's wearing an army-green blazer. His mouth is closed. But look at his eyes; they are black and small, crowded together. It's a disgruntled expression—he's like an aging film director who's not quite sure why he keeps demanding so many extra takes— and I have to say, I'd spend good money to see him in a staring contest against our foremost contemporary expert, Dr. Russell A. Barkley: the loser being the first to stop appearing so aggrieved.

Dr. Breggin is one of the most prominent voices on ADHD in our contemporary culture. He's testified before Congress, appeared on television programs such as *60 Minutes* and *Frontline,* and served as an expert witness in lawsuits. His argument on the pharmaceutical industry certainly has its allure. After all, these are not moral companies. Their goal is to make money—as much as possible—and profit depends on consumption. Since the early 1970s they've been advertising stimulant medications to doctors in venues like the *American Journal of Psychiatry,* and in 1997, after changes to the FDA guidelines, they began targeting consumers directly. Full-page spreads started appearing in print magazines such as *People* and *Good Housekeeping.* In one, an ecstatic mother hugs her son, who's small and adorable and is even missing a tooth. It's a Shire ad for extended-release Adderall. "Finally!" the text reads. "A real solution for ADHD."

But there's a difference between drug companies making money off the disorder—and affecting prescription rates in the process—and the idea that the industry has conspired to create ADHD out of thin air. The problem with Dr. Breggin's argument is that you also have to accept the series of assumptions it stands on: there's no such thing as ADHD; drug therapy can't help; half a century's worth of research is false; and the entire mental health industry is really an agent of a pharmaceutical conspiracy. "Doctors need to define these problems as medical," he told

PBS in a 2000 interview, "for their livelihood, for their authority in the community, for their own sense of identity."

When Dr. Austin suggested that I try a sustained-release stimulant, she said to me, "It can be like night and day."

I was almost eighteen. My goals were clear. And now my psychiatrist, in her high-pitched voice, was proposing a better means of reaching them.

"Maybe now's not the best time," I told her. I was afraid of something. What? It was bigger than the past, the first time I took Ritalin. It had to do with the future: the rate at which I was moving into it.

》

By the second half of my junior year in high school I began to realize that I had a chance to attend a competitive out-of-state college. The odds were still slim. I'd been suspended, I barely got along with many of my teachers, and my grades were decent but not superior. For as long as I could remember my parents had said they'd make financial sacrifices for my education, but I couldn't really justify going somewhere across the country if California offered a similar, more affordable option.

That spring I signed up for honors classes and started studying for the SATs. I tried to avoid getting any more JUGs, which was easier than it had been; the teachers assigned to upperclassmen weren't as strict.

When the probation was lifted, I tried out for varsity baseball. But I didn't make the team. Instead, Mr. Amundsen, my former health teacher, suggested I start a lunchtime club that focused on rock music from the 1960s and '70s. "I can be the advisor," he told me. "It'll be fun. We'll show concerts. You can make T-shirts." What he didn't say: extracurricular activities were important in the college application process.

I placed a notice in the school's daily announcements, and the first meeting was held in his classroom. Eventually a boy I didn't recognize came in and sat down, then another. Soon enough we had a crowd of about half a dozen. "Welcome to the first meeting of the Classic Rock Club," I told everyone.

"Your announcement mentioned that we'd get to watch concerts," one of the boys said. He had an enormous Adam's apple that seemed to drag his neck forward. "I suggest we start with *Woodstock*."

"We can screen them in the amphitheater next to the library," another offered. His hair was oily and thin, and I couldn't tell if he was a freshman or a senior. "They have a projector and everything."

"Did you already apply for funding?" a third asked. "You know the deadline's coming up, right?"

It turned out that these young men spent much of their time at school involved in clubs like jazz, film, and chess. I'd always been caught up in Bellarmine's more prominent pastime—athletics—but a surprising amount of money had been set aside for students who weren't interested in sports.

We established a viewing schedule: *Woodstock* first, then *Monterey Pop,* and after that films like *Tommy* and *Easy Rider* and *The Rolling Stones Rock and Roll Circus.* The funding came through. I rented the necessary videos. We chose a T-shirt design: the cover to Jimi Hendrix's *Axis: Bold as Love.* It was a variegated poster of the Hindu godheads onto which the band members' images had been rather egregiously superimposed. I printed out a large color copy and brought it to a local specialty shop. This was my second attempt at making my own clothing, and as I handed the clerk the album image I was struck by the memory of writing my name, in childish letters, across all those shirts in junior high.

The clerk had questions about materials, the printing process, and positioning. I didn't know what to answer. Afterward I was sure I'd messed up, but when I opened the box a week later, the shirts were brilliant. You could see everything: the album's pink and orange background, Ganesh's brawny trunk, even the far-off look in Jimi's eyes.

I kept wondering what Steven Kelley and Ike Stipe would've thought. At the time I didn't talk to my fellow club members about any-

game of musical chairs. The lanes were constantly ending and reforming, and in the battle for space I'd accidentally cut someone off, or forget to merge, or fail to let in the traffic from the on-ramp. Once in a while, as if waking from a trance, I'd notice a car riding my tail. My response was always to slow down even more—because *fuck them* for bullying me.

This happened once on my way back from school: a pickup got right on my rear so I went the same steady speed as the van to my left. In the mirror I could see the driver; he was screaming and gesturing. I held the pace. But he accelerated onto the shoulder, and as he got about halfway past me, he pulled his car into mine. We were going to collide. I hit the brakes. Thankfully the rest of the traffic had seen what was going on and dropped back. Up ahead, through the dust, I realized that the pickup had slowed. The driver was waiting for me. He hung out of his window and shouted wildly, his huge mustache pulled sideways by the wind. My hands went numb, the light making unknown shapes in the interstate, and when the pickup finally started forward again I didn't understand: where had I been going and how was I expected to return there, now?

By the end of my junior year I hated everything about driving. My next accident occurred just before Bellarmine got out for the summer. I'd become friends with a kid on my recreational baseball team, Doug Eckersley: he went to the nearby public school, played the drums, and liked to argue about sports; at his house on the weekend we'd spend hours going back and forth over topics like who was the best American League shortstop in history.

On a clear evening in May we headed to a party in downtown Los Gatos. I agreed to drive. We planned to park near the shops on Main Street and then walk to the house in case the cops showed up later. But it was a busy weekend and there weren't many spots. Eventually we pulled into a small lot. It was full. I backed up quickly, without looking over my shoulder. On our way in I hadn't realized that a small, expensive sports car, its top down, was parked illegally along the lot's entrance. Now, as we smashed into it, I had no idea what was going on; the rear of my vehicle lifted upward and I started screaming. "Pull forward!" Doug yelled. But I just hit the pedal and jammed us deeper into the delicate car. Finally he reached over and shifted for me, and we managed to get free.

"What do we do?" I shouted.

Doug got out and checked the damage, and when he climbed back in he said, "Dude, just go."

We drove to an automotive shop a few miles away. Every set of headlights looked like a cop's. Remarkably, my Cutlass was only slightly dented—my back wheel had inflicted most of the damage—but the sports car had left its cherry-red finish across my bumper and fender. We bought a tub of Turtle Wax, and under a streetlight we spent a half hour scrubbing away the evidence. Doug worked methodically. By the time we were finished you could hardly tell what'd happened.

That night I dreamed about sirens, knocks on the door, and policemen with bright mirrors where their faces should've been. For the next few days I was sure that every time the phone rang my mother was going to burst into my room and shout, "I know what's going on!"

A few weeks later, driving to pick up my sister at her friend's house, I passed a body shop in Los Gatos. The cherry-red sports car was parked out front. Its hood and front bumper were stripped away. You could see the frame and, beneath, its engine: a hard, greasy heart.

»

When school got out that summer I took the SATs for the first time. Back then there were only two parts, math and verbal, and on each you could score up to 800 points. I needed to get a combined total of 1250, at the very least.

It was held on a weekend morning at San Jose State University. I left a half hour early but I got lost, and by the time I found the right building, everyone else was already seated. Then the proctor passed out a booklet of questions. The clock started. In the surrounding rows, young men and women from across the valley began working.

I opened the booklet and read the first math problem. It was simple.

But instead of coming up with my own result, as I'd done on practice exams, I looked at the possible answers listed below and started working backward. Suddenly, with the right calculations, they all seemed viable, and even when I narrowed it down to a pair I couldn't find a way to discriminate. The same thing happened on the next problem, and the ones after. Soon my time was almost up. I was forced to fill out a third of the Scantron form at random.

The verbal section went the same way. It was like listening to the sound of something that won't stop falling through the sky above you; I'd suddenly lost any sense of the difference between values that, in my normal life, had arranged naturally.

You were allowed to take the test twice, and the second score could cancel out the first. But I'd failed in a way that felt strangely familiar—comforting. I drove home, the freeway like an aqueduct, its sea-colored overpasses, the sun burnishing the foothills; I was passing through the center of San Jose, one of the few places I'd ever really known.

》

When I told my parents I'd bombed the SATs, my father said, "You don't usually fuck up on tests. Right?" My mother smiled. "It's just that your standards are so high," she assured me.

Dr. Austin explained that she saw it all the time. "Most kids express what they know on an important exam, but others have to work harder to control their reaction to the situation, which can be overwhelming."

Hearing this, I felt embarrassed, and stupid, and confused. But during our sessions, Dr. Austin tried to address my issues in a larger sense, and afterward it no longer seemed like I was the only teenager in the world seeing a psychiatrist. Maybe this was part of growing up—the realization that your concerns aren't so different from everyone else's—but it also reflected a significant statistical development: by the time I was in my last year of high school, more people than ever had been diagnosed with ADHD.

In 1980, the *DSM-III* passage on "ADD" read, "The disorder is common. In the United States, it may occur in as many as 3% of prepubertal children." But twenty years later, the fourth edition of this manual had revised the prevalence to "3% to 7%." So the number of children with ADHD had grown from hundreds of thousands to millions. Why?

The easiest explanation has to do with the way its symptoms are identified. Diagnosing mental illness involves more than ratings scales, but these are a starting point, and for a long time ADHD was thought to be synonymous with hyperactivity, meaning that children who could stay in their seats weren't counted. As later versions of the *DSM* began to incorporate more categories—including the *DSM-IV*'s "Inattentive" subtype—the prevalence rose.

Another reason for the increase was related to the 1990 Individuals with Disabilities Education Act (IDEA), which offered educational incentives for someone diagnosed with ADHD. There's also the issue of misdiagnosis: a child with some other form of mental illness mistakenly identified as ADHD. But these explanations don't address a controversial question: Is it true that thousands of healthy, normal children have been incorrectly diagnosed?

The answer depends on whom you ask. For someone like Dr. Peter Breggin, it's simple: a million boys and girls have been told they're different from everyone else when, in fact, the problem has more to do with drug companies and parenting practices. In contrast, there's Dr. Russell A. Barkley, who wrote in 1998, "The actual occurrence of ADHD may not be increasing although its detection may well be, which may partly stem from a greater awareness on the part of the public about the nature of the disorder."

But prevalence is better understood when it's broken down along geographic, gender, and socioeconomic lines. In 2007, doctors from the Mayo Clinic and the Cincinnati Children's Hospital contacted over three thousand families to try to determine the scale of diagnostic and treatment rates, and they found that children from the poorest 5 percent of households were much *less* likely to be identified as ADHD and prescribed medications. In contrast, white, older, male children with health insurance received the most diagnoses.

So the number in the very highest socioeconomic brackets has gone up, but ADHD remains underdiagnosed at the opposite end of the spectrum. This seems to make sense—a family that can afford health care and sessions with a psychologist is more likely to seek out treatment—but it also draws attention to the general difficulty of predicting prevalence. To quote the latest edition of the *DSM*: "Differences in ADHD prevalence rates across regions appear attributable mainly to different diagnostic and methodological practices. However, there also may be cultural variation in attitudes toward or interpretations of children's behaviors."

»

In the fall of my senior year at Bellarmine—about a month before I was scheduled to retake the SATs—I was driving my father's new Cadillac sedan to school when I rear-ended an expensive SUV.

I'm still not sure how it happened. This other car was stopped, and if I hadn't hit it I probably would've continued through the busy intersection and run into someone else. As I approached the stop sign at perhaps fifteen miles per hour, what had silenced the alarm in my head—the one that tells us to reach for a handle rather than run into a closed door?

That summer I'd gotten back my first SAT score. It was more than 200 points lower than what I needed, and my parents had agreed to pay for a series of intensive one-on-one tutoring sessions. I'd also enrolled in five honors classes, including AP Latin and a course on the novels of William Faulkner. The goal was to get straight *A*s at the quarter mark, then send an updated transcript to prospective colleges.

I was driving my father's car that morning because he was out of town and mine was wrecked. A few weeks earlier, in a local pizza shop's parking lot, I'd backed into the concrete base of a streetlight. I struck it solidly—my trunk wouldn't open, my bumper was wedged in above the tailpipe—and as I drove home, I thought I smelled something funny, like the dust of a heater that hadn't been used in years. So I rolled up all the windows, pulled over, let the engine run, and tried to figure out what it was. Twenty minutes later I stumbled through the front door. My mother found me on the couch downstairs, and when she asked me what was wrong I went to the bathroom and gagged. It was carbon monoxide poisoning; I'd blown out the Cutlass's exhaust system.

My father's Cadillac was enormous, cream-colored, and smelled like a woman's purse—a car that might've been the height of style two decades earlier—and on the morning I rear-ended the SUV, I was still getting used to its brakes.

Maybe the accident had something to do with that. And with the recent stress. I might've even fallen asleep. In truth I don't remember. There was a *crack* and I was thrust into the morning and its sudden trouble.

The SUV pulled forward a bit. A man stepped out. He was clean-shaven, in his thirties, and dressed in a golf shirt. His car was glossy and new. He probably worked in the valley's tech industry, which had begun making millionaires out of people who looked just like him. In the next moment we were standing a few feet apart. He stepped back. "What were you thinking?" he said.

He walked over to check the damage. But I couldn't breathe; I'd been somewhere else and now I was surrounded. I'd just turned eighteen—an adult—which meant, among other things, a whole new level of responsibility. This man could sue if he wanted to, or he could say I'd injured him deliberately. He had a power I'd never thought possible, and I was terrified in a familiar way; something dear was being taken.

"Don't call the police!" I started shouting. "Please!" Tears dimmed my vision. Then it was happening as if for the very first time; the colors kicked out from their shapes until these receded too and only the emotion remained, its depth: something that fell across everything else.

When it passed I was leaning on my father's car. The clean-shaven man stood alongside. He was holding up his palms as if to calm a horse. "Hey," he said. "Is there someone you'd like me to call?"

»

At first my parents were furious about the accident, but they calmed down when they saw how guilty I already felt. Luckily the damage wasn't too bad; our insurance would cover it.

A few days later, I described what had happened to Dr. Austin and she told me that I needed to be on a stimulant. "Even if the nortriptyline helped in the past," she said, "the current dosage is too low to be effective." She explained that car crashes were a major issue for people with ADHD. She also mentioned the academic stress. "This medication can make things more manageable."

I asked her why it would work when Ritalin hadn't, and she explained that the time-release mechanism would help with the rebound effect.

That night I discussed it with my mother. She was almost forty-five years old, but she looked the same as always; in my memory, her face tends to be marked by the emotion that inhabits it. "You know I don't like those speed drugs," she said. "You just can't tolerate them, biochemically or whatever. It's because you're sensitive to medication—I'm the same way."

I felt the familiar anger: my mother was sure she was right, reality was up for interpretation, and there was nothing to stop her from using every available option to her advantage. It didn't matter now that she was the one arguing *against* medication; I wanted to tell her that the only reason I was still taking the nortriptyline was because, with so much going on, I'd thought it best to avoid the type of conflict that this conversation was sure to stir up.

But in the next moment she said, "Timmy, you're an adult now. It's your choice. I'm just glad we're talking about it together. I want you to know how impressed I've been with you lately. Your father is too. You're working so hard!"

»

Dr. Austin wrote out a prescription for Dexedrine. We tapered the nortriptyline for a week—the daily dosage was already low—and on a Saturday morning I swallowed thirty milligrams of sustained-release amphetamine.

That afternoon, I passed the time on the couch with my father watching college football. The day went by uneventfully. At dinner, my mother asked, "Is your heart racing? Do you feel jittery? Are you hungry? You haven't touched your food—can I make you some eggs?" I told her I was fine. If anything it was the opposite of what she feared: the act of switching from one task to another suddenly felt momentous.

Then it was evening. My parents and brother and sister went to bed. I was waiting for the medication to wear off, and in the meantime I popped in Stanley Kubrick's *2001: A Space Odyssey,* which I'd tried to watch once before but kept falling asleep. Now, in the stillness of our TV room, as the screen filled with images of hominids and moonscapes and a spacecraft populated by astronauts and their mild-mannered computer, I was riveted. Where were they *really* headed? What was waiting for them? Who was telling the truth and who was lying? Oh my God, THE COMPUTER IS THE VILLAIN! And now we're traveling between time and space itself—a process that, at least in Kubrick's imagination, involves a psychedelic amount of neon. At the end, as the surviving astronaut passes through the various ages of his life (he eventually morphs into some sort of moon-sized fetus), I was sure I understood everything. So what if I couldn't explain it in a medium as coarse as words; the act of looking suddenly outweighed the object of the gaze. It felt like I'd just spent the last two and a half hours holding this film inches from my face.

Next I watched The Beatles' *Yellow Submarine.* Then *2001* again. It was midnight, it was 3 a.m. I sprawled out on the couch, loose-limbed and vibrant, hardly moving. But when the sun rose I started to panic; if I'd been awake for a full day and didn't feel the least bit tired, who's to say if I'd ever fall asleep again? As the light raked the shadows from the wall I told myself, *Go to bed.*

Finally I went upstairs to my parents' room. My mother was sleeping on her side. I was about to say her name, but I didn't. I was waiting for something I couldn't explain. It felt like a premonition, or at the very least the memory of one.

As if on cue her eyes opened. "Timmy," she said. "Have you been up all night?" I didn't understand how she could've known. In the next instant she was on her way to the bathroom; she rummaged through the cupboard and found a sleeping pill. Another thirty minutes would pass until it knocked me out, but in memory the effect comes on immediately—a blankness that had been kept at bay, up until then, by the stimulant.

»

How did Dr. Austin react to my experience on Dexedrine?

She understood that most of the people who came to see her were un-comfortable with the idea of a stimulant. In my case, a full year had passed before I was even willing to consider it. "That amount of milligrams was on the low end of the spectrum for someone your size," she told me. I expected her to argue in favor of a smaller dosage—that the drug had worked, just for too long—but she didn't. "There's still the nortriptyline," she said in her delicate voice. "It seemed to help you in the past. Do you want to go back on it? We could try returning to a larger dose?"

"No," I told her. And that was that; for the first time in nearly a de-cade I wouldn't be taking a behavior-modifying drug.

We set up a time for my next appointment. I left. Outside, the af-ternoon held the light, its sky and windows facing west. But there was something else. A sound in the distance like water.

For years this was exactly what I'd wanted; I had honestly believed that a psychotropic medication would someday betray my deepest flaws to the rest of the world—that the drug was complicit in these flaws because of its attempt, however unsuccessful, to conceal them—and if I could just go off it there'd finally be nothing left to hide, I'd be *me,* and the future would come to represent the same thing it does for everyone else.

But at the time, as I walked through the parking lot to my car, I wasn't really thinking about much. Perhaps my upcoming SAT session. There was probably homework to do: a translation from the *Aeneid,* a chapter in Faulkner's *The Sound and the Fury.* What else? The strange sound in the distance? It was the wind. A current from the coastal mountains was pressing the valley to the bay, and throughout the office park, trees were shaking. Wooden pickets braced their trunks. They were pear-colored, solitary with branches, their leaves spinning quickly, discreetly, held in place by a translucence of stems. Autumn and wind and not a single leaf on the ground; it's important, I think, that I remember that.

»

If more than a hundred years have been spent researching ADHD—conducting clinical trials, honing methodology, and evaluating certain approaches against others—why is it still so difficult to diagnose and treat the disorder in a way that addresses individual circumstances?

"By the 1960s, treatment had been medicalized," Dr. Leon Eisenberg writes in "Were We All Asleep at the Switch?," a personal essay published in a 2010 issue of *Acta Psychiatrica Scandinavica.* "The first psychotropic drugs were discovered by serendipity and introduced into psychiatry. The symptom relief they brought was so startling and persuasive that there was a major shift from psychologic to pharmacological treatment."

Eisenberg is the doctor who, in 1962, conducted the first double-blind, randomized study on Ritalin and hyperactive children. Throughout his career, he advocated for a combination of different approaches to mental illness. "Psychiatric practice deals with human distress in a context that must include the psychosocial as well as the biological," he wrote in a 1973 issue of the *Lancet.* After serving as the chief of psychiatry for Massachusetts General Hospital, he joined Harvard Medical School and helped expand its Department of Social Medicine.

"Were We All Asleep at the Switch?" is dated September 15, 2009, the day of his death. He was eighty-seven years old. The text was still in the process of revision, an accompanying editor's note explains.

Eisenberg had enrolled in medical school in 1940. From the beginning he was critical of Freud's pseudoscientific approach, but in the essay he notes that psychoanalysis also "taught trainees to listen to patients and to try to understand their distress, not simply to classify their diseases or sedate them or lock them away." The strength of psychotherapy, Freud's included, was that it could help "preserve the individuality of patients."

In a section titled "The Shift from Mind to Brain," Eisenberg tells a familiar story: the discovery of effective drug treatments after World War II; successful trials; the rise of neuroscience and the decline of psychotherapy; and the publication of disease-modeled diagnostic categories in the *DSM-III*. He discusses the benefits of this shift, and he also comments on what's been lost.

"Almost 50 years later," he writes, "the pendulum has swung so far that some young psychiatrists seem to no longer listen to patients at all." From his perspective, one of the main problems has to do with an increasing reliance on primary care. In the 1980s, general practitioners and pediatricians started taking on the roles once occupied by psychiatrists: they listened to symptoms, offered diagnoses, and prescribed medications. But within the cost-based parameters of the late-twentieth-century health care system, these physicians didn't have enough time to do a thorough case history— or create the type of personal connection that psychotherapy encourages. Instead, the biological approach of general medicine was broadly applied to the field of mental illness, a shift that has caused "psychiatry to focus so exclusively on the brain as an organ that the experience of the patient as a person has receded below the horizon of our vision."

The results are what we're seeing now: misdiagnosis and overdiagnosis, and a reliance on drug therapy as the primary line of defense against disorders that, because of their nature, demand a multifaceted approach.

In the final section, Dr. Eisenberg argues that instead of fighting over the causes and treatments of something like ADHD, psychiatrists, social workers, and psychologists need to work together to fulfill their proper roles in a diversified health care system. "If we focus on meeting public need," he writes, "psychiatry will have an honorable place in medicine."

»

On a morning a few weeks after the sleepless night, I arrived at Bellarmine an hour early. The school was like a rumor of itself. Members of the water-polo team lingered near the swimming pool. A teacher walked from the lounge holding an ugly red Stanford mug. In the distance, out past the library, a crowd was gathering: each day the Jesuits performed a morning mass that lasted only half an hour and was said to include, afterward, all the doughnuts you could eat.

I was dressed in a collared shirt, khaki pants, and a pair of shoes with water stains at their tips. A representative from Northwestern University was arriving to meet prospective students, and with the help of Mr. Amundsen, I'd been assigned to greet him.

This representative had an Irish name, Mr. Finnerty, I think. He was in his fifties and wore a navy sport coat with brass buttons at the cuffs. I'd been told he wasn't just another admissions rep; in the application process he held unusual sway, and anything I could do to make a good impression might help my chances.

"Welcome to Bellarmine!" I said.

"Happy to be here!" he replied. No doubt this was the first stop in a long day of campus visits. He explained that he'd just arrived from Chicago and was still adjusting to the time change. "You kids in California always seem the sleepiest," he said, "but that's probably because I've already been awake for hours."

"I'm not sleepy!" I told him. There were still a few minutes before his presentation. I rustled up some coffee, and as we sat together in the office's common room, he asked questions about sports, the weather, and my academic background. I responded to each in absurd detail—speaking rapidly and with my hands.

Soon enough the counseling office filled up with other seniors and Mr. Finnerty started his pitch. "I know you're all considering different options," he said, "but I have to tell you, Northwestern is where it's at." He described the lakefront campus, its old stone quads, and a social life that included football tailgates and coed dorms. "Chicago's one heck of a town," he said dryly.

I glanced around at the other boys, most of whom I recognized from my honors classes. They were wearing shorts and sweatshirts and *did* look sleepy. For them, Northwestern was a backup school; their real hope was Harvard or Princeton. I knew this because they talked about it openly. One of them, a kid named Applebee, had said before our Faulkner class, "I just don't think Brown's endowment is big enough for it to be considered an elite institution, at least if we're going to define 'elite' properly."

Over the last few months I'd become obsessed with Northwestern. It was a small school, had great academics, and most importantly, was located more than two thousand miles away. My father's baby sister, Lizzie, had gone there ten years earlier and swore that the experience changed her life, and she and her husband had convinced my parents that it would be a perfect fit. But even if I achieved everything I was working for that fall, my odds of acceptance were at best fifty-fifty.

Mr. Finnerty's presentation ended about ten minutes before the first bell, and afterward I walked him out. "So," he said, "might I also interest you in a nice set of steak knives?"

I don't know how I phrased it, exactly, but I basically told him that Northwestern was the very best school in the world and *I* knew how lucky someone like me would be to go there. I talked about its journalism and history departments. I think I even brought up its classics program, which my Latin teacher had mentioned once. "And the football!" I added. "Hey, the Big Ten's no joke."

He looked at me vaguely. "Well all right," he finally said. "But I better tell you one thing. It's about the winters."

I nodded quickly. He held up his hand. "They're colder than you've ever imagined. It's something to consider. I've seen too many Californians pack it up after their first year, and I don't blame them. It's paradise here."

For an instant I saw the Bay Area as if for the first time, its mountains and aridity, a place determined by wind and tall pines, by San Jose, Oakland, and San Francisco: a city that everyone I knew considered the finest in the world. I love these aspects of my hometown now, and miss them, but at the time they were part of a place I was willing to leave forever if, by doing so, I could break the sad choreography I believed to be the past.

Mr. Finnerty and I shook hands and he departed for his next school. A few weeks later Mr. Amundsen showed me a letter he'd received. It was a formal thank-you note, but at the top, scrawled in blue ink, the Northwestern rep had added a comment: *"It was great to be welcomed so early in the morning by such an energetic young man!"*

»

A few weeks later I retook the SATs. This time I felt more prepared. For the preceding months, a pair of twentysomething tutors had been coming to my house on different days. There was a guy whose specialty was math; he had a white Labrador that would lounge without a leash in our front yard while, inside, we tackled word problems. The girl who taught the verbal section had high cheekbones and watery eyes, and we'd sit side by side at my kitchen table going through analogies and reading samples, her fingers combing her hair from her neck. They both explained that the SAT is really testing you on how good you are at *taking* tests, and we prepared for it accordingly.

This time around I arrived early. Nervousness? Confusion? The fear that it would all go like it had before? Sure, but when I walked in, the details of the room felt more familiar, and after seeing the answer sets, it was easy enough to eliminate the most obvious choices and work through what was left. The hours passed quickly.

»

As the fall progressed and Northwestern's application deadline approached, I still had one more thing left to do: finish the accompanying personal statement, the prompt for which concerned choices and consequences. I was also required to provide an explanation for any suspensions on my record, so I decided to do both at once and focus on Steven Kelley and Ike Stipe. What I wrote, mercifully, has been lost, though I found out later that my mother sent a copy of it to Father McGuire, along with the comment *When do we get to attend* your *disciplinary hearing?*

I was applying for an early decision—the odds were better since, should I be accepted, I would be required to attend—and just before the deadline my mother and I drove to the post office to send off all the necessary materials.

It was a clear autumn afternoon. I was at the wheel, my mother in the passenger seat. My brother must've been at home with my sister.

As we passed Vasona—the small lake in the middle of town that my father's grandparents, after emigrating from Genoa, had first settled alongside—she turned to me and said, "Timmy, can you believe it? Next year at this time you'll be living by yourself and going to college. It feels like only yesterday we were driving to your first day of school. Do you remember?"

I figured she was about to tell this story again, but instead she began to recount what had happened, twenty-five years earlier, when she went off to college. Her mother had dropped her at the dorm: "She just said to me, 'See you next week for Sunday dinner' and waved good-bye. I was like, whoa, what am I supposed to do now? I'd never really been on my own before. How could I have known what was going to happen? That I'd meet your father? That someday I'd have you?"

Briefly I imagined myself in her place: a strange university, its buildings, the summer heat. Could she really just drop me off and leave? And what would happen when she did?

In the next moment she said, "I was my mother's third child. It's much harder with your oldest!" Lightly, she touched her fingers to the arm I was using to steer. "Of course I don't *want* you to go. It'll be one of the hardest things. But I'm ready because you're ready—because I know you'll be successful. It's as simple as that: I can feel it in my heart."

We were pulling into the post office. I suddenly realized how long it had been since we'd spent time alone together, and afterward, driving home, we stopped for dinner at an expensive Italian market. It was almost November. There hadn't been any more car accidents or teary breakdowns, and the quarter grades had come back all A-minuses. On the SATs I'd raised my score by over two hundred.

Now it was time to wait, which is a skill my family has never mastered. You can't learn patience; if anything, you just get better at recognizing its absence: the way you feel as the deadline holds off; approaches; as it passes through the context of your own life to become, in memory, a relic—something that's managed to outlast a world beyond return.

»

On a Saturday in December, I was downstairs in the TV room when I heard our front door swing open. The notification from Northwestern was set to arrive, and I'd been waiting all morning for the mail.

I jogged over and looked out, but the mail hadn't come. It was just my mother; she'd also been waiting, and now she'd left the house and was charging down the sidewalk. If she was on an errand why wasn't she taking the car, and if it was just a leisurely walk, where was our golden retriever, Bubba, who she'd never leave behind? The only explanation was that she'd decided to head out into our neighborhood and track down the mailman herself.

A half hour later, when she came back, I asked her just what she thought she was doing.

"I can go for a walk if I want," she said.

"I know what you're up to! You think it's okay to open the letter before me?"

She laughed. "Timmy, come on. I just wanted to see if it was coming today."

I glared at her.

"Relax. I talked to the mailman. He doesn't have it."

This didn't make sense; unless it was lost it should be arriving now. My mother went upstairs, I loitered in the kitchen, and after a while I heard a *thud*. Outside, in the mailbox, I found a white envelope with my name on it.

When I stepped back through the door my mother was blocking my path. Everyone was there, my father, my brother too. "Open it!" my sister yelled. "Open it now!"

I made it into the kitchen and pulled out the letter. The grain of its paper was textured, the school's logo at the top. For a moment it felt like a ticket, the impossible kind, sent from a place that doesn't yet exist, and then I saw it as if at once, the size and shape of the text: *Congratulations.*

»

A few days later—following a dinner at our favorite Mexican restaurant, my parents having invited our entire extended family to celebrate—it dawned on me to ask my mother if, in fact, she'd known the outcome beforehand; what had really happened during her encounter with the mailman?

"I'll be honest," she finally said. "If he'd given it to me then, I probably would've opened it." In her mind, the letter's message of acceptance only confirmed something that was already true. "Anyway, what's so bad about hearing such glorious news from your mother who loves you?"

But when she'd come upon our mailman he'd been confused by her demands, and he'd rummaged through his bag a few times before telling her it wasn't there. She didn't believe him—*Check again!,* she wanted to say—but she gave up and walked home, where she tried to wait like the rest of us for the news that already was on its way.

»

When it comes to the broader narrative of ADHD, the most important questions are the kind you'd ask about your own life. How did we get here? Where are we going next? And what's the point of all the work—not just in the present, but also by the people before us, along with the ones who'll be around after we're gone?

At the end of the 1990s, the scientific community started to arrive at more of a consensus on the disorder. In 1998 the National Institutes of Health (NIH) sponsored a three-day conference that included thirty experts from varying backgrounds. Russell A. Barkley gave the presentation "ADHD: Long-Term Course, Adult Outcome, and Comorbid Disorders." Peter Breggin lectured on the "Risks and Mechanism of Action of Stimulants." Twelve hundred people attended, and afterward a thirteen-member panel "representing the fields of psychology, psychiatry, neurology, pediatrics, epidemiology, biostatistics, education, and the public" offered a joint statement.

In 1999, the most comprehensive study of ADHD to date, the Multimodal Treatment Assessment, was completed. More than six hundred children between the ages of seven and nine were observed for fourteen months. The goal was to compare the effectiveness of four different options: stimulant medication, behavior therapy, the combination of both, and standard community care.

And in 2002, Dr. Barkley published "International Consensus Statement on ADHD," which declared, "The US Surgeon General, the American Medical Association, the American Psychiatric Association, the American Academy of Child and Adolescent Psychiatry, the American Psychological Association, and the American Academy of Pediatrics, among others, all recognize ADHD as a valid disorder."

Now it was possible to offer a clearer set of answers to some of the most familiar questions. What is ADHD? A trend that continues to exist in significant numbers and produces harm. What causes it? A developmental delay that's rooted in biology and experience. What's the best way to treat it? Through a combination of different evidence-based therapies that should be adjusted to meet the demands of a child's situation. Why do we diagnose it? To recognize and alleviate the levels of conflict and stress that, over time, interfere with normal childhood development. What's the long-term goal? To help some of the most vulnerable members of society—struggling children—make it safely into adulthood.

One of my goals, here, has been to examine the mountains of material on ADHD from the point of view of a patient; to retell a narrative that in the past has been the exclusive province of the people prescribing, as opposed to receiving, treatment. But this book is also an attempt to collapse a personal space—between attention and desire, normal and disordered, between sane and crazy.

In the meantime the way I see the subject will remain inseparable from my experience with it: a childhood of drug- and psychotherapy that, in late-twentieth-century America, was accompanied by a bewildering amount of conflict.

The question, then: Is the act of telling the story, in itself, enough? Or to put it another way: Is survival the same as being healed?

Epilogue

When I open my eyes the light is coming down through the high window of our bedroom, a late-summer light. I'm completely awake, as if the dream I've been having is just a memory of the present, its orchestra of quick steps.

My son, Jack, is standing at the side of the bed. His blond head is level with mine, and I can already tell what he's thinking. "Are you excited?" I ask. Today is his first day of kindergarten.

"It's time to get up!" he tells me.

Over the past few weeks there's been an orientation session, an ice cream social, and a tour of the building where his classroom is located. We've been counting down the days.

Alongside, my wife, Brett, stirs. "Kindergarten!" she says.

"I know!" he responds.

I sit up. "I can't believe my son is so big he's going off to school!" I tell him.

"Daddy," he says. "You gotta get out of bed. I don't wanna miss the bus."

His room is across the hall from ours. There's a bright round clock near his window; it's set to turn from blue to yellow at 7:15 a.m. Each morning—even this one—he waits for its signal before crossing the hardwood floor to wake us up. Usually, Brett heads off to work and Jack and I take our time getting ready, then I drop him at child care. But today we'll all walk to the school-bus stop together.

"Daddy!" he says again. I stand up and follow him downstairs. We get dressed, eat Cheerios, and watch baseball highlights on the computer. He feeds our two cats and I refill their water. For a moment it feels like any other morning. Then it's time to go. The door opens onto the humidity, its earthy haze, the sun hidden behind the branches of our neighborhood's trees.

For the last few years we've been living in a suburb of Washington, DC. I teach composition at a nearby university. My students are mostly seniors: smart, down-to-earth young adults who in many cases work full-time to pay their tuition. My wife and I met as undergraduates at Northwestern. She works at a laboratory in Maryland as a scientist on NASA's satellite missions to the moon, Mercury, and the asteroid belt; part of her job is to analyze the images the probes send back—the way light reflects from a planet or asteroid's surface—and then use the data to explain the region's geologic history. She's often traveling to conferences and meetings, which means that for perhaps a week out of each month it's just me and Jack: I'll drop him off, pick him up, pitch him a few Wiffle Balls in our front yard, heat dinner, stream an episode of a kids' show on the Internet, and then we'll read a book together while he strokes the ears of his favorite stuffed animal, a floppy bunny, and the clock by the bed counts down toward the moment it will turn blue again.

»

Whenever I find myself talking to people about my childhood experience with medication, one of the first questions tends to be *So, do you still have ADHD?*

By the time I was in my midtwenties the behavioral problems from childhood had for the most part transformed. Now one of the main issues was restlessness. I felt it often. An example: I'd be sitting in a crowded room, listening to a speaker at the front, and as my mind kept racing away from the topic at hand, I'd tap my fingers, bounce my knee, and whisper something to the person on my right—until a woman a few rows ahead would suddenly turn and tell me to quiet down, to which I'd respond that *she* should be quiet, and then we'd be shouting . . .

Another aspect had to do with something that was especially tough after my son was born. When Brett would be traveling and I was home with Jack, the tasks I needed to accomplish would come together in a single obstacle; there seemed to be no way to arrange these things in their natural order and start my progression through them.

A few years ago, after I found myself in the middle of one of those difficult stretches that had so often occurred while I was growing up, I started seeing a psychiatrist again, and we talked about going back on a stimulant.

I was reluctant, of course, but I couldn't help but wonder: Would things be different if, this time, I was the one who controlled the process?

I decided to try a low daily dosage of instant-release amphetamine salts (Adderall). At this amount I could tolerate the drug well enough. But was it beneficial?

A stimulant medication works—when taken at a therapeutic dosage—by making the world around you more immediate. It's as if the distance between you and the object of your gaze is emptied of interference, and the task at hand begins to resemble an ongoing, well-constructed argument; why break off on a tangent if it's unrelated to what you're trying to accomplish? Which is one of the reasons these drugs are dangerous. They change the shape of reality in a manner that makes doing something you don't want to do easier, and they work this way for everyone.

At first, I tried taking the amphetamine in small doses throughout the day; it affected me for most of the time I was awake. The sense of immediacy it brought on seemed to help. I felt calmer within my body. Suddenly I could sit in a library and do research in a way that hadn't been possible. Coming home, I wasn't so overwhelmed. But even at such a low dosage I didn't like how it made me appear obsessive and brooding, something I'd never been, and at night, when it wore off, I felt irritable, my appetite diminished and my normal sleep patterns disrupted.

Soon enough I started to remember: I *hate* taking a drug for my behavior, especially a stimulant. It wasn't just the physical discomfort, or the issue of needing extra help to function, or the struggle to define improvement. By agreeing to go on the amphetamine, I felt like I was reducing something exceedingly complex to a set of symptoms. Even the term "ADHD" began to sound easy. Is it ever possible to explain yourself in a medical fashion and not come off like you're making excuses?

Eventually I tried to look at things in a more environmental light: How could I recognize, ahead of time, certain situations that the medication might help alleviate? Like when my wife was traveling; or if I needed to sit through a daylong orientation session; or drive in traffic to a child's birthday party at an ice rink, where I'd be responsible for my son's safety while hundreds of people shouted and jostled in a small, poorly lit space. As the months passed I began to understand that, for me at least, the drug worked best and caused the least amount of harm when I took it under specific circumstances.

There are other ways to replicate these benefits. I try to exercise five days a week, which goes a long way toward burning off the sense of restlessness, and I work a job that lets me fulfill its tasks at my own pace. I'm still taking the amphetamine, but each day I aim to limit myself to 5 milligrams, the effects of which will last for about three hours.

Not that it always turns out this way. I'll often take a larger amount, especially if I'm traveling, or have too many papers to grade, or need to reread an article in a densely worded turn-of-the-century medical journal by one of our favorite British doctors . . .

The truth is I'm playing all of this by ear. Even if these current measures help, the reality is that at some point they won't. Taking a stimulant drug is an attempt to put something off. You could say the same about psychotherapy, or an environmental change, about treatment in general; in all likelihood, whatever it is that's fucked up your life in the past will return to fuck it up again, and despite the message of most personal narratives—that living to tell the tale means you've also overcome the obstacles therein—a prior experience with mental illness is of limited defense against its future approach. If anything, you learn to recognize just how much you stand to lose.

》

Jack steps outside first and Brett and I follow him through the cool envelope of our house's air-conditioning. Then the humidity hits us. We live just off of one of the busiest streets in Maryland, but the school bus comes to a safe, quiet pocket of our neighborhood, about a five-minute walk away.

Jack's looking ahead, toward our destination, and I reach for my phone and snap a picture; I've promised to take some for my parents, who at this moment are asleep in California.

Needless to say, my mother is not happy about how far away we currently live. She and my father are still in Los Gatos, about to turn sixty. Recently they sold our childhood house and moved into a condominium downtown, where they can walk to nearby restaurants and coffee shops. My father is the coach of the local high school's baseball team. My mother, after twenty-five years of rheumatoid arthritis, suffers from a severe immune deficiency, and she spends a few days out of each week in bed with a cold or infection. She would've loved to be here for Jack's first day of school, but airplane travel is especially difficult.

I take a brief video; in it you can hear me telling Jack to stop, wave, and say, "Hi Grandma and Grandpa, I'm going to my first day of school!" He does so dutifully. Then he glances over his shoulder.

"Let's race to the end of the block," I tell him. I take off. He follows, the backpack weighing him down, and by the time we're at the corner he's panting.

"Look," I say. Down the street, parents and children have gathered on a large tract of grass. Brett catches up with us and we walk over. It suddenly strikes me as an absurd proposition; why in your right mind would you agree to wait patiently for an enormous yellow machine that exists for the sole purpose of taking away your child?

As Brett and I introduce ourselves to the other parents, Jack runs to join the pack of kids. The bus stop is meant for kindergarten-through-fifth graders, and there are perhaps a dozen children of all different ages waiting to get on board. Some of the older girls, perched on the curb, are staring intently in the expected direction. A few younger boys are chasing one another. Jack is spinning in circles with another kindergartner, and every so often they freeze, like a pair of enormous squirrels, to glance with anticipation up the street.

Then someone starts shouting and we all look over at once; the yellow hull of the bus is angling forward, its lights in steady flashes.

The children line up. Kindergartners are supposed to get on first, but a few of them are clinging to their parents. During orientation, the principal told us that it might take a couple of days for a new student to get used to the situation, and we shouldn't worry if on the first morning our son changes his mind about the bus.

The school he's attending is a public one. There's an on-site psychologist, a large parent-teacher organization, and various after-hours clubs and activities. During the orientation I watched as one of the mothers approached a teacher and said, "I just want you to know that I personally asked for my daughter to be in your classroom. Her older brother is on the autism spectrum; he's in middle school now but it's been tough, and even though she hasn't been diagnosed herself, she has a hard time in situations when there's so much going on, and all the other parents said that you're just so calm and good with kids who need a bit more attention so I wanted to introduce myself . . ."

Jack's at the front of the line now. The doors are open. The driver rests his palm on the wheel. There's only one path: up the lead-colored steps and into the aisle, its dimness.

He walks onto the bus and, perched at the entrance, looks back. I give him a thumbs-up. He smiles and climbs the rest of the steps. Then he turns down the aisle and is lost beneath the tint of the daytime windows.

Brett grabs my arm. When I look at her I realize she's crying.

"What's the matter?"

She shields her face and whispers, "He's just a baby! What's he doing going off to kindergarten all by himself?"

And as the children pile on and the doors grind together I understand exactly what she means. For a moment, imagining it from Jack's perspective, I'm terrified; all I can see are the many things that can go wrong.

Then the bus folds in its stop sign and quiets the pattern of its lights, and the engine revs and a gear shifts as our son is carried off.

Afterward there is silence, and light, the street made sudden by both. Other parents cross into the space the bus has left behind. They're blinking, looking around. Now they're saying good-bye. Brett puts her arm through mine. A blue, humid morning. In a seat on a crowded aisle Jack is traveling to his first day of school.

ACKNOWLEDGMENTS

This book would not exist without the help of a great number of thoughtful, talented people:

My agent, the outstanding Kathleen Anderson; my expert and patient editor, Trish Todd; and the excellent team at Simon & Schuster, including Molly Lindley, Andrea DeWerd, and Sarah Reidy.

My core group of excellent readers: Nick Kowalczyk, Matt Davis, and Andre Perry.

The instructors whose support I've been lucky enough to receive throughout the years: Reginald Gibbons and Josh Weiner in Chicago; Robert Shapard, Susan Schultz, Joe Stanton, and Robert Sullivan in Honolulu; Patricia Foster, Jo Ann Beard, Stephen Kuusisto, David Hamilton, Bonnie Sunstein, and Robin Hemley in Iowa City; and the faculty and staff of the Professional Writing Program in College Park.

The friends and experts whose assistance proved invaluable during the book's long composition and production: Dr. Debra Suda, Dr. Edward Hallowell, Betty Parsons, Laurie, Clay Hopper, Jim Turner, Stewart Moss, K. E. Semmel, Leigh Saffold, Nate Brown, Dylan Nice, Tom Hope, Jen Percy, Cutter Wood, Joseph Tiefenthaler, and M. Thomas Gammarino.

My family: the cousins and aunts and uncles of the Denevi clan; Chris; Mikey, Katie, Ed, and Penny; Lee, Lewis, and Palmer (who suggested the book's eventual title!); my parents, who've remained patient and selfless throughout, despite being asked to read multiple drafts of a story that places them at the center of its action; and Brett and Jack, whose unconditional love and support are beyond measure.

I'm also grateful to the MacDowell Colony and the Virginia Center for the Creative Arts for their generous financial support.

I was once told that publishing a book is too large an endeavor for a single person to accomplish, and after going through this process for the first time I can't help but agree; writing is a collaborative form, and your final product is inseparable from all the people who've helped you along the way. To the many individuals who sacrificed their time so that this project might reach its completion: Thank you!

NOTES

Chapter One

5 *the Feingold diet:* For a 2012 review of studies refuting the dietary factor in ADHD, see Millichap et al., "The Diet Factor." For the earlier studies, see Conners, *Food Additives*, and National Advisory Committee on Hyperkinesis and Food Additives, *Final Report*.

6 *The latest* Diagnostic and Statistical Manual of Mental Disorders (DSM): American Psychiatric Association (APA), *DSM-V* (2013): 60. The 2013 edition of the *DSM* specifies between adult and childhood symptoms to a much greater extent than previous versions, but for the passage quoted, only the diagnostic criteria targeting childhood behavior has been included.

6 *six out of nine possible symptoms:* According to the *DSM-V,* these symptoms should appear before the age of twelve, be present in multiple settings, cause significant impairment, and exist independently of other mental disorders (60).

10 *"ADHD constitutes a failure":* From Barkley's introduction to Weyandt, *An ADHD Primer,* iv.

10 *"the most recent diagnostic label"*: Barkley, *Attention-Deficit Hyperactivity Disorder* (2nd ed.): 3.

10 *"a framework for identifying children"*: Nigg, *What Causes ADHD?*, 46.

10 *"It's a disorder of efficiency"*: Frontline, "Medicating Kids" (April 10, 2001).

11 *"a condition that psychiatry"*: Diller, *Running on Ritalin*, 49.

11 *"The drug companies"*: Breggin's quote is from a 2000 interview on PBS's website for *Frontline*: http://www.pbs.org/wgbh/pages/frontline/shows/medicating/interviews/breggin.html (accessed November 24, 2012).

11 *3–8 percent of US children*: Experts continue to vary slightly on prevalence. A sample of recent sources: 3–5 percent: Office of the Surgeon General, *Mental Health* (1999); 3–7 percent: *DSM-IV, rev.* (2000); 7.2 percent: Centers for Disease Control and Prevention, *MMWR: Morbidity and Mortality Weekly Report* (2010); 4–8 percent, American Academy of Child and Adolescent Psychiatry (AACAP), "AACAP Official Action: Practice Parameter for the Assessment and Treatment of Children and Adolescents with Attention-Deficit/Hyperactivity Disorder," *Journal of the American Academy of Child and Adolescent Psychiatry* 46, no. 7 (2007): 894–921; 5 percent, *DSM-V* (2013).

11 *affects boys at a much higher ratio*: For a recent review on gender and other prevalence statistics, see Polanczyk and Jensen, "Epidemiologic Considerations," 245–60.

11 *follow-up studies*: For a summary of studies, see Weiss and Hechtman, *Hyperactive Children*; see also Gittelman-Klein et al., "Hyperactive Boys," 937–47.

12 *a 1902 presentation*: Still, "Goulstonian Lectures," 1008–12, 1079–82, 1163–68.

12 *Still was born in 1868*: Biographical information is drawn from Farrow, "Sir George Frederick Still (1868–1941)," 777–78.

16 *The encephalitis epidemic*: Kessler, "History of Minimal Brain Dysfunction," and Ebaugh, "Neuropsychiatric Sequelae," 89–97.

16 *frontal lobe ablation studies*: Blau, "Mental Changes," 722–69.

16 *minimal brain damage*: Strauss and Lehtinen, *Psychopathology and Education*.

16 *millions of American children*: One of the recent estimates for the number of US children with ADHD is 5.4 million, from the CDC's 2010 *MMWR*.

17 *"Hyperkinetic Reaction of Childhood"*: APA, *DSM-II*, 1968.

21 *overall brain volume is less:* Castellanos et al., "Quantitative Brain Magnetic
    Resonance Imaging," 607–16; see also Swanson and Castellanos, "Biological
    Bases of ADHD," 7-1-7-20; and Castellanos et al., "Anatomic Brain Abnor-
    malities," 1693–96.

21 *a deficit in communication:* See Cook et al., "Association of Attention Deficit
    Disorder," 993–98; see also E. H. Cook Jr., M. A. Stein, and B. L. Leventhal,
    "Family-Based Association of Attention-Deficit/Hyperactivity Disorder and
    the Dopamine Transporter," *Handbook of Psychiatric Genetics,* eds. K. Blum
    and E. P. Noble (New York: CRC Press, 1996): 297–310; and Barkley, *Atten-
    tion-Deficit Hyperactivity Disorder* (3rd ed.).

22 *overwhelmingly inherited:* See Faraone et al., "Efficacy of Methylphenidate,"
    24–29; see also Gilger et al., "Etiology of Comorbidity," 343–48.

22 *"For comparison":* From the section "ADHD Facts" on Barkley's website:
    http://www.russellbarkley.org/content/adhd-facts.pdf (accessed November 24,
    2012).

22 *"These types of genetic influences":* Nigg, *What Causes ADHD?,* 218.

22 *"We do not have evidence that":* Pennington, *Diagnosing Learning Disorders,*
    157.

23 *up to 20 percent:* See Mick et al., "Case-Control Study," 378–85; Brennan et
    al., "Prenatal and Perinatal Influences"; and Nigg et al., "Prenatal Smoking
    Exposure," 362–69.

Chapter Two

33 *only a few hundred years ago:* This historical account is based on facts from
    the section "Historical Views and Breakthroughs" in Mash and Wolfe, *Ab-
    normal Child Psychology*; and from "The Birth of Psychiatry" and "The
    Asylum Era" in Shorter, *A History of Psychiatry.*

34 *eight thousand patients:* Shorter, *A History of Psychiatry,* 45.

34 *"Psychiatry was at a dead end":* Ibid., 65.

34 *Enter Sigmund Freud:* Freud's biographical information is drawn from Freud,
    Freud Reader.

35 *a 1909 case study:* Freud, "Analysis of Phobia in a Five-Year-Old Boy," from
    Complete Psychological Works, 5–148.

35 *The analyst would observe:* Diller, *Running on Ritalin,* 4–5, 219.

37 *"the middle childhood stage":* Teeter, *Interventions for ADHD,* 111.

39 *the Emma Pendleton Bradley Home:* The details of the hospital's history are drawn from Jones, *Legacy of Hope,* 7, http://www.bradleyhospital.org /WorkArea/DownloadAsset.aspx?id=23096.

40 *Amphetamine was first isolated:* Shorter, *Before Prozac,* 25; see also Edeleano, "Ueber einige derivate," 616–22.

40 *Available under the trademark Benzedrine:* Cho and Segal (eds.), *Amphetamine and Its Analogs,* 439–57.

40 *a controlled study:* Bradley, "Children Receiving Benzedrine," 577–85.

41 *Bradley had studied:* Work, H. H., "George Lathrop Bradley and the War over Ritalin," *COSMOS Journal,* 2001, http://www.cosmosclub.org/web/journals /2001/work.html.

41 *a picture of him:* Brown, "Images in Psychiatry: Charles Bradley, M.D., 1902–1979," 968.

46 *fewer than a dozen studies:* Safer, "Drugs for Problem School Children," 491.

46 *Bradley's own 1950 follow-up:* Bradley, "Benzedrine and Dexedrine," 24–37.

46 *many of his European followers had fled:* Jahoda, "Migration of Psychoanalysis."

46 *would come to staff:* Grob, *From Asylum to Community,* 32.

46 *and occupy the academic chairs:* Sarason, *American Psychologist,* 215–16.

46 *solidifying their influence:* For more details on the rise of psychoanalytic theory during this time period, see Shorter, *A History of Psychiatry,* 170–74.

47 *a new drug:* Much of the history of chlorpromazine is based on facts from Caldwell, "History of Psychopharmacology," 20–30.

47 *"anxious, Mediterranean-type":* Swazey, *Chlorpromazine in Psychiatry,* 79; the quote is Laborit's.

47 *provided to Laborit for testing:* Antihistamines were initially discovered in the 1930s by the Swiss-born chemist Daniel Bovet, who was working for Rhône-Poulenc. Bovet would eventually win a Nobel Prize for his research into allergies, but at the time, Rhône-Poulenc was hoping to develop antihistamines to use during surgery. Laborit was aware of Bovet's work; he'd contacted

Rhône-Poulenc and suggested that they adapt a new antihistamine to better stabilize the central nervous system. The company created chlorpromazine, and after assessing its effectiveness on laboratory rats, they provided it to him for testing (Healy, *Creation of Psychopharmacology,* 78–81).

47 *These results:* Delay et al., "Traitement des états d'excitation et d'agitation," 267–73.

47 *In American mental hospitals:* Swazey, *Chlorpromazine in Psychiatry,* 201–7.

47 *The first detailed study:* Freed and Peifer, "Prolonged Administration of Chlorpromazine," 22–26.

48 *chlorpromazine's most serious side effect:* Caldwell, "History of Psychopharmacology," 34–35.

52 *a pair of papers:* Laufer et al., "Hyperkinetic Impulse Disorder; and Laufer and Denhoff, "Hyperkinetic Behavior Syndrome."

52 *Methylphenidate was synthesized:* Panizzon, "La preparazione di piridil-e," 1748–1756.

52 *He called it Ritalin:* The background on methylphenidate's discovery is drawn from Shorter's *Before Prozac,* 39–40.

52 *Ritalin's chemical properties:* Sample et al., *Psychopharmacologic Drugs: A Pocket Reference,* 67.

52 *introduced to the American market as an antidepressant:* Ferguson et al., "Methylphenidate (Ritalin)," 1303–4.

52 *An early advertisement:* Singh, "Not Just Naughty," 134–45. (The specific advertisement is pictured on 145 and cited *AJP,* 1964.)

52 *amended Ritalin's usage:* As Ilina Singh notes in her above-mentioned essay, "Not Just Naughty," "Novartis (formerly CIBA) has been only marginally helpful to scholars attempting to piece together a history of the most famous stimulant drug, Ritalin." The best source for the date of Ritalin's approval for childhood disorders comes from the author Larry Diller's personal communication in 1996 with Todd Forte, a public relations officer for Novartis (*Running on Ritalin,* 25).

52 *The first major report:* Conners and Eisenberg, "The Effects of Methylphenidate," 458–64.

53 *the most rigorous clinical trial:* Landau, M., "Leon Eisenberg: Dedicated to

Letting the Outsider In," *Focus,* February 22, 2008, http://archives.focus.hms
.harvard.edu/2008/022208/profile.shtml.

53 *Keith Conners:* This biographical information is drawn from Mayes et al., *Medicating Children,* 60.

53 *the first detailed, long-term study:* Eisenberg, "The Autistic Child in Adolescence," *American Journal of Psychiatry* 112, no. 8 (1956): 607–12.

53 *shouted him down:* Eisenberg, "Mindlessness and Brainlessness," 498.

53 *"It's time to stop":* Mayes et al., *Medicating Children,* 60 (via a phone interview with Eisenberg).

53 *Eisenberg's parents:* This biographical information is drawn from C. Ireland, "Harvard Medical School Fetes Scholar, Names Chair," *Harvard Gazette,* June 25, 2009, http://news.harvard.edu/gazette/story/2009/06/harvard
-medical-school-fetes-scholar-names-chair/.

53 *In a photograph:* This image was featured in Eisenberg, "Were We All Asleep at the Switch?" 96.

53 *a 1960 study:* Cytryn et al., "Tranquilizing Drugs," 113–29.

54 *They both received grants:* Mayes et al., *Medicating Children,* 60–63.

54 *150,000 and 200,000 American children:* US Congress, House of Representatives, Subcommittee of the Committee on Government Operations, *Federal Involvement in the Use of Behavior Modification Drugs on Grammar School Children of the Right to Privacy Inquiry,* 91st Congress, 2nd Session (Washington, DC: Government Printing Office, September 29, 1970), 16.

54 *Born in 1842:* Biographical information is drawn from R. Goodman, "William James," *The Stanford Encyclopedia of Philosophy* (Spring 2011 edition), ed. E. N. Zalta, http://plato.stanford.edu/archives/spr2011/entries/james/.

55 *"an altar to an unknown god":* W. James, "The Dilemma of Determinism," in *The Will to Believe,* 147.

55 *a researcher from South Carolina:* The material on Watson is drawn from Karier, *Scientists of the Mind,* 106–53.

55 *"a doctor, lawyer, artist":* Watson, *Behaviorism,* 82.

55 *his theory of operant conditioning:* Mash and Wolfe, *Abnormal Child Psychology,* 8–9, 49.

55 *applied to more extreme cases:* Ibid., 9.

56 *"Bobo doll experiment":* Bandura, "Transmission of Aggression," 575–82.

56 *applying this new treatment:* Personal communication, Laurie Hamilton, March 18, 2011.

56 *"What treatment":* Paul, "Strategy of Outcome," 109–18.

60 *repeatable, evidence-based results:* Members of the American Psychoanalytic Association had tried to produce scientific evidence to support their therapies starting in 1948. But in 1957, the research produced by their Central Fact-Gathering Committee was deemed "potentially misleading," and the committee "recommended that members keep this report confidential." *American Psychoanalytic Association Bulletin* 14 (April 1958): 362; see also Shorter's *A History of Psychiatry,* 311; in contrast, as early as 1952, a study by Maudsley Hospital psychologist Hans Eysenck showed that Freud's treatment was not statistically effective (Eysenck, "The Effects of Psychotherapy," 321–22); later, in 1964, a study at Camarillo State Hospital showed that psychotherapy was vastly inferior in comparison to drug therapy for treating schizophrenia (May and Tuma, "Psychotherapy and Stelazine," 362–69).

60 *researching identical twins:* See Kety, "Types and Prevalence of Mental Illness," 345–62; Kety and Ingraham, "Genetic Transmission," 247–55; and Kety et al., "Mental Illness in the Biological and Adoptive Relatives," 442–55.

60 *Subsequent studies:* For the study on bipolar disorder, see Bertelsen et al., "A Danish Twin Study," 330–35; for a summary of twin studies on a variety of disorders, see Plomin, "Genetic Risk," 101–38.

60 *"objects of disbelief":* Shorter, *A History of Psychiatry,* 313.

60 *the drug's effect on* everyone: Weiss and Laties, "Enhancement of Human Performance," 1–36.

61 *produce a sense of euphoria:* Hardman and Limbird (eds.), *Pharmacological Basis of Therapeutics,* 221.

61 *banned in Sweden:* Perman, "Speed in Sweden," 760.

61 *fear of a similar epidemic:* Schmeck, H., "Federal Drug Agency Plans a 3-Phase Drive to Curb the Misuse of 'Pep Pills,'" (*New York Times,* August 3, 1970).

61 *front-page news:* Maynard, "Omaha Pupils."

61 *5–10 percent:* An August 10, 1970, issue of the *Medical News* cited this number as inaccurate: 5–10 percent of children in *special-education programs*—not the entire school district—were thought to be on medication.

61 *promised a congressional hearing:* W. Smith, "Behavior Drugs Given Pupils," *The Harvard Crimson,* Thursday, July 2, 1970, http://www.thecrimson.com /article/1970/7/2/behavior-drugs-given-pupils-pthe-city/.

61 *other media outlets:* E. T. Ladd, "Pills for Classroom Peace?" *Saturday Review* (November 21, 1970): 66–68, 81–83.

61 *Comprehensive Drug Abuse Prevention and Control Act:* US Congress, House of Representatives, *Federal Involvement in the Use of Behavior Modification Drugs on Grammar School Children; Comprehensive Drug Abuse Prevention and Control Act,* Public Law 91-513, 84 Stat. 1236 (October 27, 1970).

62 *Schedule II:* "Methylphenidate (A Background Paper)," Drug and Chemical Evaluation Section, Office of Diversion Control, Drug Enforcement Administration, Department of Justice, Washington, DC (October 1995).

62 *first advertisement recommending Ritalin:* Singh, "Not Just Naughty," 141 (the advertisement is pictured on 145 and cited: *AJP,* 1971).

62 *his own follow-up articles:* Feingold, "Hyperkinesis and Learning Disabilities," 797–803.

62 *more rigorous studies:* Millichap and Yee's 2012 review article in *Pediatrics* states that, at most, "an occasional child might react adversely to dyes and preservatives in foods and might benefit from their elimination"; selected earlier studies include Harley et al., "Hyperkinesis and Food Additives," 818–28; and National Advisory Committee, *Final Report to the Nutrition Foundation.*

63 *parent associations sprouted up:* Barkley, *Attention-Deficit Hyperactivity Disorder* (2nd ed.): 15.

63 *new laws:* Diller, *Running on Ritalin,* p. 27.

63 *more than 120 studies:* Swanson et al., "Stimulant Medications," 265–322.

63 *up to 600,000 children:* From Sprague, "Principles of Clinical Trials," 109; this number was higher than other estimates; in the 1981 study "Prevalence of Drug Treatment for Hyperactivity and Other Childhood Behavior Disorders," the number of children diagnosed with the disorder—not including

treatment—is cited as 400,000 (Gadow and Loney, eds., *Psychosocial Aspects*).

63 *an article in* Science: Rapoport et al., "Dextroamphetamine," 560–63.

66 *A number of new studies:* One of the earliest studies to compare components of behavior therapy with drug therapy: Gittelman-Klein et al., "Relative Efficacy of Methylphenidate," 261–79; see also Brown et al., "Methylphenidate and Cognitive Therapy," 69–88; and for a general review of studies, see Abikoff, "An Evaluation," 171–216.

Chapter Three

77 *In the same 1902 lecture:* Still, "Goulstonian Lectures," 1902.

78 *widespread educational reforms:* The details on British educational reform are drawn in parts from these chapters: "A Survey of the Evolution of ADHD and Pediatric Stimulant Use, 1900–1980," in Mayes et al., *Medicating Children*; "The Concept of Mental Deficiency or Retardation," Tredgold et al., in *Tredgold's Mental Retardation*; and "Feeble-Mindedness in Children—Mentally Defective Children," in Tredgold, *Mental Deficiency (Amentia)*.

78 *three grades of impairment:* Tredgold's *Mental Retardation*, 6–7.

78 *Alfred Frank Tredgold:* This biographical information is from Thomson, "Tredgold, Alfred Frank (1870–1952)," *Oxford Dictionary of National Biography.*

79 *a picture of him:* This photograph is from the title page of *Tredgold's Mental Retardation.*

79 *Tredgold offered his own solution:* Tredgold, *Mental Deficiency (Amentia),* 174–200.

86 *resembled the British:* This history of American educational practices is drawn from the chapter "The Emergence of Special Classes," in Winzer, *History of Special Education,* 322–36.

87 *his 1914 book:* Wallin, *Mental Health of the School Child,* 387–92.

87 *emphasized manual training:* On p. 333 of *The History of Special Education,* Dr. Margret Winzer of the University of Lethbridge writes that in these early-twentieth-century American special-ed classrooms, children "engaged in making rugs, scrubbing brushes, raffia baskets and mats, or Swiss lace."

87 *their 1947 book:* Strauss et al., *Psychopathology and Education,* 1–4, 127–200.

95 *"with few notable exceptions":* Ibid., 131.

96 *a system-wide sense of inequality:* This assessment of postwar specialized educational practices is drawn from Winzer's *The History of Special Education,* 379–80.

96 *failed to offer clear proof:* In fact, a series of studies starting in 1968 would prove the opposite. Some of these studies include Bradfield et al., "The Special Child in the Regular Classroom," 384–90; Bruininks et al., "Social Acceptance of Mildly Retarded Pupils," 377–83; Dunn, "Special Education for the Mildly Retarded," 5–22; and Myers, "The Efficacy of the Special Day School," 3–11.

96 *by almost two million:* Winzer, *The History of Special Education,* 376: "Between 1948 and 1968 the number of children in public school special education classes in the United States went from 357,000 to 2,252,000, or from 1.2 to 4.5 percent of the total enrollment in kindergarten to grade twelve."

96 *two options:* Ibid., 376.

96 *a series of lawsuits:* These lawsuits include *Diana v. State Board of Education* [in California] (1970); *Kentucky Association for Retarded Citizens v. Kentucky* (1974); and *Panitch v. State of Wisconsin* (1974). Source: Melcher, "Law, Litigation, and Handicapped Children," 126–30.

96 *the 1972 case: Pennsylvania Association for Retarded Children v. Commonwealth of Pennsylvania,* 334 F. Supp. 1257 (DC ED Pa. 1971), 343 F. Supp. 279 (ED. Pa. 1972): 1–33.

96 *were discriminatory: Mills v. Board of Education* [for the District of Columbia], 348 F. Supp. 866 (D. DC 1972): 1–7.

97 *Congress began holding hearings:* Sealander, *Failed Century,* 272.

97 *the Education for All Handicapped Children Act:* Public Law No. 94-142, 89 Stat. 773, "Statement of Findings and Purpose" (November 14, 1975): 3–22.

100 *"abominably cruel":* O'Connor, *An Only Child,* 16.

104 *"rage reaction":* Hallowell et al., *Driven to Distraction,* 15–16.

106 *according to the law's definition:* These definitions of "handicapped" are from the House of Representatives' official report on the law, which was passed as HR 7217: US Congress, House of Representatives, Committee on Education and Labor, "Education for All Handicapped Children Act of 1975," 94th Congress, 1st Session (June 26, 1975): 7–10.

106 *weren't receiving extra help:* Barkley et al., "The Adolescent Outcome of Hyperactive Children," 546–57.

106 *revising the 1975 law:* Much of this history detailing EHA's revision in the form of the IDEA Act is from the chapter "ADHD and the Politics of Children's Disability Policy" in Mayes et al., *Medicating Children.*

106 *opposed ADHD's inclusion:* These groups included the National Association of State Directors of Special Education, the National Education Association, the National Association of School Psychologists, and the Council for Exceptional Children (from Mayes et al., *Medicating Children,* 109).

106 *During congressional hearings:* US Congress, House, Committee on Education and Labor, Subcommittee on Select Education, *Hearings on the Reauthorization of the EHA Discretionary Programs,* 101st Congress, 2nd session, (1990): 60–99.

106 *the revised version:* Public Law No. 101-476, 104 Stat. 1142 (October 30, 1990).

107 *OSEP issued a memorandum:* Davila et al., *Clarification of Policy.*

107 *a legitimate disorder:* As Rick Mayes, Catherine Bagwell, and Jennifer Erkulwater state on p. 111 in *Medicating Children,* OSEP's clarification helped increase awareness in three ways: "First, the rule clarification alerted many teachers and school administrators to the fact that ADHD was indeed a qualifying disorder for special education. Also, the publicity surrounding the rule change itself could have increased awareness of the disorder among teachers and education officials, leading them to pay closer attention to children who may be eligible. Moreover, the Department of Education's announcement encouraged states to do a more thorough job of identifying students with subtle impairments like ADHD and to locate children with disabilities at an earlier age in order to provide preventative and adaptive services."

107 *three qualifying categories:* Enrollment between 1991 and 2001 would increase by 28 percent under the "Learning Disabled" category, from 2.2 to 2.9 million; 18 percent under "serious emotional disturbance," from 400,000 to 473,000; and almost 400 percent under "other health impairment," from 58,700 to 290,000. From US Department of Education, *To Assure the Free Appropriate Public Education of All Children with Disabilities* (Washington DC, 2002): 11–20.

111 *an older drug:* The details on nortriptyline are drawn from Kelsey et al., *Principles of Psychopharmacology,* 319–23; Sample et al., *Psychopharmacologic*

Drugs, 30–35; Barchas et al., *Psychopharmacology,* 190, 441–42; and David Healy, *The Creation of Psychopharmacology,* 227–30.

111 *occasionally prescribed to adolescents:* The 1987 report "Medication for Children with an Attention Deficit Disorder," released by the American Academy of Pediatrics, Committee on Children with Disabilities and the Committee on Drugs, in *Pediatrics* 80, stated that "tricyclic antidepressants also ameliorate the symptoms of attention deficit in selected patients" (758).

115 *overdose symptoms:* Information on overdose symptoms comes from Rosenbaum and Kou, "Are One or Two Dangerous?" 160–74; and Woolf et al., "Tricyclic Antidepressant Poisoning," 203–33.

Chapter Four

117 *Tricyclic antidepressants:* The history of tricyclics is drawn from Edward Shorter's chapter "The Second Biological Psychiatry" in *A History of Psychiatry*; David Healy's *The Creation of Psychopharmacology,* 227–30; and from the chapter "The First Drug Set" in Shorter's *Before Prozac.*

117 *seemed to alleviate severe symptoms:* Kuhn first presented his results at the Second Congress of World Psychiatry in 1957; afterward he published this presentation in the September 1957 issue of *Schweizerische Medizinische Wochenschrift,* 1135–40.

118 *examining its effectiveness on childhood disorders:* For example, Poussaint and Ditman, "A Controlled Study of Imipramine (Tofranil)," 283–90.

118 *a pair of studies:* Rapoport, "Childhood Behavior," 635–42; and Rapoport et al., "Imipramine and Methylphenidate Treatments," 789–93.

118 *the use of tricyclic antidepressants was reexamined:* Some of the studies on tricyclics and ADHD in the 1980s include Werry et al., "Imipramine and Methylphenidate," 27–35; Biederman et al., "Desipramine in the Treatment," 359–63; and Pliszka, "Tricyclic Antidepressants," 127–32.

118 *A 1983 study:* Garfinkel et al., "Tricyclic Antidepressant and Methylphenidate Treatment," 343–48.

118 *tricyclics as an alternative treatment option:* American Academy of Pediatrics, "Medication for Children with an Attention Deficit Disorder," 759.

118 *Nortriptyline was introduced:* Shorter, *Before Prozac,* 223.

118 *Its most common side effects:* The aspects of nortriptyline's chemical makeup are drawn from Barchas et al., *Psychopharmacology,* 190, and Kelsey et al., *Principles of Psychopharmacology,* 321.

118 *nortriptyline could be a decent fit:* The 1993 study "Nortriptyline in the Treatment of ADHD," conducted by doctors from Harvard Medical School and Massachusetts General Hospital and published in the *Journal of the American Academy of Child and Adolescent Psychiatry,* noted that "surprisingly, NT has received little attention" as a viable option for adolescents who responded poorly to stimulants. The study focused on "treatment-resistant" cases and found that in over three-fourths of them, nortriptyline brought about "moderate to marked improvement." They eventually concluded that "more work needs to be done to disentangle the anti-ADHD and antidepressant effects" (Wilens et al., "Nortriptyline in the Treatment of ADHD," 343–49).

122 *"The serious danger":* Still, "Goulstonian Lectures," 1167.

123 *nothing less than apocalyptic:* The following quotes and summaries are drawn from Tredgold's *Mental Deficiency (Amentia),* 524–40.

123 *increased fertility:* Tredgold wrote: "I think it has long been recognized by psychiatrists that the birth-rate of psychopathic families tends to be high" (*Mental Deficiency,* 524).

124 *wasn't some conspiracist:* This biographical information is drawn from Thomson's article on Tredgold in the *Oxford Dictionary of National Biography.*

131 *an article for* Psychiatry: Fromm-Reichmann, "Treatment of Schizophrenics by Psychoanalytic Psychotherapy," 263–73.

132 *it had a significant impact:* As Edward Shorter writes in *A History of Psychiatry,* "Generations of American mothers had to suffer unwarranted approaches as 'schizophrenogenic mothers'" (177).

132 *Anna Freud:* This biographical information is drawn from Yorke, "Freud, Anna (1895–1982)," http://www.oxforddnb.com/view/article/31126.

132 *ADHD was a response to the unconscious apprehension that children felt:* see Mash and Wolfe, *Abnormal Child Psychology,* 7; and Rafalovich, *Framing ADHD Children,* 36–37.

132 *her 1932 book:* Klein, *The Psycho-Analysis of Children,* 144 (originally published as *Die Psychoanalyse des Kindes* in 1932).

133 *Dr. Spock's book:* Spock, *Baby and Child Care.*

133 *"The most important thing":* Ibid., p. xv.

133 *a very specific conception:* As the psychiatrist Larry Diller explains on p. 179 in *Running on Ritalin,* "Spock brought psychoanalytic sensitivities to American child rearing in a readable, accessible form" and advocated a theory of children as "blank slates of psychological health on which parents could all too easily leave damaging marks."

138 *a new ideology:* The history of the antipsychiatry movement is drawn from Shorter's *A History of Psychiatry;* Healy's *The Creation of Psychopharmacology;* and the chapter "Stuck in the Cuckoo's Nest" in Judith Warner's *We've Got Issues.*

138 *"The movement's basic argument":* Shorter, *A History of Psychiatry,* 274.

138 *The French philosopher:* Foucault, *Madness and Civilization.*

138 *"It is customary to define psychiatry":* Szasz, *Myth of Mental Illness,* 262.

139 *He chronicled his experiences:* Laing, *The Divided Self,* 117, 156, and 177.

139 *"just a wanderer and logging bum":* Kesey, *One Flew over the Cuckoo's Nest,* 20.

139 *Conrad published "The Discovery":* Conrad, "The Discovery of Hyperkinesis, 12–21.

140 *influenced an entire generation of sociologists:* In his introduction to the 2004 *Framing ADHD Children,* the sociologist Adam Rafalovich has a section titled "Acknowledging Peter Conrad," in which he talks about Conrad's influence in the field (3–6).

141 *These authors claimed:* Schrag and Divoky, *Myth of the Hyperactive Child;* the quotes are from pp. 71, 72, and 228–29.

141 *a 1975 Noteworthy Title:* "A Selection of Noteworthy Titles," New York Times Book Review, *New York Times* (December 7, 1975).

147 *the founder of the Church of Scientology:* The history of Scientology is drawn from Lawrence Wright's article "The Apostate" in *The New Yorker* (February 14, 2011): 84–111.

147 *"Our most spectacular feat":* Phelan, "Have You Ever Been a Boo-Hoo?"

148 *On its website:* http://www.cchr.org/about-us/what-is-cchr.html (accessed August 30, 2012).

148 *"hidden key players":* http://www.cchr.org/quick-facts/introduction.html; and: http://www.cchr.org/cchr-reports/behind-terrorism/introduction.html (accessed August 30, 2012).

148 *petitioned state legislators:* Shorter, *A History of Psychiatry,* 282–84.

148 *more than a dozen lawsuits:* Schafer and Krager, "Effect of a Media Blitz," 1004–7.

148 *an enormous amount of attention:* Ibid., 1004.

149 *as much as 39 percent:* Safer and Krager note that this statistic is specific to Baltimore County in Maryland, the region in which they had been document-ing Ritalin consumption for more nearly two decades, but it can also serve to represent the general effect of the lawsuits and media attention on stimulant use nationally; they write: "The rate of medication usage for HA/I children in Baltimore County schools, after a steady and continuing rise between 1971 and 1987, dropped 39% in 1989 and 1991 from its 1987 peak. This occurred after a threatened local lawsuit and a critical national and local media blitz concerning Ritalin. Similar effects following critical media assaults have been observed with birth control pills in the early 1970s and recently with fluoxetine (Prozac)"; and "Strong circumstantial evidence suggests that the prominent 1989 and 1991 declines in the initiation of stimulant medication for hyperac-tive/inattentive students were related to the apprehension of parents and in-volved professionals generated by the methylphenidate media blitz and the threatened lawsuit" (ibid., 1007, 1004).

149 *an estimated 25,000 followers:* This statistic is presented in Wright's "The Apostate" (106), and is drawn from the survey of American religious affilia-tions in *The Statistical Abstract of the United States.*

Chapter Five

170 *because their brains hadn't properly evolved:* Still, "Goulstonian Lectures," 1011.

170 *"Now the essence of mental defect":* Tredgold, *Mental Deficiency,* 186.

171 *"We should therefore not":* Barkley, *Attention-Deficit Hyperactivity Disorder* (1st ed.): 5–6.

177 *a 1957 article:* Laufer and Denhoff, "Hyperkinetic Behavior Syndrome," 463–74.

177 *Stella Chess published "Diagnosis":* Chess, "Diagnosis and Treatment," 2379–85.

178 *"Hyperkinetic Reaction": DSM-II.*

185 *published their findings:* Douglas, "Stop, Look and Listen," 259–82 (this article was originally presented as the keynote address to the Canadian Psychological Association in 1971).

185 *concentration was not affected by physical activity:* "There does not seem to be a simple negative relationship between efficiency in attending and the amount the child moves" (Douglas, "Stop, Look and Listen," 267).

186 *continued to follow up:* Weiss and Hechtman, *Hyperactive Children Grown Up.*

187 *still prevalent:* Weiss and Hechtman's study originally followed a control group and 104 hyperactive children from 1962 to 1965 at Montreal's Children's Hospital. At the fifteen-year follow-up, the doctors were still in touch with seventy-six of the subjects (70–71).

187 *"While hyperactive adolescents":* Ibid., 319.

187 *The same went for "stimulant-treated":* Ibid., 242–50.

187 *"in general, studies":* Ibid., 319.

187 *"What was the matter":* Ibid., 310.

188 *"My dignity and self-esteem":* Ibid., 311.

193 *"Effort of attention":* Still gives this quote by James on p. 1166 of his "Goulstonian Lectures"; the full quote—"Effort of attention is thus the essential phenomenon of will"—can be found in James's *Principles of Psychology* (450).

193 *began to reexamine:* Some of these studies include Barkley, "Do As We Say, Not As We Do: The Problem of Stimulus Control and Rule-Governed Behavior in Attention Deficit Disorder with Hyperactivity" (paper presented at the Highpoint Hospital Conference on Attention Deficit and Conduct Disorders, Toronto, 1984); Draeger et al., "Visual and Auditory Attention," 411–24; and Sergeant and van der Meere, "The Diagnostic Significance of Attentional Processing," 151–66.

194 *when it came to the "perception . . .":* This quote is from p. 26 of the 1998 edition of Barkley's *ADHD Handbook.*

194 *"a deficit in responding"*: Ibid., 26.

194 *less susceptible to "reinforcement"*: Ibid., 26.

194 *He argued that its root cause:* Ibid., 27.

194 *summarized these findings:* These statistics are drawn from the section "Developmental Course and Adult Outcome" (186–218) and from "Nature and Diagnosis: Associated Problems" (121–24) in the 1998 edition of Barkley's *ADHD Handbook.*

195 *a longitudinal study:* The various results of Terman's longitudinal study can be found in the multiple volumes of his book *Genetic Studies of Genius,* which has been published by Stanford University Press over the last century; Barkley writes, "The follow-up study of [Terman's] group indicated that the most significant childhood personality characteristic predictive of reduced life expectancy by all causes was related to impulsive, undercontrolled personality characteristics"; for a fuller follow-up study on Terman's subjects, see Friedman et al., "Psychosocial and Behavioral Predictors of Longevity," 69–78.

195 *"the risk for reduced longevity":* Barkley's 1998 *ADHD Handbook,* 124.

195 *first started researching:* The biographical information on Barkley is taken from his personal website: russellbarkley.org (accessed November 24, 2012).

Chapter Six

206 *the medications themselves:* This information on stimulants is drawn from Kelsey et al., *Principles of Psychopharmacology,* 240–42.

206 *time-release technology:* The background on sustained-release pills is from Mayes et al., *Medicating Children,* 33; and Barkley's *ADHD Handbook,* 532.

206 *a shift in the pharmaceutical industry:* The history of drug companies and childhood drugs is mostly drawn from Judith Warner's *We've Got Issues,* 135–38; and the chapters "The Transformation of Mental Disorders in the 1980s" and "The Backlash against ADHD and Stimulants" in Mayes et al., *Medicating Children,* 70–95, 152–56.

207 *the Hatch-Waxman Act:* This law is formally known as the Drug Price Competition and Patent Term Restoration Act, Public Law 98-417, September 24, 1984.

207 *the Food and Drug Administration Modernization Act:* The 1997 FDA Mod-

ernization Act amended the Federal Food, Drug, and Cosmetic Act, Public Law 75-717, which was originally passed on June 25, 1938.

207 *nearly $2 billion:* Lehmann, "Extension Likely," 4.

207 *their earnings skyrocketed:* As Shorter points out in *A History of Psychiatry,* "by 1995 doctors were writing 6 million prescriptions for Ritalin a year" (290).

207 *increased fourfold:* Olfson et al., "National Trends," 514–21.

207 *biggest success stories:* Rodgers, "ADHD Med Reformulated," 31–32.

207 *half the expected prevalence:* According to the above mentioned study by Olfson and his colleagues, between 1987 and 1996, stimulant use increased from 0.6 to 2.4 percent of children, which accounts for about half of the disorder's expected prevalence rate in the population (Olfson et al., "National Trends").

207 *one of the most profitable in the world:* "Introduction," *Medicating Modern America: Prescription Drugs in History,* eds. A. Tone and E. S. Watkins (New York: New York University Press, 2007), 1.

207 *graduated from Harvard:* The following biographical information on Peter Breggin is from his website, www.breggin.com, and from a copy of his résumé posted there: http://breggin.com/resume.pdf (accessed November 24, 2012).

207 *"Diagnosing a child with":* Breggin, *Talking Back to Ritalin,* 171.

208 *the "Psychopharmaceutical Complex":* Ibid., 248.

208 *a picture of Dr. Breggin:* http://breggin.com/index.php?option=com_content&task=view&id=1&Itemid=41 (accessed November 24, 2012).

208 *Served as an expert witness:* In one of these lawsuits, a 1997 case in Milwaukee County, Judge James W. Rice wrote: "Dr. Breggin's observations are totally without credibility. I can almost declare him, I guess from statements that floor me, to say he's a fraud or at least approaching that. . . . He's untrained. He's a member of no hospital staff. He has not since medical school participated in any studies to support his conclusions except maybe one. . . . I can't place any credence or credibility in what he has to recommend in this case" (Order and Decision from Proceedings held before the Honorable James W. Rice, Reserved Circuit Court Judge Presiding, Case No. 93-FA-939-763, *Jacqueline D. Schellinger v. Neal C. Schellinger,* July 2, 1997, pp. 70–71; this quote, edited as such, appeared in Warner's *We've Got Issues,* 23).

208 *advertising stimulant medications to doctors:* Singh, "Not Just Naughty," in *Medicating Modern America,* 141.

208 *changes to the FDA guidelines:* As Judith Warner states in *We've Got Issues,* "Prior to 1997, the pharmaceutical industry didn't advertise much on TV, because the FDA required broadcast advertisements to include full information about drug side effects. This changed when the Food and Drug Administration Modernization Act (which also loosened regulations on off-label drug promotion) altered the rules for broadcast ads so that advertisers had only to mention major side effects and refer viewers to their doctors or to a toll-free number" (246).

208 *a Shire ad:* Singh, "Not Just Naughty," 144; the advertisement is pictured on this page and cited as "*Good Housekeeping,* 2004."

208 *"Doctors need to define":* This quote is from Breggin's interview on PBS's website for *Frontline:* http://www.pbs.org/wgbh/pages/frontline/shows/medicating/interviews/breggin.html (accessed November 24, 2012).

215 *"The disorder is common":* from the 1980 *DSM-III.*

215 *"3% to 7%":* from the 2000 *DSM-IV* (text rev.).

215 *from hundreds of thousands to millions:* In Gadow and Loney's *Psychosocial Aspects of Drug Treatment for Hyperactivity,* the prevalence in 1980 was estimated at 400,000; in the 1996 study "More Frequent Diagnosis of Attention Deficit-Hyperactivity Disorder," by Swanson et al., the prevalence in 1990 was estimated at 900,000 (p. 994); and in the CDC's 2010 *MMWR,* the number was estimated as high as 5.4 million.

215 *the prevalence rose:* Warner, *We've Got Issues,* 52.

215 *"The actual occurrence of ADHD":* Barkley, *ADHD Handbook* (2nd ed.), 86.

215 *prevalence is better understood:* For recent studies on this subject, see Cox et al., "Geographic Variation," 237–43; Stevens et al., "Ethnic and Regional Differences," 318–25; Stevens et al., "Race/Ethnicity and Insurance Status," 88–96; and Radigan et al., "Medication Patterns for Attention-Deficit/Hyperactivity Disorder," 44–56.

215 *contacted more than three thousand families:* Froehlich et al., "Prevalence, Recognition, and Treatment," 857–64.

216 *"Differences in ADHD prevalence":* DSM-V, 62.

221 *a personal essay:* Eisenberg, "Were We All Asleep at the Switch?" 89–102.

221 *"Psychiatric practice deals with":* Eisenberg, "The Future of Psychiatry," 1371–75.

221 *After serving as the chief of psychiatry:* This biographical information is from B. Marquard, "Dr. Leon Eisenberg, at 87; Affirmative Action Advocate" (*Boston Globe,* October 11, 2009), http://www.boston.com/bostonglobe/obituaries/articles/2009/10/11/dr_leon_eisenberg_87_affirmative_action_advocate_at_harvard_medical/.

222 *critical of Freud's pseudoscientific approach:* The same 2009 article in the *Boston Globe* offered a quote from Eisenberg on psychoanalysis: "How could you use a treatment that would take so long per person when the burden of mental illness was so high? And second, there was no real evidence it worked."

222 *the roles once occupied by psychiatrists:* As Mayes, Bagwell, and Erkulwater write in *Medicating Children,* "With the growth of managed care, which discouraged expensive referrals to specialist physicians (such as child psychiatrists), pediatricians increasingly diagnosed ADHD and prescribed stimulants themselves. As a result, psychosocial problems were becoming the centerpiece of pediatric primary care by the end of the 1980s, the most common chronic condition that pediatricians treated, surpassing asthma and heart disease" (93).

229 *a three-day conference:* National Institutes of Health, "Consensus Development Conference Statement," 1–37.

229 *Multimodal Treatment Assessment:* MTA Cooperative Group, "A 14-Month Randomized Clinical Trial," 1073–86.

229 *Barkley published "International Consensus":* Barkley, "International Consensus Statement on ADHD," 89–111.

BIBLIOGRAPHY

Abikoff, Howard. "An Evaluation of Cognitive Behavior Therapy for Hyperactive Children." In *Advances in Clinical Child Psychology,* vol. 10, edited by Benjamin B. Lahey and Alan E. Kazdin, 171–216. New York: Plenum Press, 1987.

American Academy of Pediatrics: Committee on Children with Disabilities and Committee on Drugs. "Medication for Children with an Attention Deficit Disorder." *Pediatrics* 80, no. 5 (1987): 758–60.

American Psychiatric Association (APA). *Diagnostic and Statistical Manual of Mental Disorders.* 2nd ed. (1968); 3rd ed. (1980); 4th ed. (1994); 4th ed. text rev. (2000); 5th ed. (2013). Washington, DC: American Psychiatric Association.

Bandura, Albert, Dorothea Ross, and Sheila A. Ross. "Transmission of Aggression through Imitation of Aggressive Models." *Journal of Abnormal and Social Psychology* 63 (1961): 575–82.

Barchas, Jack D., Philip A. Berger, Roland D. Ciaranello, and Glen R. Elliott, eds. *Psychopharmacology: From Theory to Practice.* New York: Oxford University Press, 1977.

Barkley, Russell A. *Attention-Deficit Hyperactivity Disorder: A Handbook for Diagnosis and Treatment.* 1st ed. (1990); 2nd ed. (1998); 3rd ed. (2005). New York: Guilford.

———. "International Consensus Statement on ADHD." *Clinical Child and Family Psychology Review* 5, no. 2 (2002): 89–111.

Barkley, Russell A., Mariellen Fischer, Craig S. Edelbrock, and Lori Smallish. "The Adolescent Outcome of Hyperactive Children Diagnosed by Research Criteria: An 8-year Prospective Follow-up Study." *Journal of the American Academy of Child and Adolescent Psychiatry* 29, no. 4 (1990): 546–57.

Bertelsen, A., Bent Harvald, and Mogens Hauge. "A Danish Twin Study of Manic-Depressive Disorders." *British Journal of Psychiatry* 130 (1977): 330–51.

Biederman, Joseph, David R. Gastfriend, and Michael S. Jellinek. "Desipramine in the Treatment of Children with Attention Deficit Disorder." *Journal of Clinical Psychopharmacology* 6, no. 6 (1986): 359–63.

Blau, Abram. "Mental Changes Following Head Trauma in Children." *Archives of Neurology & Psychiatry* 35, no. 4 (1936): 723–69.

Blum, Kenneth, and Ernest P. Noble, eds. *Handbook of Psychiatric Genetics.* Boca Raton, FL: CRC Press, 1996.

Bradfield, Robert H., Josephine Brown, Phyllis Kaplan, Edward Rickert, and Robert Stannard. "The Special Child in the Regular Classroom." *Exceptional Children* 39, no. 5 (1973): 384–90.

Bradley, Charles. "The Behavior of Children Receiving Benzedrine." *American Journal of Psychiatry* 94 (1937): 577–85.

———. "Benzedrine and Dexedrine in the Treatment of Children's Behavior Disorders." *Pediatrics* 5, no. 1 (1950): 24–37.

Breggin, Peter. *Talking Back to Ritalin: What Doctors Aren't Telling You about Stimulants and ADHD,* rev. ed. Cambridge, MA: Perseus Books, 2001.

Brennan, Patricia A., Emily R. Grekin, and Sarnoff A. Mednick. "Prenatal and Perinatal Influences on Conduct Disorder and Serious Delinquency." In *Causes of Conduct Disorder and Juvenile Delinquency,* edited by Benjamin B. Lahey, Terrie E. Moffitt, and Avshalom Caspi. New York: Guilford, 2003.

Brown, Ronald T., Martha Ellen Wynne, and Rute Medenis. "Methylphenidate and Cognitive Therapy: A Comparison of Treatment Approaches with Hyperactive Boys." *Journal of Abnormal Child Psychology* 13, no. 1 (1985): 69–87.

Brown, Walter A. "Images in Psychiatry: Charles Bradley, M.D., 1902–1979." *American Journal of Psychiatry* 155, no. 7 (1998): 968.

Bruininks, Robert H., J. Rynders, and John E. Gross. "Social Acceptance of Mildly Retarded Pupils in Resource Rooms and Regular Classes." *American Journal of Mental Deficiency* 78, no. 4 (1974): 377–83.

Caldwell, Anne E. "History of Psychopharmacology." In *Principles of Psychopharmacology*, 2nd ed. Edited by William G. Clark and Joseph Del Giudice. New York: Academic Press, 1978.

Castellanos, F. Xavier, Jay N. Giedd, Wendy L. Marsh, Susan D. Hamburger, A. Catherine Vaituzis, Daniel P. Dickstein, Stacey E. Sarfatti, et al. "Quantitative Brain Magnetic Resonance Imaging in Attention-Deficit Hyperactivity Disorder." *Archives of General Psychiatry* 53, no. 7 (1996): 607–16.

Castellanos, F. Xavier, Wendy S. Sharp, Rebecca F. Gottesman, Deanna K. Greenstein, Jay N. Giedd, and Judith L. Rapoport. "Anatomic Brain Abnormalities in Monozygotic Twins Discordant for Attention Deficit Hyperactivity Disorder." *American Journal of Psychiatry* 160, no. 9 (2003): 1693–96.

Centers for Disease Control and Prevention (CDC). "Increasing Prevalence of Parent-Reported Attention-Deficit/Hyperactivity Disorder among Children—United States, 2003 and 2007." *MMWR: Morbidity and Mortality Weekly Report* 59, no. 44 (2010): 1439–43.

Chess, Stella. "Diagnosis and Treatment of the Hyperactive Child." *New York State Journal of Medicine* 60 (1960): 2379–85.

Cho, Arthur K., and David S. Segal. *Amphetamine and Its Analogs: Psychopharmacology, Toxicology, and Abuse*. San Diego: Academic Press, 1994.

Conners, C. Keith. *Food Additives and Hyperactive Children*. New York: Plenum Press, 1980.

Conners, C. Keith, and Leon Eisenberg. "The Effects of Methylphenidate on Symptomatology and Learning in Disturbed Children." *American Journal of Psychiatry* 120, no. 5 (1963): 458–64.

Conrad, Peter. "The Discovery of Hyperkinesis: Notes on the Medicalization of Deviant Behavior." *Social Problems* 23, no. 1 (1975): 12–21.

Cook, Edwin H. Jr., Mark A. Stein, Matthew D. Krasowski, Nancy J. Cox, Deborah M. Olkon, John E. Kieffer, and Bennett L. Leventhal. "Association of Attention-Deficit Disorder and the Dopamine Transporter Gene." *American Journal of Human Genetics* 56, no. 4 (1995): 993–98.

Cox, Emily R., Brenda R. Motheral, Rochelle R. Henderson, and Doug Mager. "Geographic Variation in the Prevalence of Stimulant Medication Use among Children 5 to 14 Years Old: Results from a Commercially Insured US Sample." *Pediatrics* 111, no. 2 (2003): 237–43.

Cytryn, Leon, Anita Gilbert, and Leon Eisenberg. "The Effectiveness of Tranquilizing Drugs Plus Supportive Psychotherapy in Treating Behavior Disorders of Children: A Double-Blind Study of Eighty Outpatients." *American Journal of Orthopsychiatry* 30, no. 1 (1960): 113–29.

Davila, Robert R., Michael L. Williams, and John T. MacDonald. *Clarification of Policy to Address the Needs of Children with Attention Deficit Disorders within General and/or Special Education*. Washington, DC: US Department of Education, 1991.

Delay, Jean, Pierre Deniker, and J. M. Harl. "Traitement des états d'excitation et d'agitation par une méthode médicamenteuse dérivée de l'hibernothérapie [Therapeutic method derived from hiberno-therapy in excitation and agitation states]." *Annales Médico-Psychologiques* 110 (1952): 267–73.

Diller, Lawrence H. *Running on Ritalin: A Physician Reflects on Children, Society, and Performance in a Pill*. New York: Bantam, 1998.

Douglas, Virginia I. "Stop, Look and Listen: The Problem of Sustained Attention and Impulse Control in Hyperactive and Normal Children." *Canadian Journal of Behavioural Science* 4, no. 4 (1972): 259–82.

Draeger, Sonya, Margot Prior, and Ann Sanson. "Visual and Auditory Attention Performance in Hyperactive Children: Competence or Compliance." *Journal of Abnormal Child Psychology* 14, no. 3 (1986): 411–24.

Dulcan, Mina K., and R. Scott Benson. "AACAP Official Action: Summary of the Practice Parameters for the Assessment and Treatment of Children, Adolescents, and Adults with ADHD." *Journal of the American Academy of Child and Adolescent Psychiatry* 36, no. 9 (1997): 1311–17.

Dunn, Lloyd. "Special Education for the Mildly Retarded—Is Much of It Justifiable?" *Exceptional Children* 35, no. 1 (1968): 5–22.

Ebaugh, Franklin G. "Neuropsychiatric Sequelae of Acute Epidemic Encephalitis in Children." *American Journal of Diseases of Children* 25, no. 2 (1923): 89–97.

Edeleano, Lazar. "Ueber einige Derivate der Phenylmethacrylsäure und der Phenylisobuttersäure." *Berichte der Deutschen Chemischen Gesellschaft* 20, no. 1 (1887): 616–22.

Eisenberg, Leon. "The Autistic Child in Adolescence." *American Journal of Psychiatry* 112, no. 8 (1956): 607–12.

———. "The Future of Psychiatry." *The Lancet* 302, no. 7842 (1973): 1371–75.

———. "Mindlessness and Brainlessness in Psychiatry." *British Journal of Psychiatry* 148 (1986): 497–508.

Eisenberg, Leon, and Laurence B. Guttmacher. "Were We All Asleep at the Switch? A Personal Reminiscence of Psychiatry from 1940 to 2010." *Acta Psychiatrica Scandinavica* 122, no. 2 (2010): 89–102.

Eysenck, Hans J. "The Effects of Psychotherapy: An Evaluation." *Journal of Consulting Psychology* 16, no. 5 (1952): 319–24.

Faraone, Stephen V., Thomas Spencer, Megan Aleardi, Christine Pagano, and Joseph Biederman. "Meta-Analysis of the Efficacy of Methylphenidate for Treating Adult Attention-Deficit/Hyperactivity Disorder." *Journal of Clinical Psychopharmacology* 24, no. 1 (2004): 24–29.

Farrow, S. J. "Sir George Frederick [*sic*] Still (1868–1941)." *Rheumatology* 45, no. 6 (2006): 777–78.

Feingold, Ben F. "Hyperkinesis and Learning Disabilities Linked to Artificial Food Flavors and Colors." *American Journal of Nursing* 75, no. 5 (1975): 797–803.

———. *Why Your Child Is Hyperactive.* New York: Random House, 1975.

Ferguson, John T., Frank V. Z. Linn, John A. Sheets Jr., and Mervyn M. Nickels. "Methylphenidate (Ritalin) Hydrochloride Parenteral Solution: Preliminary Report." *Journal of the American Medical Association* 162, no. 14 (1956): 1303–4.

Foucault, Michel. *Madness and Civilization: A History of Insanity in the Age of Reason.* Paris: Plon, 1961.

Freed, Herbert, and Charles A. Peifer. "Treatment of Hyperkinetic Emotionally Disturbed Children with Prolonged Administration of Chlorpromazine." *American Journal of Psychiatry* 113, no. 1 (1956): 22–26.

Freud, Sigmund. *The Standard Edition of the Complete Psychological Works of Sigmund Freud. Volume X (1909).* London: Hogarth Press, 1955.

———. *The Freud Reader,* edited by Peter Gay. New York: W. W. Norton, 1989.

Friedman, Howard S., Joan S. Tucker, Joseph E. Schwartz, Carol Tomlinson-Keasey, Leslie R. Martin, Deborah L. Wingard, and Michael H. Criqui. "Psychosocial and Behavioral Predictors of Longevity: The Aging and Death of the 'Termites.'" *American Psychologist* 50, no. 2 (1995): 69–78.

Froehlich, Tanya E., Bruce P. Lanphear, Jeffery N. Epstein, William J. Barbaresi, Slavika K. Katusic, and Robert S. Kahn. "Prevalence, Recognition, and Treatment of Attention-Deficit/Hyperactivity Disorder in a National Sample of US Children." *Archives of Pediatrics & Adolescent Medicine* 161, no. 9 (2007): 857–64.

Fromm-Reichmann, Frieda. "Notes on the Development of Treatment of Schizophrenics by Psychoanalytic Psychotherapy." *Psychiatry* 11, no. 3 (1948): 263–73.

Gadow, Kenneth D., and Jan Loney, eds. *Psychosocial Aspects of Drug Treatment for Hyperactivity.* Boulder, CO: Westview Press, 1981.

Garfinkel, Barry D., Paul H. Wender, Leon Sloman, and Irene O'Neil. "Tricyclic Antidepressant and Methylphenidate Treatment of Attention Deficit Disorder in Children." *Journal of the American Academy of Child Psychiatry* 22, no. 4 (1983): 343–48.

Gilger, Jeffrey W., Bruce F. Pennington, and John C. DeFries. "A Twin Study of the Etiology of Comorbidity: Attention-Deficit Hyperactivity Disorder and Dyslexia." *Journal of the American Academy of Child and Adolescent Psychiatry* 31, no. 2 (1992): 343–48.

Gittelman-Klein, Rachel, Salvatore Mannuzza, Ronald Shenker, and Noreen Bonagura. "Hyperactive Boys Almost Grown Up. I. Psychiatric Status." *Archives of General Psychiatry* 42, no. 10 (1985): 937–47.

Gittelman-Klein, Rachel, Donald F. Klein, Howard Abikoff, Sidney Katz, Audrey C. Gloisten, and Wendy Kates. "Relative Efficacy of Methylphenidate and Behavior Modification in Hyperkinetic Children: An Interim Report." *Journal of Abnormal Child Psychology* 4, no. 4 (1976): 361–79.

Grob, Gerald N. *From Asylum to Community: Mental Health Policy in Modern America.* Princeton, NJ: Princeton University Press, 1991.

Hallowell, Edward M., and John J. Ratey. *Driven to Distraction: Recognizing and Coping with Attention Deficit Disorder from Childhood through Adulthood.* New York: Touchstone, 1995.

Hardman, Joel G., and Lee E. Limbird. *Goodman & Gilman's The Pharmacological Basis of Therapeutics,* 9th ed., edited by Perry B. Molinoff, Raymond W. Ruddon, and Alfred Goodman Gilman. New York: McGraw-Hill, 1996.

Harley, J. Preston, Roberta S. Ray, Lawrence Tomasi, Peter L. Eichman, Charles G. Matthews, Raymond Chun, Charles S. Cleeland, et al. "Hyperkinesis and Food Additives: Testing the Feingold Hypothesis." *Pediatrics* 61, no. 6 (1978): 818–28.

Healy, David. *The Creation of Psychopharmacology.* Cambridge, MA: Harvard University Press, 2002.

Jahoda, Marie. "The Migration of Psychoanalysis: Its Impact on American Psychiatry." In *The Intellectual Migration: Europe and America 1930–1960,* edited by Donald Fleming and Bernard Bailyn. Cambridge, MA: Harvard University Press, 1969.

James, William. *The Will to Believe and Other Essays in Popular Philosophy* (1897). Cambridge, MA: Harvard University Press, 1979.

Jones, Brian C. *Legacy of Hope: A Profile of America's First Mental Health Hospital for Children on its 75th Anniversary.* Providence, RI: Bradley Hospital, 2006.

Karier, Clarence J. *Scientists of the Mind: Intellectual Founders of Modern Psychology.* Urbana: University of Illinois Press, 1986.

Kelsey, Jeffrey E., D. Jeffrey Newport, and Charles B. Nemeroff. *Principles of Psychopharmacology for Mental Health Professionals.* Hoboken, NJ: Wiley, 2006.

Kesey, Ken. *One Flew over the Cuckoo's Nest.* New York: Viking, 1962.

Kessler, Jane W. "History of Minimal Brain Dysfunction." In *Handbook of Minimal Brain Dysfunctions: A Critical View,* edited by Herbert E. Rie and Ellen D. Rie. Hoboken, NJ: Wiley, 1980.

Kety, Seymour S., David Rosenthal, Paul H. Wender, and Fini Schulsinger. "Mental Illness in the Biological and Adoptive Families of Adopted Schizophrenics." *American Journal of Psychiatry* 128, no. 3 (1971): 302–6.

Kety, Seymour S., David Rosenthal, Paul H. Wender, and Fini Schulsinger, "The Types and Prevalence of Mental Illness in the Biological and Adoptive Families of Adopted Schizophrenics," in *The Transmission of Schizophrenia: Proceedings of the Second Research Conference of the Foundations' Fund for Research in Psychiatry,* Dorado, Puerto Rico, June 26 to July 1, 1967. David Rosenthal and Seymour S. Kety, eds. New York: Pergamon Press, 1968, pp. 345–62.

Kety, Seymour S., Paul H. Wender, Bjørn Jacobsen, Loring J. Ingraham, Lennart Janson, Britta Faber, and Dennis K. Kinney. "Mental Illness in the Biological and Adoptive Relatives of Schizophrenic Adoptees: Replication of the Copenhagen Study in the Rest of Denmark." *Archives of General Psychiatry* 51, no. 6 (1994): 442–55.

Kety, Seymour S., and Loring J. Ingraham. "Genetic Transmission and Improved Diagnosis of Schizophrenia from Pedigrees of Adoptees." *Journal of Psychiatric Research* 26, no. 4 (1992): 247–55.

Klein, Melanie. *The Psycho-Analysis of Children.* London: Hogarth Press, 1975.

Kuhn, Roland. "Über Depressive Zustände mit einem Iminodibenylderivat." *Schweizerische Medizinische Wochenschrift* 87 (1957): 1135–40.

Laing, R. D. *The Divided Self.* New York: Pantheon, 1969.

Laufer, Maurice W., and Eric Denhoff. "Hyperkinetic Behavior Syndrome in Children." *Journal of Pediatrics* 50, no. 4 (1957): 463–74.

Laufer, Maurice W., Eric Denhoff, and Gerald Solomons. "Hyperkinetic Impulse Disorder in Children's Behavior Problems." *Psychosomatic Medicine* 19, no. 1 (1957): 38–49.

Lehmann, Christine. "Extension Likely for Law Encouraging Medication Studies in Children." *Psychiatric News,* July 20, 2001.

Lehmann, Heinz E. "Tranquillizers and Other Psychotropic Drugs in Clinical Practice." *Canadian Medical Association Journal* 79, no. 9 (1958): 701–8.

Mash, Eric J., and David A. Wolfe. *Abnormal Child Psychology.* 4th ed. Belmont, CA: Wadsworth, CENGAGE Learning, 2010.

May, Philip R. A., and A. Hussain Tuma. "The Effect of Psychotherapy and Stelazine on Length of Hospital Stay, Release Rate and Supplemental Treatment of Schizophrenic Patients." *Journal of Nervous and Mental Disease* 139 (1964): 362–69.

Mayes, Rick, Catherine Bagwell, and Jennifer Erkulwater. *Medicating Children: ADHD and Pediatric Mental Health.* Cambridge, MA: Harvard University Press, 2009.

Melcher, John W. "Law, Litigation, and Handicapped Children." *Exceptional Children* 43, no. 3 (1976): 126–30.

Mick, Eric, Joseph Biederman, Stephen V. Faraone, Julie Sayer, and Seth Kleinman. "Case-Control Study of Attention-Deficit Hyperactivity Disorder and Maternal Smoking, Alcohol Use, and Drug Use During Pregnancy." *Journal of the American Academy of Child and Adolescent Psychiatry* 41, no. 4 (2002): 378–85.

Millichap, J. Gordon, and Michelle M. Yee. "The Diet Factor in Attention-Deficit/ Hyperactivity Disorder." *Pediatrics* 129 (2012): 330–37.

MTA Cooperative Group. "A 14-Month Randomized Clinical Trial of Treatment Strategies for Attention-Deficit/Hyperactivity Disorder." *Archives of General Psychiatry* 56, no. 12 (1999): 1073–86.

Myers, James K. "The Efficacy of the Special Day School for EMR Pupils." *Mental Retardation* 14, no. 4 (1976): 3–11.

National Advisory Committee on Hyperkinesis and Food Additives. *Final Report to the Nutrition Foundation.* New York: Nutrition Foundation, 1980.

National Institutes of Health. "Consensus Development Conference Statement: Diagnosis and Treatment of Attention-Deficit/Hyperactivity Disorder (ADHD)." *Journal of the American Academy of Child and Adolescent Psychiatry* 39, no. 2 (2000): 182–93.

Nigg, Joel T. *What Causes ADHD?: Understanding What Goes Wrong and Why*. New York: Guilford, 2006.

Nigg, Joel T., and Naomi Breslau. "Prenatal Smoking Exposure, Low Birth Weight, and Disruptive Behavior Disorders." *Journal of the American Academy of Child and Adolescent Psychiatry* 46, no. 3 (2007): 362–69.

O'Connor, Frank. *An Only Child*. New York: Knopf, 1961.

Office of the Surgeon General. *Mental Health: A Report of the Surgeon General.* Rockville, MD: US Department of Health and Human Services, 1999.

Olfson, Mark, Steven C. Marcus, Myrna M. Weissman, and Peter S. Jensen. "National Trends in the Use of Psychotropic Medications by Children." *Journal of the American Academy of Child & Adolescent Psychiatry* 41, no. 5 (2002): 514–21.

Panizzon, Leandro. "La Preparazione di Piridil-e Piperidil-Arilacetonitrili e di Alcuni Prodotti di Trasformazione (Parte I)." *Chimica Acta* 27 (1944): 1748–56.

Paul, Gordon L. "Strategy of Outcome Research in Psychotherapy." *Journal of Consulting Psychology* 31, no. 2 (1967): 109–18.

Pennington, Bruce F. *Diagnosing Learning Disorders: A Neuropsychological Framework*. 2nd ed. New York: Guilford, 2009.

Perman, Einar S. "Speed in Sweden." *New England Journal of Medicine* 283, no. 14 (1970): 760–61.

Phelan, James. "Have You Ever Been a Boo-Hoo?" *Saturday Evening Post,* March 21, 1964.

Pliszka, Steven R. "Tricyclic Antidepressants in the Treatment of Children with Attention Deficit Disorder." *Journal of the American Academy of Child and Adolescent Psychiatry* 26, no. 2 (1987): 127–32.

Plomin, Robert. "Genetic Risk and Psychosocial Disorders: Links Between the Normal and Abnormal." In *Biological Risk Factors for Psychosocial Disorders,* edited by Michael Rutter and Paul Casaer. Cambridge, UK: Cambridge University Press, 1991.

Polanczyk, Guilherme, and Peter Jensen. "Epidemiologic Considerations in Attention Deficit Hyperactivity Disorder: A Review and Update." *Child and Adolescent Psychiatric Clinics of North America* 17, no. 2 (2008): 245–60.

Poussaint, Alvin F., and Keith S. Ditman. "A Controlled Study of Imipramine (Tofranil) in the Treatment of Childhood Enuresis." *Journal of Pediatrics* 67, no. 2 (1965): 283–90.

Radigan, Marleen, Peter Lannon, Patrick Roohan, and Foster Gesten. "Medication Patterns for Attention-Deficit/Hyperactivity Disorder and Comorbid Psychiatric Conditions in a Low-Income Population." *Journal of Child and Adolescent Psychopharmacology* 15, no. 1 (2005): 44–56.

Rafalovich, Adam. *Framing ADHD Children: A Critical Examination of the History, Discourse, and Everyday Experience of Attention Deficit/Hyperactivity Disorder.* Lanham, MD.: Lexington Books, 2004.

Rapoport, Judith L. "Childhood Behavior and Learning Problems Treated with Imipramine." *International Journal of Neuropsychiatry* 1, no. 6 (1965): 635–42.

Rapoport, Judith L., Monte S. Buchsbaum, Theodore P. Zahn, Herbert Weingartner, Christine Ludlow, and Edwin J. Mikkelsen. "Dextroamphetamine: Cognitive and Behavioral Effects in Normal Prepubertal Boys." *Science* 199, no. 4328 (1978): 560–63.

Rapoport, Judith L., Patricia O. Quinn, Gail Bradbard, and K. Duane Riddle. "Imipramine and Methylphenidate Treatments of Hyperactive Boys: A Double-Blind Comparison." *Archives of General Psychiatry* 30, no. 6 (1974): 789–93. doi:10.1001/archpsyc.1974.01760120049008.

Rodgers, Katie. "ADHD Med Reformulated: An Old Drug Reenters Market." *Drug Topics* 140, no. 6 (1996): 31.

Rosenbaum, Tina G., and Maybelle Kou. "Are One or Two Dangerous? Tricyclic Antidepressant Exposure in Toddlers." *Journal of Emergency Medicine* 28, no. 2 (2005): 169–74. doi:10.1016/j.jemermed.2004.08.018.

Safer, Daniel J. "Drugs for Problem School Children." *Journal of School Health* 41, no. 9 (1971): 491–95. doi:10.1111/j.1746-1561.1971.tb05156.x.

Safer, Daniel J., and John M. Krager. "Effect of a Media Blitz and a Threatened Lawsuit on Stimulant Treatment." *Journal of the American Medical Association* 268, no. 8 (1992): 1004–7.

Sample, Richard G., G. John Di Gregorio, and Robert J. Wicks. *Psychopharmacologic Drugs: A Pocket Reference.* Philadelphia: Stickley, 1978.

Sarason, Seymour Bernard. *The Making of an American Psychologist: An Autobiography.* San Francisco: Jossey-Bass, 1998.

Schrag, Peter, and Diane Divoky. *The Myth of the Hyperactive Child: And Other Means of Child Control.* New York: Pantheon, 1975.

Sealander, Judith. *The Failed Century of the Child: Governing America's Young in the Twentieth Century.* Cambridge, UK: Cambridge University Press, 2003.

Sergeant, Joseph, and Jaap van der Meere. "The Diagnostic Significance of Attentional Processing: Its Significance for Future ADD + H Classification—A Future DSM." In *Attention Deficit Disorder: Clinical and Basic Research,* edited by T. Sagvolden and T. Archer. Hillsdale, NJ: Erlbaum, 1989.

Shorter, Edward. *A History of Psychiatry: From the Era of the Asylum to the Age of Prozac.* Hoboken, NJ: Wiley, 1997.

———. *Before Prozac: The Troubled History of Mood Disorders in Psychiatry.* New York: Oxford University Press, 2008.

Singh, Ilina. "Not Just Naughty: 50 Years of Stimulant Drug Advertising." In *Medicating Modern America: Prescription Drugs in History,* edited by Andrea Tone and Elizabeth Siegel Watkins. New York: New York University Press, 2007.

Spock, Benjamin. *Baby and Child Care.* New York: Pocket Books, 1968.

Sprague, Robert L. "Principles of Clinical Trials and Social, Ethical, and Legal Issues of Drug Use in Children." In *Pediatric Psychopharmacology: The Use of Behavior Modifying Drugs in Children,* edited by John S. Werry. New York: Brunner/Mazel, 1978.

Stevens, Jack, Jeffrey S. Harman, and Kelly J. Kelleher. "Ethnic and Regional Differences in Primary Care Visits for Attention-Deficit Hyperactivity Disorder." *Journal of Developmental and Behavioral Pediatrics* 25, no. 5 (2004): 318–25.

———. "Race/Ethnicity and Insurance Status as Factors Associated with ADHD

Treatment Patterns." *Journal of Child and Adolescent Psychopharmacology* 15, no. 1 (2005): 88–96.

Still, George Frederic. "The Goulstonian Lectures on Some Abnormal Psychical Conditions in Children." *The Lancet* 159, no. 4104 (1902): 1008–12, 1079–82, 1163–68.

Strauss, Alfred A., and Laura E. Lehtinen. *Psychopathology and Education of the Brain-Injured Child,* vol. 1. New York: Grune & Stratton, 1947.

Swanson, James M., and F. Xavier Castellanos. "Biological Bases of Attention Deficit Hyperactivity Disorder: Neuroanatomy, Genetics, and Pathophysiology." In *Attention Deficit Hyperactivity Disorder: State of the Science, Best Practices,* edited by Peter S. Jensen and James R. Cooper. Kingston, NJ: Civic Research Institute, 2002.

Swanson, James M., Marc Lerner, and Lillie Williams. "More Frequent Diagnosis of Attention Deficit-Hyperactivity Disorder." *New England Journal of Medicine* 333, no. 944 (1995).

Swanson, James M., Keith McBurnett, Diane L. Christian, and Tim Wigal. "Stimulant Medications and the Treatment of Children with ADHD." In *Advances in Clinical Child Psychology,* vol. 17, edited by Thomas H. Ollendick and Ronald J. Prinz, 265–322. New York: Plenum Press, 1995.

Swazey, Judith P. *Chlorpromazine in Psychiatry; A Study of Therapeutic Innovation.* Cambridge, MA: MIT Press, 1974.

Szasz, Thomas S. *The Myth of Mental Illness: Foundations of a Theory of Personal Conduct.* New York: Harper, 1961.

Teeter, Phyllis Anne. *Interventions for ADHD: Treatment in Developmental Context.* New York: Guilford, 1998.

Thomson, Mathew. "Tredgold, Alfred Frank (1870–1952)." In *Oxford Dictionary of National Biography.* Oxford: Oxford University Press, 2004.

Tredgold, Alfred Frank. *Mental Deficiency (Amentia).* 4th ed. New York: William Wood, 1922.

Tredgold, Alfred Frank, Roger Francis Tredgold, and Kenneth Soddy. *Tredgold's Mental Retardation.* Baltimore: Williams and Wilkins, 1970.

Wallin, John Edward Wallace. *The Mental Health of the School Child: The Psycho-Educational Clinic in Relation to Child Welfare; Contributions to a New Science of Orthophrenics and Orthosomatics.* New Haven: Yale University Press, 1914.

Warner, Judith. *We've Got Issues: Children and Parents in the Age of Medication.* New York: Riverhead, 2010.

Watson, John B. *Behaviorism.* New York: People's Institute, 1925.

Weiss, Bernard, and Victor G. Laties. "Enhancement of Human Performance by Caffeine and the Amphetamines." *Pharmacological Reviews* 14, no. 1 (1962): 1–36.

Weiss, Gabrielle, and Lily Trockenberg Hechtman. *Hyperactive Children Grown Up: Empirical Findings and Theoretical Considerations.* New York: Guilford, 1986.

Werry, John S., Michael G. Aman, and Eileen Diamond. "Imipramine and Methylphenidate in Hyperactive Children." *Journal of Child Psychology and Psychiatry* 21, no. 1 (1980): 27–35.

Weyandt, Lisa. *An ADHD Primer.* Boston: Allyn and Bacon, 2001.

Wilens, Timothy E., Joseph Biederman, David E. Geist, Ronald Steingard, and Thomas Spencer. "Nortriptyline in the Treatment of ADHD: A Chart Review of 58 Cases." *Journal of the American Academy of Child & Adolescent Psychiatry* 32, no. 2 (1993): 343–49.

Winzer, Margret A. *The History of Special Education: From Isolation to Integration.* Washington, DC: Gallaudet University Press, 1993.

Woolf, Alan D., Andrew R. Erdman, Lewis S. Nelson, E. Martin Caravati, Daniel J. Cobaugh, Lisa L. Booze, Paul M. Wax, et al. "Tricyclic Antidepressant Poisoning: An Evidence-Based Consensus Guideline for Out-of-Hospital Management." *Clinical Toxicology* 45, no. 3 (2007): 203–33.

Wright, Lawrence. "The Apostate." *The New Yorker,* February 14, 2011.

Yorke, Clifford. "Freud, Anna (1895–1982)." In *Oxford Dictionary of National Biography.* Oxford: Oxford University Press, 2004.

ABOUT THE AUTHOR

Timothy Denevi received his MFA in nonfiction from the University of Iowa. He has been awarded fellowships by the MacDowell Colony, the Virginia Center for the Creative Arts, and the Community of Writers at Squaw Valley. He lives near Washington, DC, and is the Nonfiction Visiting Writer in the MFA program at George Mason University.